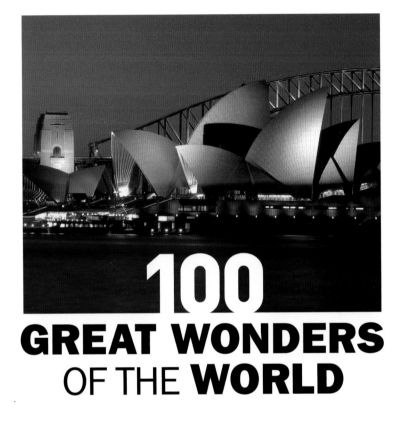

100
GREAT WONDERS
OF THE **WORLD**

Metro Books
122 Fifth Avenue
New York, NY 10011

ISBN: 978-1-4351-3001-2

Printed and bound in Dubai

10 9 8 7 6 5 4 3 2 1

PAGE 1 The Sydney Opera House (see pages 214–217).
BELOW A view from the Convent of Roussanou, one of the Monasteries of the Metéora (see pages 56–57).

Created by AA Publishing, a trading name of AA Media Ltd, whose registered office is Fanum House, Basing View, Basingstoke, Hampshire, United Kingdom RG21 4EA. Registered Number 06112600

Writers: Dr John Baxter, Rosemary Burton, Richard Cavendish, Dr Peter Clarkson, Dr Elizabeth Cruwys, Dr Beau Riffenburgh and Nia Williams

Revised and updated by Anne Locke and Andrew McIlwraith

Managing Editor: David Popey
Designer: Austin Taylor
Picture researcher: Wilf Matos
Proofreader: Alison Moore
Indexer: Marie Lorimer
Image manipulation and internal repro: Sarah Montgomery
Production: Rachel Davis
Cartography provided by the Mapping Services Department of AA Publishing

100
GREAT WONDERS
OF THE WORLD

A COLLECTION OF THE WORLD'S AWE-INSPIRING PLACES, BUILDINGS AND LANDSCAPES

METRO BOOKS
NEW YORK

CONTENTS

Introduction 6

EUROPE 10

The Great Fjords 12
Volcanic Iceland 14
The Giant's Causeway 16
Edinburgh Castle 18
Stonehenge 20
The Waddenzee 21
The Camargue 22
Versailles 24
SUPER SITE **The Eiffel Tower** 26
The Pont du Gard 30
Grand' Place 31
Neuschwanstein 32
Golden Lane 34
Wieliczka Salt Mines 35
The Danube Delta 36
The Hofburg 37
The Kapellbrücke 38
The Matterhorn 40
The Colosseum 42
The Leaning Tower of Pisa 44
The Grand Canal 46
SUPER SITE **St Peter's Basilica** 48
FEATURE **RENAISSANCE EUROPE** 52
The Parthenon 54
Metéora Monasteries 56
The Alhambra 58
The Sagrada Família 60
The Kremlin 62
The Great Palace 64
The Trans-Siberian Railway 66

ASIA 68

Pamukkale 70
The Blue Mosque 72
Nemrut Dag 74
The Dead Sea 75
SUPER SITE **Jerusalem** 76
Petra 80
Burj Khalifa 82
SUPER SITE **The Great Wall of China** 84
The Forbidden City 88
The Guilin Hills 90
The Three Gorges Dam 92
SUPER SITE **The Taj Mahal** 94
The Red Fort 98
Potala Palace 99
FEATURE **HOUSES OF WORSHIP** 100
The Himalayas 102
Itsukushima Shrine 104
Beppu 105
Mount Fuji 106
Borobudur 108
Angkor Wat 109
Wat Phra Keo 110
Ayutthaya 112

AFRICA 114

The Temple of Karnak 116
SUPER SITE **The Great Pyramid** 118
The River Nile 122
Carthage 124
Fez Medina 126
The Great Sahara 128
The East African Rift Valley 130
Lake Nakuru 132
FEATURE **GREAT LANDSCAPES** 134
Mount Kilimanjaro 136
The Congo River 138
Madagascar 140
Victoria Falls 142
The Okavango Delta 144
Table Mountain 146

NORTH AMERICA 148

The Canadian Pacific Railway 150
Niagara Falls 152
SUPER SITE **The Statue of Liberty** 154
The Lincoln Memorial 158
Mount Rushmore 160
The Empire State Building 162
FEATURE **GREAT ARCHITECTURE** 164
Zion National Park 166
The Hoover Dam 168
The Golden Gate Bridge 170
The Devil's Tower 172
Yosemite National Park 174
The Grand Canyon 176
Redwoods and Giant Sequoias 178
Meteor Crater 179
The Everglades 180
The Hawaiian Islands 182

CENTRAL & SOUTH AMERICA 184

Teotihuacán 186
Chichén Itzá 188
FEATURE **GREAT CIVILIZATIONS** 190
Tikal 192
Angel Falls 194
The Nazca Lines 195
SUPER SITE **Machu Picchu** 196
The Amazon Basin 200
Iguaçu Falls 202
Galapagos Islands 204
The Inca Trails 206
Tierra del Fuego 208

AUSTRALASIA & OCEANIA 210

Easter Island 212
SUPER SITE **Sydney Opera House** 214
Uluru (Ayers Rock) & Kata Tjuta 218
SUPER SITE **The Great Barrier Reef** 220
FEATURE **FEATS OF ENGINEERING** 224
Glaciers of the Southern Alps 226
Rotorua 228

ANTARCTICA 230

Mount Erebus 232
FEATURE **THE ELEMENTS** 234
Deception Island 236

Index 238
Acknowledgements 240

INTRODUCTION

EACH LANDSCAPE AND STRUCTURE in this book is a source of wonder. Even in a time of mass and instantaneous communication, when images of the globe's farthest and most remote reaches can be transmitted to screens in every continent, feats of human ingenuity and skill and the extremes of the natural world can still astonish. The manmade achievements celebrated here span thousands of years of human history, while the Earth's natural splendors illustrate millions of years of upheaval, movement, and erosion.

The desire to build

ABOVE A small train of camels crossing the Erg Chebbi sand dunes, which stretch into the Sahara (see pages 128–129).

BELOW Watch towers on a section of the Great Wall of China near Simitai (see pages 84–87).

Across the world there has always been a delight in the spectacular and an urge to embellish the surface of the earth with the tallest, heaviest, largest constructions that imagination and technology would allow, from Stonehenge to the Three Gorges Dam. Burj Khalifa in Dubai rises 828m (2,717ft) from the ground. It dwarfs the Empire State Building in New York City, which, for more than 40 years, enjoyed the prestige of being the world's highest building. Like the elegant Eiffel Tower and the soaring spires of medieval cathedrals, these structures show what human beings can achieve when they aim for the skies.

Some wonders are marvels of engineering, conquering distance and taming nature. The Trans-Siberian and the Canadian Pacific railways represent the pioneering impulse to cover vast distances and establish links across apparently impenetrable terrain. Some wonders, such as Stonehenge and the Great Wall of China, are equally astonishing structures, completed without the benefit of modern machinery. Others illustrate the power of faith to overcome the challenges presented by seemingly inaccessible places—like the Metéora

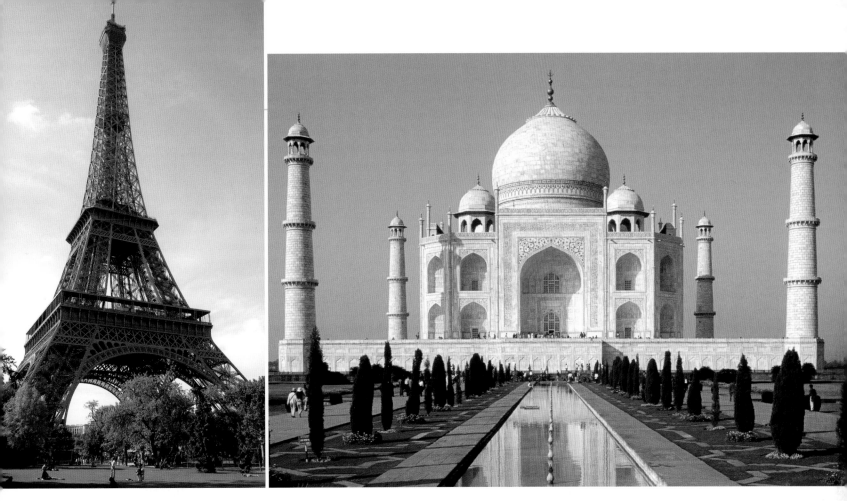

monasteries in Greece, and the mysterious religious settlement at Machu Picchu, built by the Incas. Power and status have prompted the raising of monuments too, from the colossal, scattered statues of Nemrut Dag to the stone faces of American presidents hewn into Mount Rushmore. The more enigmatic the structure, the more awe-inspiring it seems. Was Stonehenge used an an observatory or a place of healing? How were the gigantic patterns in the desert at Nazca laid out before the era of flight? Who lived in the Mayan temple-cities, in the jungles of the Yucatán? And what is the significance of the stone figures gazing mutely from Easter Island? A dozen theories can be found for every question, but these ancient manmade wonders keep their secrets safe.

Paradise on earth

Many vast constructions in stone and marble display the glory of royalty, from Versailles to the Kremlin. Some became gilded prisons—like the Forbidden City of the Chinese emperors in Beijing, or the Potala Palace of the Dalai Lamas at Lhasa—in which the ruler could be isolated, kept apart from real life. Such buildings may also be attempts to create an earthly paradise. 'If there is a paradise on Earth,' said Shah Jehan, builder of the Red Fort in Delhi, 'it is this, it is this, it is this.' The Alhambra in Spain was designed with the same intention, and at the Palace of Versailles, Louis XIV's architects and landscape designers set out to build a palace of ideal proportions, which would demonstrate not only the Sun King's majesty, but also the order of the world.

ABOVE Two of the world's most recognizable modern wonders, the Eiffel Tower (pages 26–29) and the Taj Mahal (pages 94–97), are also astounding feats of architectural engineering.

BELOW An image of King Antiochus I, enthroned more than 2000 years ago on the mountain top at Nemrut Dag in Turkey (see page 74).

ABOVE The El Capitan Cathederal Rocks as seen from Valley View in Yosemite National Park (see pages 174–175).

The same is true of great religious buildings—cathedrals, mosques and temples—created as symbols of the divine order. The colossal temple-mountains of the East, such as Borobudur in Java and Angkor Wat in Cambodia, are stone lessons on the true nature of the universe. They demonstrate the indefatigable human ambition to match earthly wonders with wonders of the human spirit.

Hence the importance of orientation: of aligning a building with the order of the world. The Great Pyramid in Egypt was built so that its four sides accurately faced north, east, south and west. On the other side of the world, 3,000 years later, the city of Teotihuacán in Mexico was laid out in similar fashion. Sometimes orientation was used to spectacular symbolic effect. At Chichén Itzá, also in Mexico, the steps and terraces of the pyramid-temple represent the days and months of the year, so that at the spring and autumn equinoxes the shadows and patterns of sunlight made it look as if its serpent-god was coiling and writhing its way out of the temple.

Glories of nature

Many of the sites explored in this book represent the attempts of humankind to travel across land and sea, or to make a mark on previously uninhabited territory. Yet it is not long since whole continents on Earth remained more or less unexplored by humanity. Antarctica is the world's largest and least-populated wilderness, and much of the ocean floor is still a mystery. Our small planet, one of millions of objects in the galaxy, which is itself one of millions of galaxies in the universe, is an astoundingly beautiful place. Think of the Grand Canyon (the vast gorge in the Arizona Desert, worn more than 1.6km (1 mile) deep by the Colorado River), the bewildering array of life among the corals of the Great Barrier Reef, the delicate beauty of snow-topped Mount Fuji and the fiery rage of the young Hawaiian volcanoes.

Extremes of nature have always been a source of fascination. The formidable peaks of the Himalayas, the world's highest mountains, have provided daunting goals for mountaineers —not only the highest peak of all, Mount Everest, but the sheer ascents of Annapurna I and Nanga Parbat, the highest and longest wall climbs, respectively, in existence. The Dead Sea marks the lowest point on the Earth's land surface and attracts crowds of visitors to marvel at its strange clusters of mineral salts and to wallow in the mudbaths and hot springs at its southern reaches. The world's biggest desert, the Great Sahara, is astonishing for the range of landscapes and life contained within its 9 million sq km (3.5 million square miles), though best known for the ethereal beauty of its sweeping, golden sand dunes. And in the same continent the world's longest river, the Nile, flows more than 6,436km (4,000 miles) across Africa to its delta, one of the most fertile places on Earth, where fields and crops are irrigated by its waters today as they have been for thousands of years.

The changing world

Nature is always changing, as is evident from the growing Hawaiian Islands and Iceland's steaming vents. The drift of continents, the ravages of weather, and the natural extinction and evolution of species continues inexorably from millennium to millennium. Other changes, not always positive, have been brought about by human activity, hastening the pace of change and damage. The Amazonian rainforest—only one example of many endangered forests around the globe—is being felled and cleared at an alarming rate, before many native plants and animals have even been identified. Average temperatures are rising, at least in part as a result of industrial emissions, and extreme weather events such as storms and floods are becoming more common: the cumulative impact is felt across the world, from the equator to the polar ice caps. Some species are on the verge of extinction as their habitats disappear. Increased travel, itself an element in these changes, has however also opened the eyes of millions to the effects of climate change on the wonders of their planet.

BELOW Some wonders of the world comprise whole regions or countries. Here, a Coquerel's Sifaka clings to a branch in the Madagascan rainforest (see pages 140–141).

As for manmade monuments, cities and temples, they will crumble in time and be replaced by new wonders. Their remains may linger to perplex future generations, just as the ruined legacies of past ages, half-smothered by jungle growth, eroded by weather or pilfered for new structures, continue to intrigue us today. Sometimes the ravages of war threaten to destroy our wonders before their time, as at Angkor Wat, where scarring and bullet holes tell of recent hostilities. Sometimes the actions of individuals, governments or states are blamed for the defacement of great buildings. An example is Athens, where controversy still rages over the removal by Lord Elgin of part of the classical frieze from the city's landmark, the Parthenon.

Earth and beyond

Looking ever outward and upward, mankind continues its search for the astounding and the extreme, for new challenges to meet and for new technologies. The great adventure into space has brought us images of previously unimaginable wonders such as giant, spiraling columns of stardust, planets of fire, planets of ice, the birth of stars and stars on the point of death. But however many marvels we discover beyond our world, and no matter how many other worlds there may be, there is no denying the beauty of our own. There is also no denying its fragility. Some of the greatest sites celebrated in this book are endangered, even as new wonders of the universe are being discovered.

EUROPE

The Great Fjords 12

Volcanic Iceland 14

The Giant's Causeway 16

Edinburgh Castle 18

Stonehenge 20

The Waddenzee 21

The Camargue 22

Versailles 24

The Eiffel Tower 26

The Pont du Gard 30

Grand' Place 31

Neuschwanstein 32

Golden Lane 34

Wieliczka Salt Mines 35

The Danube Delta 36

The Hofburg 37

The Kapellbrücke 38

The Matterhorn 40

The Colosseum 42

The Leaning Tower of Pisa 44

The Grand Canal 46

St Peter's Basilica 48

Renaissance Europe 52

The Parthenon 54

Metéora Monasteries 56

The Alhambra 58

The Sagrada Família 60

The Kremlin 62

The Great Palace 64

The Trans-Siberian Railway 66

SINCE THE GREAT STONES OF STONEHENGE WERE RAISED more than 4,000 years ago there have been many great feats of design and engineering in Europe—some intended to induce awe, fear or respect, some to glorify deities and some to glorify monarchs and emperors. From the 5th century BC until the 4th century AD the Greek and Roman civilizations exerted a profound influence on Western culture. In Athens the Parthenon, temple of its protecting goddess, symbolized the Greek ascendancy, and when Roman power extended across Europe and North Africa, the Colosseum provided an impressive monument to imperial grandeur and savagery. After the fall of Rome in AD 476 a new Western European civilization emerged, bringing with it soaring cathedrals and palaces, while in Granada the Muslim conquerors of southern Spain built a paradise on Earth among the shaded courts of the Alhambra.

The genius of Greece and Rome took hold of Europe afresh during the Renaissance. Later in Rome, at the heart of Western Christendom, the vast Basilica of St Peter heralded the grandiose

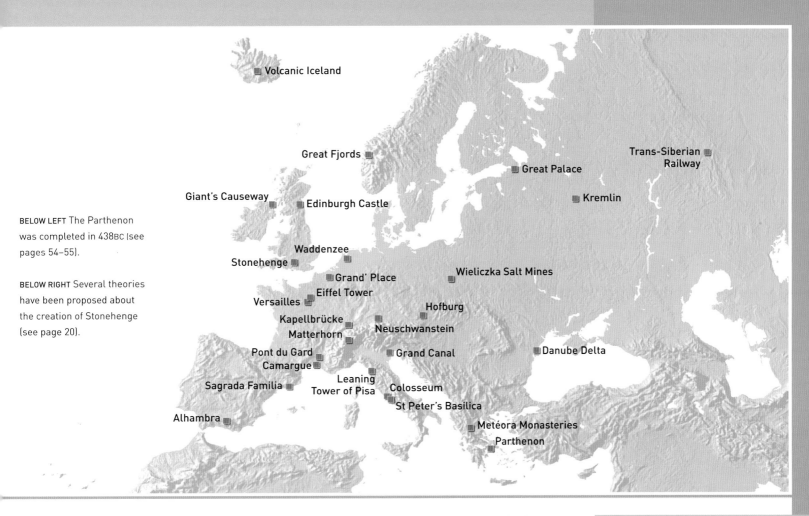

Volcanic Iceland

Great Fjords

Trans-Siberian Railway

Great Palace

Giant's Causeway

Kremlin

Edinburgh Castle

BELOW LEFT The Parthenon was completed in 438BC (see pages 54–55).

Waddenzee

Stonehenge

Grand' Place

Wieliczka Salt Mines

BELOW RIGHT Several theories have been proposed about the creation of Stonehenge (see page 20).

Eiffel Tower

Versailles

Hofburg

Kapellbrücke

Neuschwanstein

Matterhorn

Pont du Gard

Grand Canal

Danube Delta

Camargue

Sagrada Familia

Leaning Tower of Pisa

Colosseum

St Peter's Basilica

Alhambra

Metéora Monasteries

Parthenon

Baroque style. The merchant princes of Venice, who controlled European trade with the East, constructed waterside palaces along the Grand Canal, while their northern equivalents in the Low Countries created the sumptuous Grand' Place in Brussels. Renaissance influence spread as far as Moscow, where the cathedral of St Michael the Archangel was built in the citadel of the Kremlin.

The evolution of the modern nation-state required palaces appropriate to the rulers' status. In Vienna the Hapsburg dynasty ruled an empire from the Hofburg, and Versailles made a noble setting for the Sun King, Louis XIV, and his successors in France.

A new age dawned with the 18th-century Industrial Revolution, which transformed the rural economy of Western Europe into an economy of machines, factories, teeming towns and mass production of consumer goods. The Eiffel Tower in Paris and the rails of the Trans-Siberian Railway, stretching from Moscow to the far coast of Asia, are two potent symbols of this age of machinery.

THE GREAT FJORDS

■ **Norway's coastline is so indented that its length is impossible to calculate, but it has been estimated at around 25,000km (15,500 miles).**

■ *Fjord* **is a Norwegian word meaning 'an arm of the sea', and is applied to any long, narrow land indentations flooded by the sea.**

■ **From the top of its sheer cliffs to the bottom of its waters, Sognefjord is up to 1,200m (4,000ft) deep.**

SITTING IN A SMALL BOAT between the gray and forbidding walls of the great Norwegian fjords, it is easy to see how the legends of Valhalla and the brooding Nordic gods arose. On a dull and misty day, it is also not difficult to imagine the Viking longships in these mysterious waters, oars dipping into the still water as the Norsemen headed off to explore the coasts of more gentle lands.

Scandinavia's fjords were created many thousands of years ago during the ice ages, when glaciers ground their way across the land, carving deep U-shaped valleys. Sheer cliffs at the water's edge show tell-tale signs of scratching and scouring by the ice, and the fjords are shallower at the point where they enter the sea—here, the glaciers ran out of the power necessary to gouge through the bedrock. Not all geologists accept that the fjords were formed entirely by glacial action; the beds of some of the deepest fjords, such as Sognefjord, in Norway, are considered too far below sealevel to have been wholly carved in this way.

The Norwegian coast is deeply indented with fjords from Stavanger, in the south, to the border with Russia. Bergen, easily accessible by air and by ferry, makes a good base for exploration. Unlike the country's cold and mountainous interior, the coastal climate is temperate, modified by the North Atlantic current. Some 50,000 islands lie offshore, many supporting small settlements.

Fjords lead inland, to where great ice caps once lay. Little remains of the ice cap that ruled supreme until

RIGHT Waterfalls plunge down the sheer slopes of Geirangerfjord, which jointly with Nærøyfjord was declared a UNESCO World Heritage Site in 2005.

LEFT Visitors take a trip by inflatable raft on the clear waters of Smeerenburg Fjord, off the island of Spitsbergen in the most northerly part of Norway, formerly a centre of the international whaling industry.

THE HURTIGRUTEN

The Hurtigruten is a passenger and freight service that sails regularly from Bergen to Kirkenes, in the far north, following the rugged coastline and stopping at more than 30 settlements along the way. The voyage takes seven days in all and brings communication and supplies to isolated communities, ranging from towns to hamlets, some of which are on tiny offshore islands.

Since 1893 the Hurtigruten has been an essential coastal service. When it first started, the route had never been mapped.

In recent years, its 12 vessels have also doubled as a tourist attraction, as passengers take the opportunity to enjoy the cruise past dramatic fjord scenery from the fertile south to the Arctic Circle.

FJORDS GREAT AND SMALL

Sognefjord is Norway's biggest fjord. This finger of the sea is 180km (112 miles) long, although it is rarely more than 5km (3 miles) wide. It has several branches, including Nærøyfjord, where the walls are so close that ships sailing down it seem to disappear into a tunnel.

The great fjord carves its way through barren, desolate scenery to the highest mountains in Norway. Most of the way, the flanking mountains loom over the water and it always seems to be in twilight.

One of the smallest but most spectacular fjords is Geirangerfjord, snaking along for 16km (10 miles) with waterfalls cascading down its slopes and a village at each end.

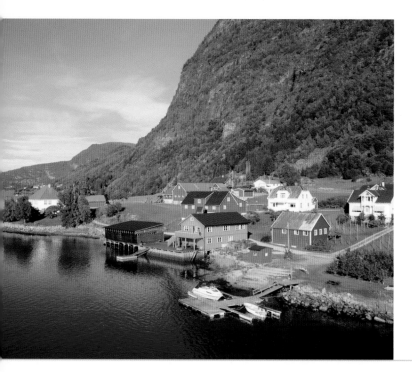

10,000 years ago, only isolated patches of ice, such as the Jostedalsbreen to the north of Sognefjorden. The pressure of the ice caps forced ice to flow seaward in individual valley glaciers. This process can be seen today at the vast Søndre Strømfjord on Greenland's west coast, where a glacier still flows over its head, producing green-blue icebergs.

In Norway the fjords make communication by land difficult, for villages that may lie just a few miles apart by boat are sometimes hundreds of miles apart by road. In the past many settlements had no land communications at all because the steep-sided fjords made permanent roads impossible. Some remote places still rely on the sea-going vessels of the Hurtigruten service for contact.

LEFT Around Sognefjord, colorful wooden houses cluster between the cliffs and the water.

SEE ALSO

Patagonia page 209

VOLCANIC ICELAND

■ **Iceland's highest point is Hvannadalshnúkur, 2,119m (6,952ft) up, on the volcanic massif of Öræfajökull in the south.**

■ **Hraunhafnartangi, the northernmost point of Iceland, just touches the Arctic Circle.**

■ **In 1963 a fissure eruption created Surtsey, a new island off the south coast.**

ICELAND IS A LAND like no other. Only the southern coastal plains support much vegetation, and most of the country's farms are found here. The interior of the country is a barren, lunar-looking landscape, almost uninhabited, especially in winter. The vast majority of the country's population of about 320,000 lives in the capital, Reykjavik.

LEFT Birthplace of icebergs: at the Jökulsárlón glacial lagoon, icebergs break away from a glacier and cluster drifting in a deep lake until they float away to sea.

RIGHT Near Reykjavik, a meandering river has over time cut down through the mountain rock to create a dramatic valley landscape.

Iceland is a volcanic island with no native natural building materials such as wood. There are few stone buildings here, and the roofs are mainly corrugated iron. The land itself is still being built by nature—constantly pulled into two parts because of its position. It lies across the vast undersea split known as the mid-Atlantic ridge, which is stretched as Greenland and Scotland continue to move apart and cause sudden upheavals and volcanic eruptions.

The opening of the Atlantic Ocean began some 180 million years ago, and Greenland began to separate from

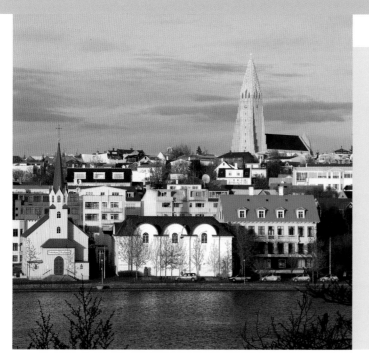

SETTLEMENT IN ICELAND

In the ninth and tenth centuries AD, settlers from Scandinavia and from Norse communities in Britain arrived at Iceland, the last European country to be settled. The first to make a home here was Ingólfur Arnarson, a Norwegian chieftain, who set up a farm on the present site of Reykjavik in 874. In 930 Icelandic society was firmly established and the Althingi (parliament) was instituted, meeting once a year to adopt laws and deliver judgments.

Icelandic adventurers discovered Greenland in the late tenth century, and in about 1000 Leifur Eiríksson was the first recorded European to set foot on the American continent.

LEFT The Hallgrímskirkja church punctuates Reykjavik's skyline.
RIGHT Reykjavik's statue of Leifur Eiríksson, a gift from the United States government in 1930.

Scotland 60 million years ago, giving rise to the Tertiary volcanic provinces of the north of Ireland, northwest Scotland and southeast Greenland. The oldest rocks in Iceland are less than 60 million years old, and the island has continued to grow since that time, piling sheet upon sheet of lava from long fissure eruptions that provided the foundation for the active volcanoes of today. Despite the internal heat of Iceland, the island was covered by a sheet of ice during the last ice age and the remnants of that sheet form the ice caps and glaciers seen here today. Of the 102,797sq km (39,690 square miles) or so that Iceland covers, about 11.5 percent is made up of ice caps and glaciers.

Vatnajökull, on the southeast of Iceland, is the largest ice cap in Europe, covering many geothermal sources. One gives rise to Grimsvötn, a unique lake within the ice cap with a surface that is normally frozen solid. The source of the Jökulsá á Fjöllum River lies beneath the northern part of Vatnajökull, with hot springs under the ice keeping a chimney open to the lake above. In 1983 a canoeing expedition lowered its boats down the chimney and then paddled through the ice tunnel to the open river and down to the North Atlantic Ocean.

SEE ALSO
- *Beppu* page 105
- *Deception Island* page 236
- *The Hawaiian Islands* page 182

EXPLOSIVE LANDSCAPE

Evidence of volcanism is everywhere, from the major active volcanic cones such as Hekla (major eruption in 1947, lesser eruptions in 1991 and 2000) to extinct craters, many with spectacular lakes and extensive hot-spring areas. These springs range from sulfurous pools of boiling mud to crystal clear, turquoise-blue siliceous springs and geysers. Stóri Geysir (Great Geyser) at Geysir has given its name to all other spouting springs, and although it spouts less frequently today, it still performs spectacularly.

Hot water is Iceland's geological resource and its value has long been recognized. Reykjavik is centrally heated by the island's subterranean hot water, which is pumped to all public and domestic buildings.

THE GIANT'S CAUSEWAY

■ There are about 40,000 basalt columns making up the Giant's Causeway.

■ The tallest columns rise about 12.2m (40ft) from sea level.

■ At some points in the cliffs they are 27.4m (90ft) thick.

■ Molten basalt has been recorded flowing downhill at speeds of more than 48km (30 miles) per hour.

THE STRANGE COLUMNS OF the Giant's Causeway in County Antrim, Northern Ireland, seem to have been fashioned as part of a vast, manmade architectural monument. Wedged tightly together, they descend in tiers, forming irregular stepping stones from the cliffside and out into the sea. Most of the columns are strictly hexagonal, though some have four, five, seven or eight straight sides. Their creation is, inevitably, the theme of legend, but in fact they were the result of the reshaping of an active landscape.

In the early days of the North Atlantic Ocean, the newly formed seaway flowing between the recently separated continents of North America and Europe was a still-developing feature: the body of the North Atlantic was in place, but its edges were still being formed and re-formed. The western coast of Greenland separated from Canada about 80 million years ago but the southeastern coast was still firmly attached to the opposing northwestern coast of the British Isles. Some 20 million years later

FINGAL'S CAVE

Columnar basalts are not confined to Northern Ireland, and another of the best-known examples of this phenomenon is in the Inner Hebrides, off Scotland's west coast.

On Staffa, the columns are well developed over a large part of the island, and a huge cave where the sea has eroded the columns is known as Fingal's Cave, named for a mythical giant.

Fingal's Cave has figured in many poems and novels over the centuries, and a rather rough boat trip to the island in 1829 by the composer Felix Mendelssohn inspired his famous orchestral overture known as *The Hebrides*.

LEFT The width of a column—typically about 46cm (18in)—depends on how quickly the lava cooled.

ABOVE Visitors can cross the site by walking over the columns to The Island, at the edge of the sea.

these coasts began to separate and there were major volcanoes on what are now the islands of Skye, Rum, Mull and Arran, on the Scottish mainland at Ardnamurchan Point, and also to the south in Ireland at Slieve Gullion, Carlingford and Mourne. These ancient volcanoes must have been splendid sights in their prime, but the greatest record of this episode lies in the flood, or plateau, basalts. Basalt is a particularly hot, fluid lava, able to spread across large areas relatively easily, and constitutes the bulk of lava features found in this whole volcanic area.

Hot liquids contract as they cool, and molten lava is no exception. However, when lava eventually cools sufficiently to crystallize, it tends to crack in a regular pattern, usually a hexagonal design similar to the cracks

THE MYTH OF THE GIANT'S CAUSEWAY

Legend has it that the Giant's Causeway was built by the Irish giant Finn Mac Cool, who drove the columns into the seabed one by one so that he could walk to Scotland to fight his rival Finn Gall. When his work was finished, Finn Mac Cool decided to take a rest. Meanwhile, Finn Gall walked across to Ireland to size up his opponent, and was amazed and frightened by the size of the sleeping giant, especially after Mac Cool's wife told him that this was, in fact, only the giant's baby.

Fearing for his life at the thought of how big the baby's father might be, Finn Gall beat a hasty retreat, destroying the causeway behind him. All that remains of it today is on the Antrim coast.

formed in the bottom of a muddy pond that dries out in a hot summer. The significant difference with lava is that the cracks extend right down through the flow from top to bottom. The result is a distinctive network of basalt columns, all packed incredibly closely together with just the thinnest of gaps in between. The causeway was first publicized by the Bishop of Londonderry, who visited in 1692. It became known as the 'eighth wonder of the natural world', attracting visitors in increasing numbers, while scholarly societies in Dublin and London long debated whether it had been formed by humans or by nature—or indeed by giants.

SEE ALSO

■ *The Devil's Tower* page 172
■ *Uluru (Ayer's Rock)* page 218

EDINBURGH CASTLE

■ **The One O'Clock Gun is fired every day except Sunday at 1pm and is used by locals as an infallible time-check.**

■ **The Scottish crown dates from 1540 and is of Scottish gold set with 94 pearls, 10 diamonds and 33 gems.**

■ **A small fountain in the Esplanade marks the spot where those convicted of witchcraft were killed.**

THE HIGH BASALT ROCK that looms over Edinburgh has probably been the site of a fort since the Iron Age. Edwin, King of Northumbria, rebuilt the original fortifications in the seventh century and some 400 years later Malcolm III and his queen, Margaret, took up residence there. Only one building, named after the Queen, remains from that period: St Margaret's Chapel, the oldest surviving structure in the city. Robert the Bruce had the castle's defences destroyed in 1314 to prevent its use as a stronghold by the English.

The castle, now seen by about a million visitors a year, is a conglomeration of buildings added, embellished

ABOVE A map of Edinburgh in 1588, shortly after the castle defences were strengthened, showing how the fortress dominated the city.

and rearranged over the course of around 700 years. An L-shaped keep, known as King David's Tower, was built at the southeast corner of Castle Rock and later partly incorporated into the 16th-century Half Moon Battery, which was raised on a platform for the defence of the castle's northeastern flank. The King's Lodging and great hall were added in the 15th and 16th centuries and altered in the 17th century. Making up the fourth side of the square of palace buildings within the castle complex is the Scottish National War Memorial, constructed shortly after World War I. Another wing contains the banqueting hall and the Great Hall, meeting place of the Scottish

THE ESPLANADE

For three weeks in August the Castle Esplanade, the ceremonial parade ground outside the castle entrance, hosts the Edinburgh Military Tattoo, a world-famous military and musical display.

The Esplanade was built in 1753. In the early 19th century it was widened and given walls and railings, signifying the castle's transition from military barracks to symbolic landmark. The castle is always guarded, though, and acts as the headquarters of the Scottish Division and several regiments, as well as housing military museums.

The first Edinburgh Tattoo was presented on the Esplanade in 1950 and since then more than 12 million people have joined the audience at the castle. In addition, some 100 million television viewers tune in to watch it every year.

parliament until 1693, and the royal apartments are ranged along the eastern side of Palace Yard.

Among the royal apartments is the tiny room where Mary, Queen of Scots gave birth to the future King James VI of Scotland and James I of England in 1566. She had fled to the castle to have her child in safety after the shocking murder of her secretary and suspected lover, David Rizzio (1533–66), by a band of conspirators who included the Queen's own husband, Henry Stuart, Lord Darnley. In 1603, on the death of the childless Elizabeth I, James succeeded to the throne of England and moved his court to London. From then on Edinburgh Castle, former royal residence, became an occasional stopover for monarchs and served largely as a military fortress and prison. During the wars with France in the 18th and 19th centuries, French prisoners of war were held in its vaults and the graffiti they etched into the walls can still be seen.

The Scottish regalia—crown, scepter and sword of state—were walled up here after the union of Scottish and English parliaments in 1707, and are now on display in the stone-vaulted Crown Room.

MONS MEG

This mighty cannon was made for the Duke of Burgundy in Belgium in 1449. The Duke duly passed it on to his nephew, King James II of Scotland, who employed it in 1455 against his enemies the Douglas family at their stronghold, Threave Castle, bringing a two-month siege to an abrupt end. Mons Meg's last action came in the 17th century when the cannon exploded while firing a salute.

For more than 70 years the cannon was kept in the Tower of London, but the writer Sir Walter Scott called for its return to Scotland in the 19th century and Meg found a retirement home at Edinburgh Castle in 1829.

BELOW View of St Cuthbert's Church, with the castle and the Old Town perched high above.

SEE ALSO
■ *The Hofburg*
page 37
■ *Neuschwanstein*
page 32

STONEHENGE

- Stonehenge is at the heart of a vast landscape of Neolithic and Bronze Age ceremonial monuments.

- The sandstone uprights are made of super-hard sarsen stone from the nearby Marlborough Downs.

- The bluestones within the sandstone ring are thought to have been transported from the Preseli Mountains of South Wales, possibly on rafts along water routes.

ONE OF MANY THEORIES about Stonehenge suggests that it was an observatory used to calculate the passage of time, since the entrance and the center of the inner horseshoe of stones are aligned with the midsummer and midwinter sun. Recent discoveries of high-status burials nearby suggest that it was a place of healing. Whatever their original purpose, these giant monoliths from another age still evoke a powerful atmosphere. There were several building phases, spanning nearly a thousand years. First, around 3000 BC, a circular ditch and bank were created, possibly with a ring of 56 massive wooden posts inside. Some 500 years later, bluestones were arranged in two concentric arcs inside the ditch. These were replaced around 2100 BC with huge sandstone blocks topped with lintels. Within this circle was a horseshoe arrangement of trilithons (two upright stones supporting a lintel). The bluestones were reinstalled to form a horseshoe and a circle inside the sandstone ring.

AVEBURY

A few miles from Stonehenge, at Avebury in Wiltshire, is a stone circle thought to be the largest in the world. A huge ditch around the outer stone circle encloses an area of nearly 12ha (30 acres).

Created between about 2850 and 2200 BC, the monument consisted of an estimated 247 standing stones forming an outer circle surrounding two smaller circles; another 97 or so pairs formed an avenue probably used as a processional route.

In medieval times the stones were objects of suspicion, and many were broken up or buried. Excavations in the 1930s found the body of one of the demolition team crushed beneath the one he was toppling. Many of the stones visible today have been re-erected.

LEFT The circle formed by Stonehenge is best viewed from above.

THE WADDENZEE

- The Waddenzee extends across some 500km (310 miles), from the Netherlands to Denmark.

- Its waters are 2–3m (7–10ft) deep.

- It is home to more than 10,000 species of plant and animal.

ABOVE In winter, about 130,000 barnacle geese migrate annually from northern Russia to feed on the marshes of the Waddenzee.

BELOW The watery landscape of the Waddenzee is constantly changing, shaped by the forces of rivers, the tides and the wind.

THE WADDENZEE IS ONE of Europe's most important and productive wetland areas. The shallow waters and extensive intertidal areas of sand and mud flats, shallow sandbanks, and salt marsh are protected from the forces of the North Sea by a string of offshore islands. More than 10 million birds from as far afield as northeast Canada, Greenland, Iceland and Siberia congregate here to feed, and many birds breed here during the summer, especially on the many remote islands. More than 100 species of fish, and common and grey seals, also live around the Waddenzee for at least part of the year.

Much of the coastline of the southern North Sea is under considerable development pressure. The construction of ports and embankments to protect against rising sea levels has resulted in the loss of much of the original salt marsh. Nonetheless, what remains still represents the most extensive wetland area in Europe.

VULNERABLE WILDLIFE

The population of the common seal in the Waddenzee, as elsewhere in the North Sea, has severely reduced in recent years. A ban on seal hunting and a reduction of some pollutants had led to an increase in numbers to 10,000 by the early 1980s, but in 1988 large numbers of dead common seals with distemper virus were reported. It is thought that the accumulation of manmade compounds and pesticides in the seals' bodies had reduced the effectiveness of their immune systems and made them more susceptible to such infections. Around 60% of the Waddenzee seals died. Numbers recovered, but the virus struck again in 2002, halving the population. The remaining population is thought to be immune to distemper, and is increasing slowly, but its reproduction level is low.

SEE ALSO
- *The Camargue* page 22
- *The Danube Delta* page 36
- *The Okavango Delta* page 144

THE CAMARGUE

- The Camargue lies at the mouth of the River Rhône, in the Golfe des Saintes-Maries in the South of France.

- It extends over 1,466 sq km (566 square miles).

- More than 300 species of migrant birds have been recorded here. Nesting birds include the collared pratincole, which breeds nowhere else in France.

THIS HUGE COASTAL WETLAND area is one of the most important of its type in Europe. When the Roman and Greek empires were at the height of their powers, the Mediterranean coast supported a mosaic of wetlands, which remained largely intact until the 19th century. Large areas were then drained to create agricultural land and to destroy the breeding grounds of the mosquito. As a result, very little remains, but the Camargue has survived more or less intact—although human intervention, such as the development of the salt pans, has brought changes to the landscape.

LEFT A summer visitor: the collared pratincole, a wading bird that migrates to the Camargue from tropical Africa.

RIGHT The Camargue is one of the few European habitats for the greater flamingo.

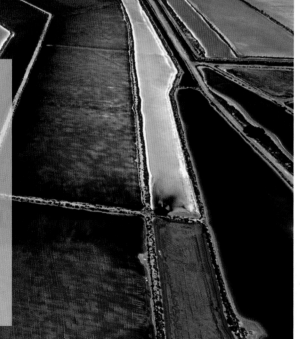

SALT PANS

One of the easiest ways of obtaining salt, historically an important trading commodity, is by allowing the sun to evaporate sea water, which leaves a residue of salt and other trace elements. In the salt pans of the Camargue, sea water is moved by pumps through a series of shallow ponds or pans, becoming more and more salty at each stage, until it reaches the final pan, where the last of the water evaporates to leave the crystalline salt.

The complete predictability of this artificial system guarantees suitable conditions for birds to roost, feed and breed. It is this manmade system that has given the Camargue its importance as a major site for the greater flamingo, as well as for other avian visitors.

BRINE SHRIMPS

Very few animals can adapt to highly saline waters. Those that have done so usually occur in very large numbers, and the brine shrimp, *Artemia salina*, is no exception.

This shrimp, no more than 15mm (about ½in) long, can live in salt levels ranging from less than a third of that of sea water to over six times as much. This enables it to survive periods of inundation by fresh water as well as times of extreme drought. It achieves this feat by having a skin that is impermeable to both salt and water, and transfer of both is restricted to very confined, strictly controlled areas of its body.

The Camargue is an intricate mix of beaches, sand dunes, reed beds, brackish lakes, riverine forest and pasture lands, together with the extensive salt pans. This array of varied habitats, combined with the strategic geographic location of the Camargue, makes it a vital staging post in the migration routes of many bird species. Millions of ducks, geese and waders visit each year from as far afield as Siberia and northern Europe. Some of these birds are merely transient visitors on longer journeys; others come here to nest and breed, attracted by the combination of suitable roosting sites and the adjacent feeding areas. Ducks spend a large part of the day in relative safety on the many brackish ponds in the region. In the early morning and late evening they can fly to the nearby marshes to feed. Many of these marshes are privately managed for wild fowling, an important part of the traditional economy of the area. Tens of thousands of birds, mainly ducks, are shot during the hunting season.

The unusual conditions of very high salinity created by the salt pans make the area especially suitable for the brine shrimp, an important food for some species of bird, particularly the pink or greater flamingo. These strikingly beautiful birds are a symbol of the success of the management of the Camargue: since 1944 the number of breeding pairs of greater flamingos has risen steadily. Central to their success is the presence of secure nesting sites in the salt pans.

The Camargue is also famous for its local breed of black cattle and, more particularly, for the celebrated roaming herds of semi-wild white horses, thought to be descendants of primitive horses.

SEE ALSO
■ *The Danube Delta* page 36
■ *The Okavango Delta* page 144
■ *The Waddenzee* page 21

BELOW White Camargue horses on a beach are reflected in the shallow water.

VERSAILLES

■ The architecture of Versailles influenced the design of royal palaces across Europe.

■ The garden frontage of the palace is 640m (2,100ft) long.

■ World War I formally ended in the palace's Hall of Mirrors in 1919, where Germany and the Allied Powers signed the Treaty of Versailles.

VERSAILLES, LESS THAN 24km (15 miles) from Paris, was chosen by King Louis XIII (1601–43) as the site for a modest chateau that would serve him as a base for his hunting expeditions. His son, Louis XIV (1638–1715), also enjoyed hunting but had more elaborate plans for the estate. Dissatisfied with other palaces available (including the Louvre and the Tuileries), he decided, in 1660, to turn Versailles into a vast royal enclave. Everything was to be the ultimate in magnificence, and he would build on such a scale that eventually the whole French court could be accommodated.

Work began in 1661, and in the course of two years Louis XIV, who came to be known as the Sun King, spent a vast amount of money, provoking anguished protests from the treasury. In fact, building was to continue for decades, involving many thousands of workmen and ever-increasing expense. The original architect, Louis Le Vau, was succeeded by Jules Hardouin Mansart, who worked on Versailles for 30 years. André Le Nôtre was responsible for the landscaping, and his grand design for the gardens so surpassed the original chateau that it was decided to turn it into a far more sumptuous palace.

At the heart of the building is the Hall of Mirrors, a huge gallery with 17 windows overlooking the gardens, matched by enormous mirrors on the opposite wall. Paintings by Charles Le Brun present a flattering account of the reign of Louis XIV between 1661 and 1678; this artistic celebration of the king helped to enhance the

ABOVE The Temple of Love in the grounds of the Petit Trianon, a small palace in the Versailles grounds originally built for Louis XV's mistress, Madame de Pompadour.

OPPOSITE PAGE Le Nôtre's gardens represent the height of the French formal style, providing a spacious setting for the classical buildings of the palace complex.

OUTDOOR THEATER
Parisian nobility flocked to the gardens during the early years of the Sun King's reign, and in 1664, 1668 and 1674 the grounds became the backdrop for elaborate artistic extravaganzas, featuring operas by Lully and plays by Molière and Racine. The whole place was like a stage set, with entire re-created landscapes, such as the 'Grand Canal', with its own 'Little Venice'. This tradition of make-believe was continued by Louis XIV's successors, most notoriously by Marie Antoinette. She had her own theater built in the grounds and even created a rustic hamlet, stocked with animals and staffed by shepherds and other country people, where she and her friends could play at being peasants.

aura of royalty that Louis was determined to cultivate. Versailles became his permanent residence in 1682, and the French court was soon established there. Complex rituals developed, and precise rules of etiquette were observed. Hopeful courtiers would come to Versailles and wait, sometimes in vain, for an opportunity to witness the King's Levée or Coucher—the rising or retiring to bed.

Louis XIV died in 1715. Louis XV (1710–74) engaged the architect Gabriel to carry out further work, including building an opera salon, and the palace known as the Petit Trianon. Under Louis XVI (1754–93) a fine library was added and his queen, Marie Antoinette (1755–93), took over the Petit Trianon. But in October 1789 revolutionaries reached Versailles and the palace was invaded.

SEE ALSO

■ *The Great Palace* page 64
■ *The Hofburg* page 37
■ *Neuschwanstein* page 32

THE GARDENS

Versailles' gardens were designed to house a wealth of sculpture. The Water Parterre, in front of the Hall of Mirrors, has two lakes, each with four statues representing rivers of France. The Loire and Loiret are by Regnaudin, the Saône and the Rhône are by Tuby, the rivers Marne and Seine are by Le Hongre, and the Garonne and the Dordogne rivers are by Coysevox.

A magnificent work in lead by Tuby depicts Apollo, god of the sun, driving his horses and chariot out of a lake. The Fountain of Enceladus by Gaspard Marsy, dating from 1676, portrays the tortured figure of the Titan Enceladus virtually buried beneath rocks.

SUPER SITE
THE EIFFEL TOWER

- The entire structure weighs about 10,000 metric tons (11,000 tons) and contains around 2.5 million rivets.

- The base of the tower encloses an area of 1.6ha (4 acres).

- About three million visitors go up the tower every year.

- There are 1,665 steps to the top of the tower. Visitors now take an elevator from the second floor.

For more than a hundred years the Eiffel Tower has been synonymous with Paris, its silhouette instantly recognizable around the world. Visible throughout the city, it soars above the River Seine, opposite the Trocadéro Palace by the Pont d'Iéna. Its slender grace and strength combine in a symbol of the achievements of the industrial age—a daring demonstration of the skills and ambitions of engineers and designers in the late 19th century.

BUILDING TECHNIQUES and materials accelerated the pace of change in the 19th century, and the challenge preoccupying many engineers—and politicians—of the day was to build a structure over 300m (1,000ft) high. French engineer Gustave Eiffel (1832–1923) and his company produced plans for such a tower at the end of 1884—largely the work of Eiffel's head of research, Maurice Koechlin. When a competition was announced two years later for schemes suitable for the 1889 Paris Exposition, more than 100 were submitted, and Eiffel was chosen to create the world's tallest structure.

LEFT Eiffel's career as an engineer ranged from bridge-building to designing the internal structure of the Statue of Liberty and involvement in an attempt to build the Panama Canal.

LEFT The Champ de Mars, beneath the Tower, is a favored Paris venue that can accommodate more than half a million people at events such as televised concerts.

BELOW RIGHT The Eiffel tower under construction, July 1888. It was opened only eight months later for the Paris Exposition of 1889.

Eiffel had built a number of railroad bridges and had a reputation for solving the most technically challenging problems. He was unusual among his peers for his reliance on calculation and precision, and his understanding of environmental stresses such as windforce led to the ingenious use of filigree iron, reducing the surface area to a minimum.

Speedy construction

More than 18,000 separate components were used to construct the tower, many of them prefabricated and produced with the aid of detailed technical drawings. The tallest tower in the world was built by a team of around 250 men at a speed that still seems phenomenal:

ABOVE From the day it opened the tower became a huge tourist attraction, a symbol recognized across the world. An estimated 250 million people have now visited it.

THE HISTORY

- **1884** Eiffel produces plans for a '300m Tower'.
- **1886** Competition announced for Paris Exposition designs.
- **1887** Construction begins
- **1889** Tower opens on March 31.
- **1926-36** Illuminated Citroën advert displayed on the tower.
- **1935** Tower becomes the city's TV transmission antenna.
- **1964** Eiffel Tower proclaimed an historic monument.

just 26 months. This rapid construction was possible only because of Eiffel's ability to plan ahead with the utmost precision. The 16 piers on which the tower stands (four to each leg of the base) incorporated hydraulic jacks to allow for exact alignment when the first platform came to be built. Only very minor adjustment was necessary, but without this facility it might never have been possible to complete the building.

For all the tower's social and its curiosity value, it had a serious function from the start. Gustave Eiffel was a scientist, who recoiled from the idea that his tower was a mere ornament. He installed meteorological equipment at the top to investigate weather conditions at altitude and compare readings with those on the ground; and he also used the tower to conduct experiments in aerodynamics, constructing a wind tunnel at the base. The Eiffel Tower continued to facilitate pioneering scientific experiments, being used in radio transmission and housing the country's first radio and television stations.

SEE ALSO
■ *The Leaning Tower of Pisa* page 44
■ *The Statue of Liberty* page 154

LEFT The illuminated tower complements a pyrotechnic display. The millennium celebration of 2000 was perhaps the most spectacular occasion in its history.

RIGHT A dizzying prospect: intrepid record-breakers have climbed the tower by mountain bike, monocycle and motorbike, and descended by abseiling and parachuting.

SUPPORTERS AND DETRACTORS

When the Eiffel Tower began to rise, a group of writers and artists signed a letter protesting about the effect that it would have on the Paris skyline and claiming that it was an insult to the city's great buildings.

At one point building work was halted because of the fears of local residents that both their lives and their property were in danger: a mathematician had claimed that the whole structure would collapse before it reached 229m (750ft). Eiffel, who was already bearing the majority of the cost of the project, agreed to continue construction entirely at his own risk.

During the Paris Exposition, two million visitors felt safe enough to take the elevator to the the first, second and third platforms. Later, the first platform housed a restaurant; the author Guy de Maupassant is said to have frequented it because it was the only place in Paris from which he did not have a view of the tower. *Le Figaro* newspaper even opened an office on the second platform, 116m (380ft) up.

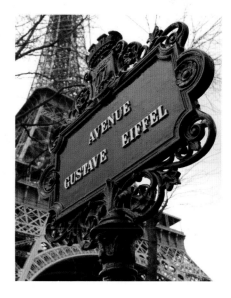

ABOVE A Paris street sign commemorates Gustave Eiffel. The elaborate style was fashionable when the tower was constructed.

THE PONT DU GARD

■ The Pont du Gard is a UNESCO World Heritage Site.

■ Only one of the lower six arches actually spans the river, and the arches in each tier are not identical.

■ The aqueduct was built with a total drop of about 17m (56ft) between the water source and the city of Nîmes.

THE PONT DU GARD was built by the Romans to carry fresh water across the Gardon River to Nîmes in southern France. Measuring 49m (160ft) high and 274m (900ft) long, it was part of an aqueduct, a water supply system of conduits and bridges, stretching 48km (30 miles) from a spring near Uzès. It was built by the Roman general and proconsul Agrippa (c.63–12 BC), probably begun in 19 BC.

The Pont du Gard has three tiers of arches: six at the bottom, 11 in the middle, and 35 along the top directly below the water channel. The builders used mortar only on the top level, and rough knobs protruding from the sides were used to attach wooden scaffolding, for carrying out maintenance work when mineral deposits accumulated in the water channel. A modern visitor center shows how the channel was built and maintained, and you can still cross the river via the bridge below.

ROMAN WATERWORKS

In the first century AD an official called Frontinus was the superintendent of Rome's water supply. The technical handbook he wrote on the subject, *De Aquis*, goes into great mathematical detail about the dimensions of pipes and the construction of aqueducts, but also gives an insight into some of the sharp practices he encountered.

He tells of landowners who intercepted the public water supply running past their fields and diverted it to irrigate their crops. Confiscation of the land in question was a possible penalty for those caught in the act. Frontinus also reveals that a secret and elaborate network of pipes was detected beneath the streets of Rome, illicitly supplying water from public sources to private premises and shops.

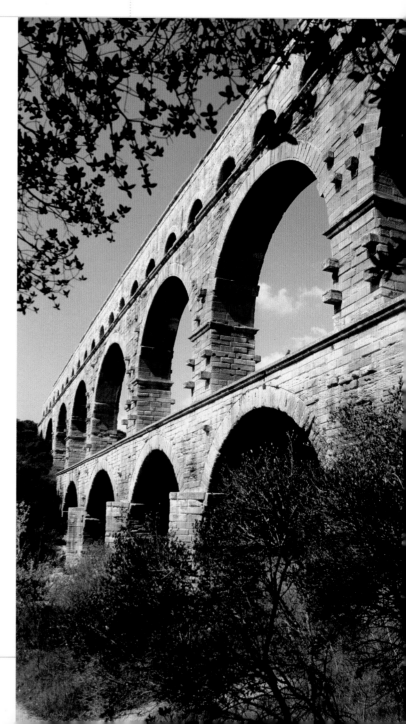

RIGHT The water channel runs along the top tier. Wide arches and pointed breakwaters on the footings enable the structure to withstand flood surges.

GRAND' PLACE

■ The original wooden guild houses on the site were replaced in flamboyant baroque style following a 36-hour French bombardment in 1695, when 16 churches and thousands of houses were destroyed.

■ There is a flower market every morning in the square, and spectacular illuminations at Christmas.

GRAND' PLACE, IN BELGIUM'S capital, Brussels, is a stage-set of pinnacles, curlicues, statues, gargoyles, medallions and heraldic beasts. Work started on the town hall, the Hôtel de Ville, which occupies most of one side, in 1402. The dazzling 91m (300ft) spire, designed by Jan van Ruysbroek, dates from the 1450s. On the façade are more than 100 statues, 19th-century replacements of the originals. Inside are sumptuously decorated rooms hung with Brussels tapestries and paintings.

The Maison du Roi, opposite the Hôtel de Ville, was once the guild house of the bakers. It was used by the Spanish-appointed governors of the Low Countries and rebuilt between 1873 and 1895 in the 16th-century style. Among the other gold-scrolled merchants' guild houses is La Louve (The She-Wolf) and No. 5, which belonged to the Guild of Archers and displays a relief of Romulus and Remus being suckled by a wolf. The gable shows a phoenix, the emblem of Brussels.

BELOW The Duke of Brabant built the Maison du Roi to rival the magnificence of the town hall and assert aristocratic power.

ABOVE Shoppers browse the morning flower market, surrounded by richly decorated guild houses.

SEE ALSO
■ *Golden Lane* page 34

MANNEKEN PIS
On the Rue de l'Etuve, not far from the Grand' Place, is the little bronze figure of a small boy passing water into the marble basin of a fountain. The 61cm (2ft) statue dates from the 19th century, but replaces much older figures. One legend about Manneken Pis has him naughtily bedewing the front steps of a wicked fairy, who retaliated by turning him to stone.

The statue is dressed up on special occasions. His first costume was presented to him in 1698 by the Elector of Bavaria, and in 1747 Louis XV of France sent him a suit of brocade embroidered in gold. More than 250 of his costumes are displayed in the Maison du Roi.

NEUSCHWANSTEIN

■ Neuschwanstein took 17 years to build.

■ Fifteen men worked for four and a half years just carving the King's bed.

■ In 1886, only three months after moving in, King Ludwig II was declared unfit to rule, and the next night was found dead in nearby Lake Starnberg.

HERRENCHIEMSEE

Ludwig bought an island in Chiemsee lake in 1873 with the idea of creating his own version of Versailles. He built a bigger and, to his mind, better Hall of Mirrors and a more sumptuous version of Louis XIV's Versailles bedroom, supposedly reserved for the use of that long-dead monarch.

The gardens were created in the French style too, but after seven years' work the money ran out and the palace was never completed. It was subsequently opened to the public.

NEUSCHWANSTEIN IS A FANTASY made real—a fairy-tale castle festooned with balconies and turrets, rising high above the trees in the Bavarian Alps. Vast and substantial, it was influenced by the work of the theatrical set designer Christian Jank, and was commissioned by King Ludwig II of Bavaria (1845–86) as a backdrop against which he might act out the stuff of German romantic legend.

King Ludwig had grown up in the nearby castle of Hohenschwangau, a medieval fortress restored by his father, Maximilian II, and decorated with wall paintings depicting, among other subjects, the legend of Lohengrin.

Ludwig appears to have identified with Lohengrin, the Knight of the Swan, and he developed an obsession with German mythology. A performance of Richard Wagner's opera Lohengrin in 1861 left him enchanted, and when he succeeded to the throne three years later, at the age of 18, one of his first acts was to summon Wagner for an audience. Now with money at his disposal and all the power of a king, Ludwig became Wagner's patron, paid his debts, and promised to provide the composer with his longed-for theater and festival, in the little town of Bayreuth. Wagner would create the German legend on stage on a grand scale and enact struggles between good and evil in front of an audience. Meanwhile, Ludwig would create a fantastic fairy-tale castle worthy in every way of the ancient German knights. But his mounting debts brought him into conflict with the Bavarian government, and he was eventually deposed in favor of his uncle. He was known as the Mad King, a dreamer with no grasp of reality, although he remained popular among the common people. His eccentric reputation was confirmed by his love of dressing up and his singular habits—he slept all day and reputedly entertained the ghost of Louis XIV at the dinner table.

LEFT Ludwig's castle has become a famous symbol of romanticism. At the height of the tourist season more than 6,000 people visit each day.

BELOW Neuschwanstein has been the location for several films and provided the inspiration for Disneyland's Sleeping Beauty Castle.

RIGHT Ludwig specified sumptuous decorations and furniture, but of the castle's 200 or more rooms only 15 were ever completely finished.

The interior of the castle is a riot of different architectural styles, a Moorish-Gothic-Baroque confection that incorporates stalactites, a throne room of outrageous Byzantine decadence, and a huge Singers' Hall, elaborately lit and intended for Wagnerian performances. Ludwig's taste for the medieval did not prevent him adding modern technology, however. The castle has an advanced heating system and a kitchen with hot and cold running water.

SEE ALSO
- *Edinburgh Castle* page 18
- *The Hofburg* page 37
- *Versailles* page 24

LINDERHOF

Ludwig had other extravagant palaces. Linderhof, near Oberammergau, stands in magnificent parkland where there are various structures including a temple of Venus and a Moorish kiosk that Ludwig bought while visiting the Paris Exhibition of 1867. Linderhof was built between 1869 and 1879, and here too the stage designer Jank was employed.

In the kiosk the king installed an outrageous peacock throne; he is said to have dined on peacock from time to time and to have requested supplies of the bird from the Shah of Persia. Most astonishing of all is the Linderhof Venusberg Grotto, an artificial cave complete with lake and stalagmites and stalactites, and decorated with a huge painting of a scene from *Tannhäuser*, Wagner's opera of 1845.

GOLDEN LANE

■ Franz Kafka (1883–1924) lived in Golden Lane between November 1916 and March 1917, and wrote many of the stories later included in *Ein Landarzt* (A Country Doctor).

■ The Hradčany castle-palace complex, once the home of the rulers of Bohemia, has more recently served as the official residence of the Czech president.

GOLDEN LANE, FORMERLY KNOWN as the Street of the Alchemists, huddles against the walls of Hradčany Castle in Prague. Its narrow, cobble-stoned street is lined with small, pastel-painted houses with diminutive doors and windows, low roofs and a crowd of chimneys. In the 1590s, in the time of the Hapsburg emperor Rudolf II, who ruled from 1575 to 1612, these houses were occupied by guards from the castle. Later the street was taken over by goldsmiths.

THE PHILOSOPHER'S STONE

Rudolf II was deeply preoccupied with alchemy, chemistry, astrology and astronomy. Born in Vienna in 1552, he was crowned King of Bohemia in 1575 and succeeded his father, Maximilian II, as Holy Roman Emperor the following year.

He suffered from frequent bouts of severe depression, and shut himself away in Prague Castle to concentrate on alchemical experiments. Meanwhile his court poet was ordered to write verse in praise of the fabled Philosopher's Stone, which reputedly turned base metals to gold and prolonged human life indefinitely. It was even said that the emperor had discovered it himself.

In 1606 his family declared him incapable of ruling and tried to install his brother in his place. After several years of internecine strife, Rudolf died in Prague in 1612.

At one end of the street is the Daliborka, a tower built in 1496. The story goes that it was named after its first prisoner, Dalibor of Kozojedy, who had joined a peasants' revolt. Imprisoned in chains, he taught himself to play the violin, which he did so sweetly that people would gather below the tower to listen. One day they waited in vain: Dalibor and his violin had been silenced. The 19th-century Czech composer Bedřich Smetana based his opera *Dalibor* on this moving story.

ABOVE Golden Lane was restored and painted in pastel colors in the 1950s, becoming a popular tourist attraction.

RIGHT The tiny scale of the cottages contrasts with the grandeur of the nearby castle and St Vitus Cathedral.

WIELICZKA SALT MINES

■ There are more than 300km (186 miles) of underground passages on nine underground levels.

■ More than 2,000 excavation chambers are linked together by the passages.

■ The chambers reach depths of 327m (1,073ft) below the surface.

LOCALS HAVE BEEN USING the naturally occuring salt in Wieliczka, near Kraków in Poland, since prehistoric times, boiling off the briny spring water to leave the salt as a deposit. From the 13th century farmers began sinking small shafts during the winter, and by the time Wieliczka's modern mines closed in the 1990s they had developed into a vast network of passages and chambers, where the rock salt had been carved by generations of miners into sculptures and statues, churches, altars and bas-reliefs.

The largest of many chapels, the Chapel of the Blessed King is a spectacular space more than 50m (164ft) long and 12m (39ft) high, scooped out of the rock 101m (331ft) below ground level.

In the 19th century brine baths there treated everything from catarrh to love-sickness, and from the late 1950s sufferers of respiratory problems could come here to benefit from the mines' microclimate. In 1996 the mines were opened for tourists to view the works of art.

MINES IN DANGER

Rock salt starts dissolving when the air around it reaches a relative humidity of about 75 percent.

During the 1980s some of the Wieliczka salt sculptures were threatened by humidity, having absorbed excess water vapor from the air that ventilates the mine. As a result their surfaces were dissolving, and it was suspected that chemicals in the atmosphere were changing the nature of the salt itself.

For nearly 10 years the mine was on the UNESCO list of World Heritage Sites in danger. Teams of scientists and engineers from Poland and the US have now installed efficient dehumidifying equipment, and there is constant monitoring of the underground chambers for potentially damaging pollutants.

SEE ALSO

■ *The Camargue* page 22
■ *The Dead Sea* page 75

BELOW A display within the mine shows figures of miners using wooden steps.

THE DANUBE DELTA

■ The Danube is the second-longest river in Europe after the Volga.

■ It flows for 2,761km (1,716 miles) from its source in the Black Forest in Germany to Romania.

■ The delta where the waters enter the Black Sea covers 6,000 sq km (2,317 square miles).

The world's largest colony of pygmy cormorants is based in the Danube delta

DELTA IN DANGER

For centuries the Danube has been a vital trade route, and for much of this time man and nature have survived in relative harmony. However, in more recent years, the Danube Delta has suffered from the commercial forces and pollution of modern civilization.

The waters of the delta and the adjacent coastal seas support a large number of fish species, many of which have been exploited. Over half the freshwater fish harvest of Romania is taken from the Danube Delta, including carp and caviar-yielding sturgeon. Increased drainage for agricultural land—which in turn has meant increased pollution—has resulted in the decline of many indigenous species. Steps are now being taken to reverse some of the damage and protect this vital ecosystem.

LEFT Scientists have identified 23 different ecosystems in the delta, which is a vast alluvial plain divided into an intricate pattern of marshes, waterways and lakes.

A VAST AREA OF WETLAND, the Danube Delta straddles the border between Romania and Ukraine. Above all else the it is famous for its bird life, with more than 300 species recorded here. About 180 species breed in the area, and the remainder—from as far apart as the Arctic, China, Siberia and the Mediterranean—use the delta as an over-wintering area or a stopover on longer migrations. Large proportions of the remaining world populations of four species in particular depend on the delta: the pygmy cormorant, of which there is a colony of around 12,000 pairs; the red-breasted goose, of which the entire world population can sometimes be found wintering in the area; 150 pairs (10 percent of the total world population) of the very rare, silvery-white Dalmatian pelican; and a substantial number of white pelicans. The floating islands and reed beds of the Danube Delta provide essential safe nesting and feeding for these two species of pelican.

THE HOFBURG

■ **The Hofburg became a regular royal residence only after 1533, when Emperor Ferdinand I made the castle his home.**

■ **The oldest part of the Hofburg palace is the Schweizerhof, which is named after the Swiss guard that garrisoned it.**

THIS SPRAWL OF BUILDINGS ranging from the 13th to the 19th centuries was the Viennese residence of the Hapsburgs, Holy Roman Emperors and subsequently rulers of the Austro-Hungarian Empire. Parts are still government offices, while others house the Hapsburg collections. Among rooms open to the public are the imperial audience chamber; the simple bedroom of Emperor Franz Josef, who died in 1916 after a reign of almost 70 years; the gymnasium where his wife, Empress Elisabeth, kept fit; and the Treasury, which houses the gem-studded 10th-century imperial crown and the Holy Lance, which reputedly pierced Christ's side on the cross. The famous Spanish Riding School, where stately white Lipizzaner horses perform, was completed in 1735.

The Albertina contains a superb collection of graphic art, and nearby is the court's parish church, the Augustinerkirche, where the ill-fated Marie Antoinette was married to the future Louis XVI, and where the hearts of Hapsburgs are interred.

CITY OF MUSIC

The Hofburg's collection of musical instruments is a reminder that no other city was home to as many great composers as Vienna. Christoph Gluck (1714–87) wrote operas for the Hapsburg court; Mozart (1756–91) and Haydn (1732–1809) both lived and composed in Vienna. Beethoven (1770–1827) settled here in 1792; and Schubert (1797–1828) lived and died here.

The city's socialites swayed to the waltzes of the Strauss family in the 19th century and hummed to the operettas of Franz Lehár (1870–1948). Brahms (1833–97) and Bruckner (1824–96) both settled in Vienna in the 1860s. Gustav Mahler (1860–1911) was director of the court opera, and Arnold Schönberg (1874–1951) and Alban Berg (1885–1935) were also sons of Vienna.

BELOW The St Michael's Wing, with its curving façade, is the main entrance to the Hofburg from the city.

SEE ALSO

■ *Edinburgh Castle* page 18
■ *Neuschwanstein* page 32
■ *Versailles* page 24

THE KAPELLBRÜCKE

■ The Kapellbrücke was badly damaged by fire in 1993 but has since been restored.

■ The Wasserturm may once have served as the lighthouse (*lucerna*) that gives the town its name.

FIRE AND RECONSTRUCTION
Shortly after midnight on August 18th 1993 a fire, probably caused by a cigarette left on a boat moored beneath, destroyed about two thirds of the bridge, sparing only the pillars, the bridgeheads and the Wasserturm. Reconstruction was rapid: within eight months the bridge was complete. Only a third of the paintings escaped damage; those that were destroyed were replicated or replaced by others that had been in storage. The $2.1 million reconstruction was funded by insurance, generous donations and revenue from a special postage stamp.

LUCERNE (LUZERN), LOCATED IN the German-speaking part of Switzerland, sits below the mountains at the northwest corner of Lake Lucerne. The town's main defense is now its main attraction: Europe's oldest wooden covered bridge, the Kapellbrücke (Chapel Bridge), built in 1333 and extending diagonally a little over 198m (650ft) across the Reuss River. Toward its southern end is the octagonal, tile-roofed Wasserturm (water tower), which has served as a prison, a torture chamber, and a treasury.

High up in the rafters of the bridge are more than 120 paintings, some surviving from the early 17th century and others replaced after the 1993 fire. They depict Lucerne's history and the brave deeds of the people of this area, who played a crucial part in the struggle for Swiss independence, and illustrate the lives and legends of Lucerne's two patron saints, St Leger and St Maurice.

Lucerne made its fortune in the 13th century, becoming a major commercial site with the opening of the Alpine route through the St Gotthard Pass between northern Italy and the Rhineland. Switzerland was the first democratic state in Europe, and the cradle of Swiss democracy was the area around Lake Lucerne. In the Middle Ages Switzerland was part of the Holy Roman Empire, but the settlements among the remote mountains and forests were largely self-governing, resisting the centralizing policies of the Hapsburg emperors.

In 1291 the representatives of three forest states, or cantons, close to the lake signed a treaty of mutual assistance. This was seen as the founding moment of

ABOVE Before the 1993 fire, the bridge had survived for more than 500 years. The reconstruction timber is lighter in color.

the Swiss Confederation, which Lucerne joined in 1332 to protect its commercial interests. Other communities joined the confederacy, and the Swiss eventually won their independence. During this period Lucerne's main fortifications were built—the bridge and the wall with its watch towers, which still stand on the Reuss.

Visible from the Kapellbrücke are the twin spires of the Church of St Leger and St Maurice, consecrated in 1644. Farther west is the Spreuerbrücke (mill bridge, see right) from 1407, which is also adorned with paintings, this time from the 17th century.

BELOW The Kapellbrücke encompasses the 13th-century Wasserturm (water tower), an octagonal fortification.

A CLOSE RELATION

Downstream, Lucerne retains another remarkable wooden covered bridge, the Spreuerbrücke. Its gables feature a set of 67 early 17th-century paintings by Kaspar Meglinger on the theme of the Dance of Death, reflecting attitudes to death at a time when the plague was rife. Dating from around 1408 and rebuilt in 1568, its zig-zag spans across the Reuss originally served to connect water mills with the baker's quarter in Pfistergasse, across the river from the medieval town—a deliberate plan to avoid fire spreading from bakers' ovens.

SEE ALSO

■ *The Golden Gate Bridge* page 170
■ *Sydney Harbour Bridge* page 217

THE MATTERHORN

- ▪ Around 30 Alpine peaks are higher than 4,000m (13,125ft).

- ▪ The Matterhorn is known in France as Mont Cervin and in Italy as Monte Cervino.

- ▪ Its summit is 4,478m (14,692 ft) high.

LEFT The Gornergrat rack railway, running from Zermatt, offers good views of the Matterhorn from its summit station, a popular starting point for hikes and skiing trips.

RIGHT AND FAR RIGHT BELOW A perfect example of a pyramidal peak, the Matterhorn dominates the skyline above the prosperous winter sports resort of Zermatt in Switzerland.

The Alps themselves were formed when the tectonic plate of Africa was forced north to collide with southern Europe. The process began about 180 million years ago, and reached a climax about 40 million years ago when the earth's crust buckled and rose to form the great spine of mountains that are the Alps. The mountains' core contains hard rocks such as granite, mica schist and gneiss, with softer rocks such as sandstones and shales at the edges. Europe's great rivers—the Rhine, the Rhône and the Danube—originate in these mountains, and famous lakes such as Maggiore and Lucerne lie in the hollows gouged by the glaciers of the last ice age.

THE MATTERHORN IS NOT the highest summit in the Alps, but it is surely the most dramatic, its classic mountain shape towering over the Italian-Swiss border. A road runs to the mountain on the Swiss side, following the River Rhône as it flows toward Lake Geneva (Lac Léman). The town of Zermatt sits under its northern face. On the Italian side there is access from Turin and Aosta.

The forces of glacial activity have formed the Matterhorn over the past two million years. Its distinctive shape is the result of ice-age glaciers grinding out vast hollows, or cirques, on each side of the mountain, and eventually converging backward to form a narrow, pointed summit, known as a pyramidal peak. The four great tapering faces of rock are so difficult to climb that an ascent was not completed until 1865.

ALPINE PEAKS

The Alpine mountains have fascinated generations of visitors for their beauty and for the climbing challenge they present. The highest mountain is Mont Blanc in France, which is 4,807m (15,771ft) high. The Jungfrau is considered one of the most spectacular of the snow-capped mountains.

The Eiger has achieved its place of importance because of the difficulty of its climbs: the almost sheer north face, 1.6km (1 mile) high, was not conquered until 1938. In Austria the towering Zugspitze is the tallest of the Bavarian Alps and is popular with skiers and climbers. In the valley below, Garmisch-Partenkirchen, site of the 1936 Winter Olympics, has a cog railway to the crest of the mountain.

SCALING THE MATTERHORN

The Matterhorn is one of the world's most climbed mountains. Every part of it has been tackled, and the most popular routes have fixed ropes, ladders and huts. However, this should not fool anyone into thinking of it as an easy climb: the Matterhorn also has one of the highest death rates—indeed, on the way down from the first successful ascent, four of Edward Whymper's party fell to their deaths.

Local guides now take most climbers along the easiest and first ascent, Hörnli Ridge and Lion Ridge, which have sections of fixed climbing aids. More experienced climbers go for the Zmutt and Furggen ridges, and the North Face presents the greatest challenge of all. Inexperienced climbers are advised to leave this mountain to the experts.

On July 14th 1865 the first successful team of climbers, led by Englishman Edward Whymper, reached the top by traversing a ridge on the Swiss side. Three days later an Italian team under the leadership of Giovanni Carrel arrived at the summit via a ridge on the Italian side. The Italians later claimed that Whymper's team had thrown rocks at them, an allegation the Englishman vigorously denied. Today cables and artificial footholds help amateurs to the top of the peak that was once the domain of the hardy few.

Another climber associated with the Matterhorn was Hermann Perren, a Zermatt guide whose ambition was to climb the Matterhorn 150 times. Tragically he fell to his death at the age of 68, a few climbs short of his goal.

SEE ALSO
■ *The Himalayas* page 102
■ *Mount Fuji* page 106
■ *Mount Kilimanjaro* page 136

THE COLOSSEUM

- The Colosseum is nearly 0.5km (0.3 mile) in circumference and more than 55m (180ft) high.

- It was built of travertine (similar to marble), tufa (a type of limestone) and brick.

- Seating and access were efficiently arranged, as spectators' ticket numbers showed which part of the stadium to enter.

THE AMPHITHEATER WAS A ROMAN design borrowed from the Greeks. Its elliptical area was surrounded by tiers of seats from which huge crowds could look safely down on spectacular displays of combat and carnage. Here gladiators fought, military displays were held and exotic animals from across the known world were exhibited and slaughtered. Rome had amphitheaters before the Colosseum, but after the great fire of AD 64 a new one was needed. Vespasian, who became emperor in AD 69, ordered the construction of a massive, permanent building that would bear his family name of Flavius and be bigger and better than any other.

Known as the Flavian Amphitheater, the new arena was built on the bed of a lake that had belonged to his predecessor Nero's absurdly opulent Golden House. The choice of site was a wise one structurally, and it also demonstrated that an era of monstrous self-indulgence was at an end. Vespasian built on as grand a scale as Nero, but he did so as a public gesture. Ironically, Nero had his posthumous revenge. Ever since the eighth century the Flavian Amphitheater has been

BELOW The floor of the arena has long disappeared, revealing the warren of passages and chambers.

CHRISTIANS AND LIONS

In 1744 the Colosseum, which had become Church property in the 13th century, was consecrated in memory of the Christians said to have died for their faith in front of crowds of baying Romans. The Colosseum has long been associated with Christian martyrdom, but there is actually very little evidence to link the two. Nonetheless, a cross stands in the arena to this day, and indeed it was its reputation and significance to the Church that eventually saved the Colosseum from obliteration.

As it was, much of its stone was plundered by the authorities for use as building material in new palaces and churches, leaving the brick shell that remains today, without its originally dazzling stone coat.

more important was the careful control of the animals. A network of passages and elevators delivered wild creatures directly to the arena from their cages below stage. Much of this infrastructure can still be seen, as can sockets and brackets for the top tier, which once held the masts from which a huge awning could be stretched over the open top. This elaborate arrangement of canvas, pulleys, and ropes was operated by sailors recruited specially for the task.

LEFT The top tier of the exterior was decorated with gilded bronze shields, and the arches were filled with statues of emperors and gods.

SEE ALSO
■ *The Pont du Gard* page 30

known as the Colosseum, a title thought to recall the colossal statue of Nero that once stood nearby. (Rather than demolish this, Vespasian had ordered a head transplant and renamed the statue Apollo).

It was opened by Vespasian's successor, Titus, in AD 80, with a ceremony that involved 5,000 wild beasts. Even then work was not complete, and it was only during the reign of the next emperor, Domitian, that the final tier was added.

The building is remarkable, and its design reveals an ingenious response to the question of crowd control. Although some 50,000 people could be accommodated, the system of staircases and corridors ensured trouble-free progress to and from the banks of seating. Still

MAN AND BEAST

In the Villa Borghese gallery in Rome are mosaics showing scenes of combat in the arena. Bulls, stags, lions and even ostriches were fair game for the *bestiarius*, a man not unlike the modern matador. Some surviving Roman amphitheaters were later used for bullfighting. The Roman fascination with exotic animals seems to date from the time when Carthaginian elephants were displayed in the city, long before the Colosseum was built.

Contests between gladiators were also part of a long tradition thought to have developed from Etruscan funeral ceremonies. Gladiatorial fights were sometimes highly professional affairs between trained and evenly matched men, and sometimes pathetic displays involving unwilling captives.

THE LEANING TOWER OF PISA

- The tower is 55m (180ft) high.

- Circular in plan, it rises in eight tiers, including the bell chamber.

- The delicate arcading surrounding the tower's six central stages may have been influenced by Byzantine or Islamic architecture.

PISA'S FAMOUS LEANING TOWER (Torre Pendente) is actually the campanile, or bell tower, of the city's cathedral, part of a magnificent ensemble of cathedral, bell tower, baptistery and cemetery. If it stood upright, its fame would probably be limited mainly to historians of art and architecture. But because it is structurally flawed, it is known throughout the world.

An inscription records that the tower was begun in 1174, but as the Pisan calendar was a year in advance of conventional dating, the true date was 1173. The original architects, Bonnano Pisano and William of Innsbruck, did not live to see the work completed—the tower had no bell chamber until the second half of the 14th century.

Some have suggested that the tower was always intended to lean, a daring demonstration of the skill of the architects. This idea is scarcely believable, and it is

LEFT Construction had reached only the third floor when the tower began to lean. Later architects attempted to correct this by building the upper floors with one side taller than the other, turning the lean into a curve.

BELOW In 2008, after more earth removal, engineers announced that the tower had stopped moving for the first time in its history. They predicted that it would be stable for at least 200 years.

CORRECTING THE LEAN

The tower started leaning very early in its history, and blocks of masonry were incorporated to try and pull it back. Between 1278 and 1360 its southward tilt is thought to have increased from just over half a degree to 1.6 degrees. This probably speeded up at an alarming rate with the addition of the seventh level and the bell chamber. At the beginning of the 20th century, the tower was 4.3m (14ft) out of perpendicular; by the end of the century it was 4.6m (15ft) out. An injection of grout in 1934 caused a 10mm (0.4in) lurch and draining groundwater in the 1970s increased the lean by 12mm (0.5in). Careful soil extraction in 1999 seems to have enjoyed more success, reducing the tilt by half a degree.

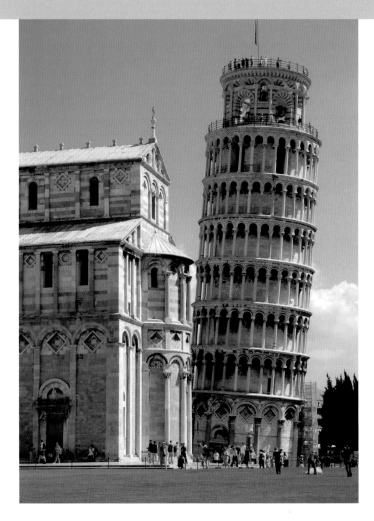

LEFT The tower leans away from the cathedral next to it.

RIGHT Marble pillars frame viewpoints for visitors. There are two fewer steps going up on the north side because of the lean.

THE TOWER COMPLEX

The tower is part of a complex of buildings in the Piazza del Duomo, which includes the *duomo* (cathedral), the baptistery and the *campo santo* (cemetery). The baptistery is a circular building of marble begun in the middle of the 12th century in Romanesque style, but with some later Gothic work. The pulpit dates from 1260 and has remarkable carvings depicting scenes from the life of Christ.

The cemetery was begun in the late 12th or early 13th century, using earth brought by ships from Calvary. Gothic arcades are decorated with frescoes and, despite troubling themes such as the Triumph of Death, Hell and the Last Judgment, this is a place with a peaceful atmosphere.

much more likely that the designers knew they would be building on less than solid ground and made some allowance for this in their plans, constructing foundations that would tolerate a certain amount of subsidence. Seeing the tower today, and experiencing the odd, disorienting sensation of being pulled to one side while climbing the 294 steps, one can only marvel at the fact that it still stands at all.

The Leaning Tower was built as the bell tower of Pisa's cathedral, which was begun a hundred years earlier, following a naval battle in 1063 in which the Pisans defeated the Saracens at Palermo. The style of architecture is known as Pisan Romanesque, and Islamic influence can once again be detected in the exterior bands of alternating red and white marble. There are arcades rising one above the other into the gable, and the dome over the crossing of the nave and the transepts was a later addition.

In 1564, the scientist Galileo was born in Pisa, and he is said to have made use of the Leaning Tower for one of his experiments, dropping objects from the top in order to demonstrate that the speed of their acceleration would be the same, regardless of weight. There is no doubt that Galileo proved this point, but whether he did so from the Leaning Tower is less certain. On the other hand, it would have offered an ideal setting for experiments with gravity, as it apparently defies gravity itself.

SEE ALSO

■ *The Eiffel Tower* page 26

THE GRAND CANAL

- The Grand Canal snakes in a broad S-shape for about 4km (2.5 miles) from the train station in the northwest of Venice to the Punt della Salute in the southeast.

- Four bridges cross the canal, with the Ponte Rialto being the oldest and best-known.

- Gondolas act as taxis on the canals.

RIGHT Gondolas passing the church of Santa Maria della Salute.

ABOVE The 16th-century Rialto Bridge is supported by around 12,000 original wooden piles.

AT THE HEIGHT OF SUMMER, with thousands of tourists swarming on and off the vaporetti (water buses), or on a damp, gray winter morning, with fog rolling in from the lagoon—under whatever conditions you see it, the Grand Canal in Venice is magical. It is difficult not to be totally overwhelmed by the city as everywhere you turn there is a building of note: a magnificent juxtaposition of brick and marble, a fine example of delicate Gothic tracery or outrageous baroque overstatement. And almost everywhere there is water, lapping the edges of the buildings, reflecting the glories of the architecture, and serving as a thoroughfare for floating traffic of every kind.

From its position among the lagoons at the head of the Adriatic, Venice built up one of the greatest commercial empires in history on the basis of its flourishing maritime trade. Water was its life, and every year on Ascension Day this was affirmed when the Doge 'married' the sea by casting a gold ring into it, in the spectacular ceremony of the Spozalizio del Mar.

Venice is built on thousands of islands, which originally were little more than mud flats. The city rose on millions of wooden piles, and a unique style of architecture evolved to suit these maritime conditions. The palaces lining the Grand Canal display Venetian grandeur of every era, from the 13th to the 20th centuries.

The visitor could journey along the canal every day for a year, even for a lifetime, and still find something new to marvel at. The 16th-century Ca' d'Oro is perhaps the most celebrated palace of all. Now an art gallery and

THE GONDOLA

Unique to Venice and a symbol of the city's romantic reputation, the gondola is artfully designed to travel in shallow water, and to carry the maximum load with the minimum draught. Eight types of wood are traditionally used in its construction. Its asymmetrical design allows it to be steered easily with one oar by one person standing at the stern.

A letter written in 1094 by the Doge Vitale Falier contains the earliest known reference to the gondola, which was probably being used, then as now, to ferry passengers around. In the 18th century there were perhaps as many as 14,000 gondolas on the canals in Venice, making these some of the busiest waterways in the world. Now there are only about 500.

open to the public again after years of restoration work, the building is a supreme example of Venetian Gothic architecture. It is said to owe its name to the fact that it was originally adorned with gilt. A slightly later and quite different building on the Grand Canal is the Palazzo Dario, with a façade studded with polychrome marble.

At the southeastern end of the Grand Canal stands the Church of Santa Maria della Salute, designed by Longhena and completed in 1687 to commemorate deliverance from a plague that afflicted the city. Each November, a bridge of boats is constructed across the canal, allowing people to walk over to the church to celebrate its annual festival.

The Fondaco dei Turchi (built at the beginning of the 13th century but heavily restored), the Ca' Giustinian (mid-15th century), the Ca' Rezzonico (17th and 18th century, now a museum), the Ca' da Mosto (13th century) ... one superbly ornamented frontage after another bears witness to the immense wealth created by generations of Venetian traders.

SEE ALSO
■ *The River Nile* page 122

PIAZZA SAN MARCO

The most beautiful street in the world leads to what Napoleon called the finest drawing room in Europe. St Mark's Square—the one and only piazza in Venice—is bordered by buildings of different dates and styles, and yet the combined effect is perfectly harmonious. The 11th-century basilica of St Mark is an astonishingly rich building with a profusion of fine mosaics and inlaid marble floors. It was originally the private chapel of the Doges of Venice, whose palace is another of the major sights of the city.

The late 15th-century clock tower has one of the first digital displays, created in 1857 to show numbers rather than a clock face. Two bronze figures strike a bell to announce the hour.

SUPER SITE
ST PETER'S BASILICA

■ St Peter's covers an area of 22,300 sq m (240,000 sq ft).

■ The dome is 138m (453ft) high and 42m (138ft) in diameter.

■ There are 284 columns in the colonnade.

■ During construction the workforce numbered up to 2,000.

Almost all the celebrated architects of 16th-century Italy had a hand in the construction of this vast church. It took 170 years for the basilica to be completed, as its plans were passed from hand to hand and its design revised or replaced. The building that stands in the heart of Rome today is awe-inspiring in its dimensions. Even more remarkable, given the saga of its construction, is the fact that it was completed at all.

ABOVE Statues of Christ and the apostles crown the 1612 façade overlooking the piazza. Commissioned by Pope Paul V, they were carved in travertine.

ST PETER'S HAS ITS ORIGINS in the martyrdom of the apostle Peter, crucified by Emperor Nero and buried in a public cemetery in about AD 64. Peter's tomb became a place of pilgrimage, and Constantine (AD 274–337), the first Christian emperor, built a basilica around it, which stood for a thousand years. When the structure began to crumble, Pope Nicholas V planned a replacement, but he died in 1455 before work began. Work on the new St Peter's was to continue for nearly two centuries, interrupted at regular intervals as yet another pope or architect died and one scheme replaced another. The subsequent design of nave, façade and portico was ill-advised and ruined the view of the dome originally planned by Bramante and reintroduced 30 years later by Michelangelo.

Bernini's contribution

The piazza in front of St Peter's was built later and much more swiftly, between 1656 and 1667. The work of

LEFT The Basilica as seen beyond the Roman bridge of Pont Sant'Angelo, which was constructed in AD 134 and later adorned with statues of saints.

RIGHT St Peter's Piazza, with Bernini's colonnades. The obelisk that marks the center was from Ancient Egypt, brought to Rome by Emperor Caligula in AD 37.

THE HISTORY

- **1506** *Donato Bramante begins construction with Greek cross plan and dome.*
- **1514–20** *Raphael put in charge and abandons dome.*
- **1539** *Antonio da Sangallo draws up a new scheme, which is not implemented.*
- **1546** *Michelangelo appointed to the project and reinstates dome.*
- **1564** *Giacomo della Porta succeeds Michelangelo and alters the design again.*
- **1626** *Church consecrated on November 18th by Pope Urban VIII.*

LEFT Michelangelo's design for the dome was inspired by the Pantheon of Ancient Rome. He included volcanic rock in the concrete shell to make it lighter.

RIGHT Bernini's baldachin, directly under the dome, is a gilded altar canopy with columns 20m (66ft) high. It is reputedly the largest piece of bronze in the world.

Giovanni Bernini (1598–1680), it has 284 Tuscan columns arranged four deep with statues of saints above. Inside St Peter's, Bernini constructed a less universally admired bronze baldachin, set canopy-like over the papal altar and supported on serpentine columns 29m (95ft) high.

It is possible to inspect St Peter's literally from top to bottom: to look down on Rome from a balcony attached to the lantern on top of the dome, and to descend beneath the high altar and view the excavations of the pagan necropolis that lay beneath the original basilica. One monument discovered here may mark the site of St Peter's grave, although there is not sufficient archeological evidence to allow conclusive arguments for or against this.

Built on a massive scale and heavily ornate in much of its internal decoration, St Peter's is, for some visitors, overly elaborate and even oppressive. It is the largest church

THE VATICAN

St Peter's stands in Vatican City, an autonomous state recognized as independent of Italy in 1929. Its head of state is the Pope, and the Vatican has its own radio and TV stations, a train station, and an entitlement to diplomatic representation abroad. Swiss Guards, in distinctive uniforms that have remained unchanged for 450 years, act as the state police force.

The buildings of the Vatican, constructed with ever-increasing grandeur during the 14th, 15th, and 16th centuries, house half a million books and what is said to be the biggest collection of ancient art anywhere in the world.

The Sistine Chapel, built for Pope Sixtus IV around 1473, is part of the complex of rooms and galleries open to the public, and it is celebrated throughout the world for its frescoes by Michelangelo, who at the time considered himself more a sculptor than a painter. Those frescoes painted between 1508 and 1512 depict biblical scenes and characters before the Flood. Twenty years after their completion the artist went on to paint the Last Judgment on the chapel's east wall.

ABOVE The Vatican's Swiss Guards wear Renaissance-style uniforms in the Medici colors of blue, red and gold, little changed since the 16th century.

ABOVE In his *Pietà* (1499), Michelangelo depicts the Virgin Mary as a beautiful young woman, although she would have been middle-aged at the time of the Crucifixion.

by area and volume in the world, capable of holding 60,000 worshippers. The initial impression on walking into the building, which stretches 189m (620ft) ahead, is sometimes one of bewilderment. There is so much to take in that it is difficult to appreciate it all at once. Unqualified admiration may not be everyone's verdict, but as a whole it excites wonder and contains some exquisite works of art, such as Michelangelo's *Pietà*, a marble statue of the Virgin Mary with the dead body of her son in her arms.

SEE ALSO
■ *Church of the Holy Sepulchre* page 79
■ *Haghia Sophia* page 73
■ *The Sagrada Família* page 60

RENAISSANCE EUROPE

In the 14th century a new generation of artists and architects began to look back to the Classical age of Greece and Rome. Over the next 200 years their ideas spread from Italy across Europe. New building designs were based on the symmetry of the circle and square, while artists developed techniques of realism in portraits and perspective.

■ **The Banqueting House on Whitehall in London was built by Inigo Jones (1573–1652) for James I as a demonstration of the principles of Palladianism.**

■ **Michelangelo's funerary monuments in the Church of San Lorenzo, Florence, depict living effigies instead of the reclining figures of medieval tradition.**

Above Leonardo da Vinci designed a flying machine: this modern replica has been constructed for a Milan museum.

Right Michelangelo's painting of the Holy Family shows powerful human figures, rather than the icon-like images of medieval religious art.

Top right The Banqueting House was built more than two centuries after the Renaissance began in Italy.

THEORY AND PRACTICE

Renaissance practitioners based their designs on the theories of Vitruvius, a first-century BC Roman engineer whose treatise *De Architectura* set out Greek architectural principles. These defined the three Orders— Doric, Ionic and Corinthian—and laid down the rule of proportions, relating all dimensions to each other arithmetically.

These rules dictated the grand Venetian church designs of Andrea Palladio (1508–80), whose work would, in turn, inspire 17th-century British architects, including Sir Christopher Wren.

Above Leonardo da Vinci (left), the ultimate 'Renaissance man', and Galileo Galilei (right), known as the father of modern science.

Right One of Michelangelo's tombs for the Medici family, in Florence. The lower sculptures represent Night and Day.

THE ITALIAN JOBS

Filippo Brunelleschi (1377–1446) set the pace with the vast dome of the cathedral in Florence. Moving away from the Gothic style, he based his work on sketches of Roman temples and basilicas. Florence became a Renaissance showpiece, attracting all of the talented artists and architects of the time.

Leon Battista Alberti (1404–72) spread the word across the rest of Italy, supervising the rebuilding of Rome under the patronage of Pope Nicholas V.

NEW WAYS

In 1505 Pope Julius II commissioned a new church over St Peter's tomb. The designer was Donato Bramante (1444–1514), a devoted adherent to Renaissance principles. His original plan for St Peter's Basilica employed the Classical rules of simplicity and the Orders, but a sequence of changes after his death culminated in a compromise that moved away from the strict use of proportion toward the flamboyance of the Baroque style.

Left Lorenzo Ghiberti's gilded bronze door panels for the Baptistery in Florence were commissioned in 1425. His use of realistic perspective and lifelike figures greatly influenced Italian artists of the early Renaissance.

SEE ALSO

■ *The Grand Canal* page 46
■ *St Peter's Basilica* page 48

THE PARTHENON

- The Parthenon stands on the Acropolis, the ancient city on a hill above modern Athens.

- It was built on the foundations of an earlier temple to Athena.

- Athena was the goddess of wisdom and the patron of Athens.

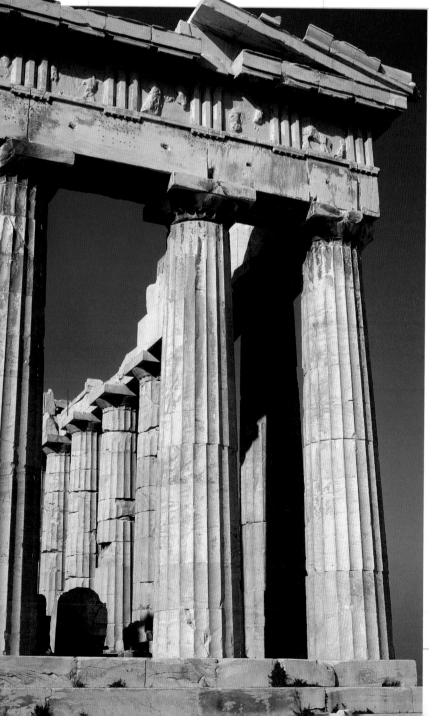

DESCRIPTIONS OF THE PARTHENON have always been littered with superlatives. This temple to Athena Parthenos, the patron deity of Athens, is regarded as the supreme example of classical architecture, an artistic and sculptural masterpiece. The building belongs to the middle of the fifth century BC. By then the Persians, who in 480 BC succeeded in storming Athens, had been decisively defeated, and the city, under the influence of the statesman Pericles, was brimming with pride and self-confidence. This mood was reflected in a lavish building project, funded by tributes exacted from Athens' allies.

THE BIG FRIEZE

If the Parthenon was a temple, it was also something of an art gallery, a perfect setting for a collection of sculpture. The pediments and entablature were covered with figures visible from outside, but the celebrated 152m (500ft)-long Parthenon frieze, half of which was removed to London by Lord Elgin and bought by the British Museum in 1816, ran around the solid outer walls of the cella at a height of about 12m (40ft).

At the new Acropolis Museum (opened 2009) parts of the frieze are displayed with views of the Parthenon beyond—and space left for the so-called Elgin Marbles if they are ever returned to Greece.

The birth of the goddess Athena was celebrated annually at Athens, and every four years there was a special ceremony involving a procession and the presentation of a new robe for the statue of the goddess. The Parthenon frieze has long been thought to represent this procession, and many of the details support such an interpretation.

Another theory is that the frieze shows the 192 Greek heroes who died fighting the Persians at the Battle of Marathon in 490 BC being presented to a whole assembly of gods, in addition to Athena.

ABOVE Athenians held a ceremonial procession to the Acropolis every four years during a festival to honour Athena.

RIGHT Six carved female figures support the Porch of the Caryatids on the Erechtheum, a temple on the north side of the Acropolis.

FAR LEFT The towering Doric columns of the Parthenon. The celebrated frieze ran round the top, with larger sculptures in the triangular pediments at each end.

The Parthenon is a temple in the Doric style, 69.5m (228ft) long and 30.5m (100ft) wide. The peristyle, or outer colonnade, enclosed an inner building, the cella, containing the shrine that housed a giant statue of the goddess, made of gold and ivory. The peristyle had 46 columns—8 visible across the front of the temple, 17 along the sides—each fluted, composed of a number of massive drums, and tapering toward the top. The columns were marble, as were the pediments and entablature they supported, but the roof of the temple was wooden. The building style had developed from that used for simple timber structures, and the Parthenon displays in stone all the elegance of those early solutions to engineering problems. But its simplicity of line and form is deceptive. The architect, an Ionian Greek called Iktinos, was a master of perspective, calculating exactly how a building must be shaped if it is to please the human eye gazing up at it from below.

The modern image of Greek temples as gleaming white buildings is a false one. The Parthenon was originally painted in bright, not to say gaudy, fashion. Subsequently it served as both Greek Orthodox and Roman Catholic churches and as a mosque. In 1687 the Turkish army was using it as a gunpowder store when besieging Venetian forces blew it up.

Repairs in the 19th century used iron pins, which corroded badly: a thorough new conservation process started in 1975 uses titanium reinforcements. Surviving stone fragments are carefully combined with specially made replacement pieces from the same quarry as the original marble. The 2004 Olympics, held in Athens, added impetus to the city's attempts to reduce air pollution around the site and across the city.

SEE ALSO
■ *Angkor Wat* page 109
■ *The Temple of Karnak* page 116
■ *Wat Phra Keo* page 110

METÉORA MONASTERIES

■ **The Greek Orthodox monasteries were strictly for monks, but there were also nunneries, such as Agios Stephanos, reached by a bridge over a terrifying chasm.**

■ **St Athanasios, who founded the Great Metéoron, came from Mount Athos in northern Greece, an important site of the Orthodox Church.**

RIGHT Roussanou Monastery was founded around 1545 and dedicated to St Barbara. Its name may refer to a hermit who once lived there.

METÉORA MEANS 'IN THE AIR', and the monasteries are indeed up in the sky—perched on sheer pillars and pinnacles of rock up to 549m (1,800ft) high on the edge of the Pindus Mountains, looking out over the valley of the Pinios River in Thessaly, in central Greece. Until the 1920s visitors either had to climb perilous and rickety ladders, 30.5m (100ft) or more long, fastened to the rock, or were hauled up by rope in a swaying net.

Supplies are still hauled up in nets, but the monasteries began attracting tourists after World War I, and especially after the 1960s, when a new road was built from the town of Kalabáka to make them easier to reach. Access now is by long flights of steps cut into the rock and across bridges over dizzying precipices. Many monks have moved away to regain privacy, and the six sites still functioning are more like museums than living communities.

Ascetics had been living on top of rock pillars in the region since the 12th century. According to legend, when St Athanasios, the founder of the principal monastery, the Great Metéoron, arrived in about 1350, he was lifted to the top of the pillar on which the monastery stands by an angel or an eagle. His pupil, Joasaph, a son of the king of Serbia, enlarged and enriched the foundation 30 or 40 years later.

THE LIFE OF PRAYER

From late in the third century AD, Christian ascetics retreated into the deserts of Egypt and Syria to lead lives of prayer and meditation. They were also well away from the growing authority of the Church. Their numbers increased in the fourth century when Christianity, now the official religion of the Roman Empire, became more identified with the power of the state.

The most famous of these early hermits was St Anthony of Egypt, celebrated for the attacks made on him by armies of evil spirits in grotesque and horrible forms, a concept that furnished a lively theme for generations of painters of devotional art.

Another famous figure was St Simeon Stylites, who spent 40 years perched on top of an 18m (60ft)-high pillar in the Syrian Mountains.

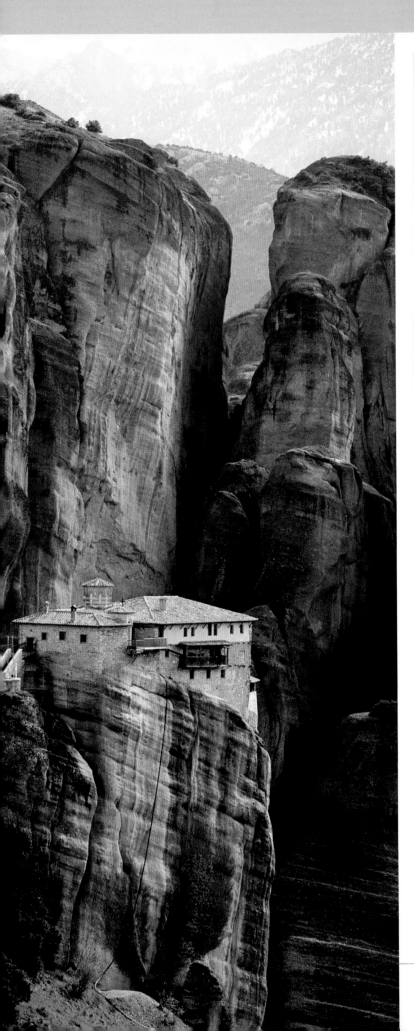

THE WILD HORSEMEN

From ancient times the broad plains of Thessaly in central Greece were well known as an important horse-breeding district. Inhabitants of the plains even entered Greek mythology. They were pictured literally as horse-men, or centaurs, each having a human head and torso growing out of the body of a horse, and were usually characterized as lusty and fond of strong drink—personifying the animal urges in human nature.

Among their numbers, however, was a rather different character—a wise old shaman named Chiron, said to have taught the heroes Achilles and Jason in their youth.

Many more communities—over 30 in all—were founded in the 15th and 16th centuries after the Turks conquered Thessaly, but a long, slow decline set in during the 17th and 18th centuries and most have not survived. In the 19th century the monasteries attracted the attention of adventurous visitors, and word of them began to spread.

Built of stone, with red-tiled roofs and wooden galleries projecting vertiginously over deep abysses, the monasteries had a cramped cell for each monk, a church and a refectory for meals. Cisterns were cut in the rock to catch rainwater. The refectory at Agios Varlaam was restored as a museum in the 1960s. At the Great Metéoron you can see the simple kitchen with its bowls and ladles. In both, the churches are adorned with frescoes depicting hell and the grisly sufferings of martyrs. The deserted monastery of Agios Nikolaos has fine 16th-century frescoes by an artist from Crete named Theophanis.

ABOVE The monasteries of Great Metéora (left) and Varlaam (right).

SEE ALSO
■ *Potala Palace* page 99

THE ALHAMBRA

■ Muhammad I ibn Nasr, founder of the Nasrid dynasty, began construction work on the Alhambra in the middle of the 13th century.

■ The royal apartments date from the reigns of Yusuf I and Muhammad V, in the second half of the 14th century.

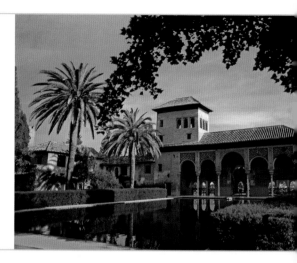

EXTERNALLY, THE ALHAMBRA IN GRANADA, southern Spain, was a fortress, a defensive stronghold with 23 towers. It was built by the Moors in the 13th century at a time when Islamic power in Spain was threatened by Christian resurgence. Internally, it was an attempt to create paradise.

The Alhambra served the Nasrid dynasty of Granada as military headquarters, administrative base and royal palace. Courtyards, corridors and water conduits combine to create a remarkable sequence of vistas. The decoration is sumptuous and ubiquitous, in the form of ceramic tiles, pierced stonework, carved foliage designs and amazingly elaborate calligraphy. There is something insubstantial and other-worldly about the exuberant muqamas vaults—riotous honeycomb-like structures suspended from wooden frames, which are themselves supported on slim columns. Verse inscriptions speak of the stars and the heavens, water runs in channels to symbolize the four rivers of the Islamic paradise, and water and light are employed by the architects as essential components in the overall design.

The Alhambra's plan is one of gardens and courtyards, with apartments opening off each of four sides. The names are evocative: the Court of Myrtles (planted in beds beside a long pool); the Hall of the Two Sisters (white marble stones set in the floor); and the Court of the Lions (with a fountain supported by 12 stone lions). The Hall of the Ambassadors, intended for royal audiences, has a carved ceiling 18.3m (60ft) above ground, an attempt to suggest the heavens.

By the mid-13th century Granada was the last major Moorish kingdom remaining in Spain. The Nasrid dynasty ruled it for 250 years under an unbroken succession of 25 sovereigns. They were notable patrons of art and learning, and attracted the great Muslim historian Ibn Khaldun to their highly civilized court.

The Nasrids finally left Granada in 1492. The emperor Charles V built his own palace within the Alhambra walls in the 16th century, but later the buildings suffered neglect, and Napoleon's forces destroyed part of the Nasrid fortress. In the 19th century, the romance of the place captured the imagination of visitors such as Victor Hugo, Théophile Gautier and Washington Irving, whose *Tales of the Alhambra* was published in 1832. It was partly their descriptions that inspired efforts to preserve the site.

SEE ALSO
■ *The Blue Mosque* page 72
■ *Fez Medina* page 126

THE MOORS IN SPAIN

Muslims came from north Africa to Spain in the year 711 and conquered the Visigoth rulers, who had their capital at Toledo. Islamic power was based in Córdoba, 160km (100 miles) from Granada, which became first an emirate and later a caliphate.

Here a remarkable mosque was built, begun in the eighth century and subsequently extended and embellished. The building was later converted into a Christian cathedral, but it still displays all the fundamental elements of Moorish architecture, with horseshoe arches, polychromatic brickwork and inscriptions taken from the Koran.

The Muslims were driven out of Córdoba during the Christian reconquest in 1236. Many escaped to Granada, where the Nasrid dynasty was then established. The last Muslim ruler of Granada was driven into exile in 1492.

THE GENERALIFE

The Generalife was a summer palace of the Nasrid royal family, built in the 14th century and once directly linked to the Alhambra by a covered walkway across a ravine. It sits on the summit of a hill known as El Sol (the sun), which is a mirror image of the hill upon which the Alhambra is built.

It was built by Aben Walid Ismail in 1318. Only two buildings survive, one at each end of the rectangular Patio de la Acequia. A long, narrow pool runs through the patio, with a stone bowl at each end. Fountains, rosebushes, colonnades and pavilions adorn the garden, which is thought to be one of the oldest of its kind in the world.

OPPOSITE PAGE TOP A still pool reflects the arches and intricate stonework of the Partal, in the upper part of the palace.

OPPOSITE PAGE BOTTOM The Alhambra citadel, with Charles V's palace and the snow-covered Sierra Nevada mountains beyond.

BELOW The Court of the Lions: the slender columns are irregularly placed to suggest the palm trees of an oasis.

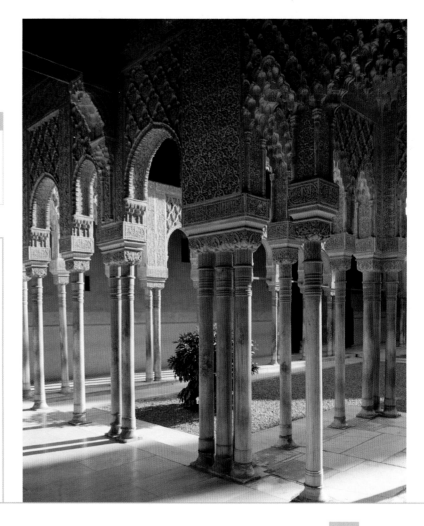

THE SAGRADA FAMÍLIA

- Gaudí was born in Reus, Spain, the son of a coppersmith.

- The 12 towers of the façades represent the 12 Apostles, and Gaudí planned another six towers, representing the four Evangelists, the Virgin Mary and Jesus Christ.

- The tallest tower—that representing Christ—is 112m (367ft) high.

WORK ON THE BASILICA of the Sagrada Família (the Church of the Holy Family), in Barcelona, began in 1884 and continues to this day. Intended as a symbol of the living Roman Catholic faith, the church was to be the focus of a complex of buildings, including schools and educational workshops. Even in its unfinished state, this huge and exuberant building is known throughout the world as a major work by the architect Antoni Gaudí (1852–1926).

Its Nativity façade takes a familiar and conventional subject of Christian art and, with no sacrifice of respect or reverence, presents it in an original, almost surreal setting. Gaudí's work reveals a Moorish influence, and has some affinities with Art Nouveau, but his was a unique approach to architecture. He treated buildings as an organic process—stone takes on a living form, and decoration grows out of it in a way that a plant might grow.

It is known that Gaudí intended the church to have three monumental façades depicting the Nativity, the Passion, and the Resurrection, and each was to have four huge towers of the type that

LEFT Under construction: much of the church remains roofless, and only one of Gaudí's three planned façades has been completed.

ABOVE Stained-glass craftsmen are still working to produce Gaudí's designs. Elsewhere, windows have clear glass to maximize the light.

PARK GÜELL

Eusebio Güell, Gaudí's patron and a rich industrialist, wanted the architect to build a whole suburb northwest of central Barcelona. The plan was never completed, but Gaudí did create a remarkable park in an area that had been without water or plants.

Here it is possible to see what Gaudí could achieve by reusing ceramic tiles. A huge curving bench is decorated with bright mosaic work, and a great dragon—looking more friendly than menacing and also created out of vivid tiles—clutches playfully at a wall near the entrance. The park also contains two very unusual entrance pavilions with mosaic-tiled roofs and a central square supported on columns that represent Gaudí's idiosyncratic version of Doric style.

were completed above the Nativity façade in the 1950s. Gaudí was a perfectionist. For his representation of the Flight into Egypt, for example, he is said to have found a working donkey and, with the owner's permission, to have made plaster casts of this animal because its weary appearance was exactly the image he wanted to portray in his sculpture. It is unlikely that the church would have retained the shade of the original stone if Gaudí had lived to complete it. He was inspired by the colors as well as the forms of natural things, and much of his work displays a riotous use of different tones, textures, and surfaces.

The architect was an accomplished artist and craftsman. He designed furniture and fashioned iron gates and railings that astonish the eye. Among his buildings in Barcelona, the Casa Batlló (said to illustrate the triumph of St George over the dragon) and Casa Milá (Spain's most controversial apartment block) are particularly striking.

There have been arguments about the feasibility of completing Gaudí's church, it is hoped that this might be achieved by 2026, the 100th anniversary of his

death. Meanwhile, the building works have become almost as much of an attraction as the structure itself. Income from tourism—which significantly increased in the years following Barcelona's 1992 Olympics—has done much to support the project.

MODUS OPERANDI

Gaudí made rough sketches rather than accurate plans of the project on which he worked, and he preferred to be on site, watching something take shape and altering it at will rather than leaving others to execute a specific design.

This method of work explains why the Sagrada Família remains incomplete. Gaudí took over the project in 1891 at a very early stage and devoted enormous energy to it, rejecting all other commissions after 1914. When he died, run over by a tram in 1926, it was impossible for anyone else to continue building in the way that he would have done.

ABOVE Tree-like interior columns change from square at the base to cylindrical at the top, from where they branch to support their load.

TOP Eusebio Güell commissioned Gaudí to design his town mansion, the only one of his buildings Gaudí saw completed.

SEE ALSO
- *Church of the Holy Sepulchre* page 79
- *Haghia Sophia* page 73
- *St Peter's Basilica* page 48

THE KREMLIN

- The Kremlin is triangular in shape, and covers 28ha (69 acres) of ground beside the Moscow River.

- The belltower of Ivan the Great is 81m (266ft) high and was completed in 1600 by Czar Boris Godunov.

- The Czar Cannon, made in 1586, weighs 40.6 tons (44.8 tons) and has the largest caliber of any cannon ever made at 890mm (35 inches)

BELOW Italian master builders completed the walls and towers of the Kremlin citadel in 1495. They enclose four palaces and four cathedrals.

RIGHT The massive Czar Cannon of 1586 was thought to be only for display. However, restorers found gunpowder inside, showing that it was fired at least once.

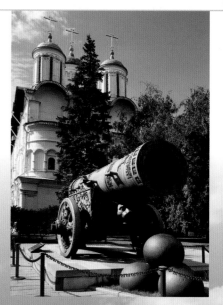

IVAN THE TERRIBLE, THE FIRST man who could justly claim to be Czar of All the Russias, was crowned in the Kremlin in Moscow in 1547. There is a kremlin, or fortress, in many an ancient Russian city, but since that moment the citadel in Moscow has been *the* Kremlin. The stronghold was the nucleus around which Moscow grew after its foundation in the 12th century. Inside are the palaces of the czars and a constellation of churches. In the aftermath of the Russian Revolution in 1917 the Kremlin became the headquarters of the Soviet government.

The towering walls were rebuilt in brick late in the 15th century. Standing up to 18.3m (60ft) high, they run for more than 1.6km (1 mile) and are punctuated by 20 towers, some with tent-shaped steeples above the gates. The main entrance is the Spassky Gate, which faces Red Square.

The Granovitaya Palata, completed in 1491, with the splendid Renaissance throne room, is still used for state occasions. The Cathedral of the Assumption, built in the

UNBURIED CAESAR

The Soviet government made its headquarters in Moscow in March 1918, and since then Russia has been ruled from the Kremlin.

Vladimir Ilyich Lenin himself moved into the 18th-century Senate building, where he lived in an austere fashion on the top floor. The clock on his study wall was kept at 8.15, the time when, desperately ill, he left the room for the last time. Lenin died on January 21 1924, and his embalmed body was displayed for veneration in a wooden pyramid in Red Square, which in 1930 was replaced by a granite mausoleum. Stalin also lay in state in the mausoleum from his death in 1953 until 1961.

AUTOCRAT OF ALL THE RUSSIAS

In 1453 the city of Constantinople, or Byzantium, fell to the Turks, marking the end of the Eastern Roman Empire and the long reign of Byzantium as the Second Rome. The Grand Dukes of Muscovy proclaimed themselves Byzantium's spiritual heirs, with their capital of Moscow as the Third Rome.

Ivan IV, 'the Terrible', inherited the Grand Duchy at the age of three, and took the reins of government at 14. At 16 he was crowned czar (Caesar); his conquests established a Russian empire. He had a savage temper, and killed his son in a rage in 1581, three years before his own death. It is said that when St Basil's Cathedral was finished, Ivan had the architect blinded so that he could never create a rival building.

1470s, was where the czars' coronations took place; the carved walnut throne of Ivan the Terrible, made in 1551, stands near the main entrance. The Cathedral of the Annunciation, rebuilt in the 1560s, was known as 'the golden-domed' because its entire roof was gilded, while the Cathedral of St Michael the Archangel, the czars' burial place, is in Russian style with Italian Renaissance influence. All three churches contain impressive frescoes and icons, and there are lesser churches close by.

The Great Kremlin Palace, subsequently the meeting place of the Supreme Soviet, was completed in 1849. From here there is access to the czars' private apartments in the 17th-century Terem Palace. The treasures amassed by the imperial family are displayed in the Armory. They range from weapons and armor to crowns and regalia, thrones, jewels, vestments, carriages, snuffboxes and Fabergé Easter eggs. The Palace of the Patriarchs of the Russian Orthodox Church, which dates from the 1650s, now houses a museum of 17th-century Russian art and culture.

Also in the Kremlin is the building used for Communist Party conferences, completed in 1961 and sunk into the ground so as not to detract from the older buildings. Immediately outside is Red Square, with the mausoleum where the body of Lenin was displayed after his death, and the onion-domed Cathedral of St Basil, built on the orders of Ivan the Terrible in the 1550s.

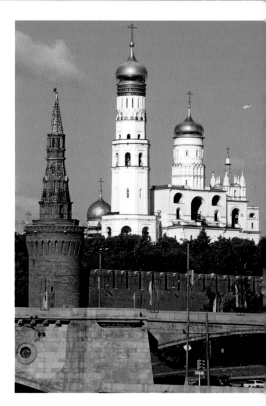

ABOVE The Church of the Twelve Apostles rivals the architecture of the Kremlin's cathedrals.

LEFT Sentinels stand guard at the Tomb of the Unknown Soldier in Alexander Garden.

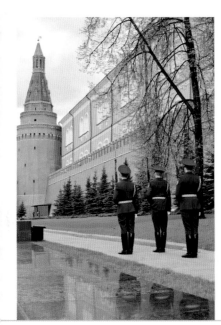

SEE ALSO

■ *The Great Palace* page 64
■ *The Hofburg* page 37

THE GREAT PALACE

- The palace waterworks require about 34,000 liters (9,000 US gal) of water per second.

- House rules at Monplaisir in Peter's time included a prohibition on guests going to bed in their riding boots.

- Catherine the Great was living here when she arranged the coup that overthrew her husband, Peter III.

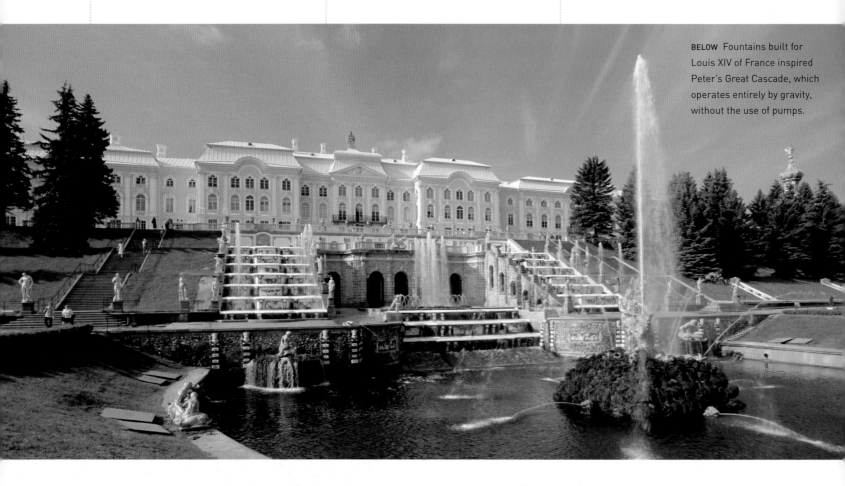

BELOW Fountains built for Louis XIV of France inspired Peter's Great Cascade, which operates entirely by gravity, without the use of pumps.

CZAR PETER THE GREAT (1672–1725) founded his new capital city of St Petersburg in 1703 (known as Leningrad for most of the 20th century, during the Soviet era).

An energetic and determined Westernizer, Peter set out to create outside the city a palace complex to rival Versailles. He planned the layout himself and assembled an army of soldiers and serfs to dig canals and channels for the dizzying array of waterworks.

In the 121ha (300-acre) park are regiments of cascades and fountains, some intended to go off unexpectedly and drench unsuspecting visitors. They cumulate in the Great Cascade, which descends seven vast steps, with fountains shooting up from each step and gilded statues of classical gods and heroes on either side. Set on a rock in a capacious basin of water is a statue of the Old Testament hero Samson, wrenching apart the jaws of a lion, from which a jet of water hurls itself 20m (66ft) into

LEFT Gilded mirrors shimmer in the palace's ballroom.

RIGHT A fountain with Neptune wrenching apart the jaws of a great fish was created to mark the end of the Thirty Years' War.

> **OTHER HOMES OF THE CZARS**
> The Alexandrovsky Palace, built in the 1790s, was the place considered as home by the ill-fated last czar, Nicholas II, who was murdered with his family by revolutionaries in 1918. A naval college in the Communist era, the palace now hosts an exhibition on the lives of the last Romanovs.
>
> Just 3km (2 miles) from Pushkin is Pavlovsk, where yet another palace of astonishing grandeur is set in a breathtaking park of 607ha (1,500 acres). It was created by the designer of the Yekaterinsky, Charles Cameron.

the air. All around is a riot of leaping, sparkling water, with grottoes and figures of dolphins, water nymphs and tritons triumphantly blowing horns, in a wildly spectacular celebration of the Russian defeat of the 'lion' of Sweden at Poltava on St Samson's Day in 1709.

The palace complex and park at Peterhof—now called Petrodvorets (Peter's Palace)—was badly damaged during World War II and has been magnificently restored since 1945. Behind the Great Cascade is the Great Palace, on a terrace looking out over the Gulf of Finland, the arm of the Baltic Sea on which St Petersburg is set. Begun in 1714 for Peter the Great, the palace was substantially enlarged and altered for his daughter, Empress Elizabeth, and later czars and czarinas have changed it in their turn.

Out in the park are smaller buildings, including Monplaisir, on the Gulf shore, where Czar Peter lived while the Great Palace was being built. The Lacquer Room, hung with lacquered papier-mâché plates showing Chinese scenes in gold on a black background, has been superbly recreated. A pavilion known as the Peterhof Hermitage—not to be confused with the great St Petersburg art museum known as the State Hermitage—has a dining room on the upper floor. Part of the table can be lowered to the ground floor to be cleared and reset by the servants.

SEE ALSO
- *The Hofburg* page 37
- *Neuschwanstein* page 32
- *Versailles* page 24

IMPERIAL GRANDEUR
Pushkin, 27km (17 miles) south of St Petersburg, is better known as Tsarskoe Selo, and was mainly laid out in the 18th century for Empress Elizabeth and Catherine the Great. Rich families from St Petersburg built houses here, and it is said to have been the first town in Europe entirely lit by electricity. It was renamed Pushkin in 1937 on the centenary of the poet's birth.

The major building is the Yekaterinsky (Catherine) Palace, or Summer Palace, created in sumptuous baroque by Rastrelli for Empress Elizabeth. The interiors were redone in the Robert Adam manner for Catherine the Great by a Scottish architect, Charles Cameron. The war-damaged palace and park have been restored, including the fabulous Amber Room, whose walls were entirely covered with amber.

THE TRANS-SIBERIAN RAILWAY

■ The Trans-Siberian was first built with a single track running 7,416km (4,608 miles) between Moscow and Vladivostok on the Sea of Japan. A second track was added later.

■ The line was built to an unusually broad gauge of 1.5m (5ft).

THE TRANS-SIBERIAN IS BY FAR the longest railway line in the world on which a regular service operates. It was built between 1891 and 1905, primarily to exploit the gold and minerals of Siberia. Political prisoners were forced to work on the line, which was also used to transport criminals and dissidents into exile. The railroad made it possible for peasants to migrate to Siberia and it led to the industrialization of this vast and remote region.

Work began simultaneously at both the Moscow and the Vladivostok ends, and the western arm reached Irkutsk in 1898. At this point passengers had to be ferried the 65km (40 miles) across Lake Baikal—frozen during the long Siberian winter—in a 3,809-tonne (4,199-ton) icebreaker, which was built in England and transported to Siberia in sections. The rail line was subsequently constructed around the southern end of the lake to cut out the ferry passage. A three-month journey had been reduced to two weeks, and would later be cut to one week.

BELOW Passing through the Siberian landscape: Chinese and Mongolian carriages such as these are used on some of the routes.

ABOVE A locomotive waiting at Vladivostock railway station. The Moscow-to-Vladivostok route has been electrified since 2002.

THE SLEEPING LAND

Siberia covers close to 13 million sq km (5 million square miles) and measures more than 6,437km (4,000 miles) across from west to east and close to 3,200km (2,000 miles) from north to south.

Its name means 'Sleeping Land' in the Tartar language, and it is full of wonders. Mammoths are preserved whole in ice, tigers prowl the remoter areas, and wolves roam the steppes. There are vast reserves of oil, coal and iron, and sinister monsters are believed to lurk in the depths of its lakes. As late as the 1940s, an unknown tribe of people was discovered by geologists.

Siberian winters last seven or eight months, and temperatures almost as low as –68°C (–90°F) have been recorded in the far north.

The timetables are in Moscow time, as are the clocks at the stations along the route, but the train passes through eight time zones, making the east coast seven hours ahead of Moscow time. Along the way it crosses rivers and negotiates mountain ranges and vast, sweeping plains blanketed with snow in winter, passing lakes, cornfields, villages and towns the railroad itself has largely created.

Much of the 1940s rolling stock was replaced in the 2000s. It has sleeping cars and a dining car that is open all day; the diner doubles as a shop, used by people from the towns and villages on the route. Starting from Moscow, the train crosses the Volga River and then heads southeast to the Ural Mountains where, 1,770km (1,100 miles) out from Moscow, it crosses from Europe into Asia. From Sverdlovsk, a major industrial town in the Urals, the line continues on to Omsk and Novosibirsk, across the Ob River, busy with cargo boats and barges, to Krasnoyarsk on the mountains south of Lake Baikal, then passes over the edge of the Gobi Desert and runs beside the Shilka River to reach Khabarovsk and Vladivostok.

Two branches now extend from Moscow to Beijing—one weekly train crossing Outer Mongolia and the Gobi Desert before entering China and passing through the Great Wall, the other (also weekly) going via Manchuria. The former journey covers 7,621km (4,735 miles), the latter 8,986km (5,584 miles) and each takes six days.

FROM BEGINNING TO END

The Trans-Siberian express trains leave Moscow from Yaroslavl Station, a remarkable Art Nouveau edifice of 1904 designed by Fedor Shekhtel. With its weird, steeply pitched roof, it looks more like the gateway to Fairyland than a train station.

At the other end of the line is Vladivostok (pictured below), a lively port that was a Soviet military base and was closed to foreigners, who had to end their journeys at Nakhodka, 80km (50 miles) north. The town was opened again in 1992 and is now thriving on trade and tourism.

LEFT A retired 1935 steam locomotive stands in a museum dedicated to the Trans-Siberian Railway in Ulan Bator, Mongolia.

SEE ALSO

■ *The Canadian Pacific Railway* page 150

ASIA

Pamukkale 70

The Blue Mosque 72

Nemrut Dag 74

The Dead Sea 75

Jerusalem 76

Petra 80

Burj Khalifa 82

The Great Wall of China 84

The Forbidden City 88

The Guilin Hills 90

The Three Gorges Dam 92

The Taj Mahal 94

The Red Fort 98

Potala Palace 99

Houses of Worship 100

The Himalayas 102

Itsukushima Shrine 104

Beppu 105

Mount Fuji 106

Borobudur 108

Angkor Wat 109

Wat Phra Keo 110

Ayutthaya 112

BELOW 300,000 people toiled to build the Great Wall of China (see pages 84–87)

EXTENDING FROM THE MEDITERRANEAN TO THE PACIFIC, Asia is the largest of the world's continents, covering about one-third of the globe's land surface. The first steps to civilization were taken in the Near East, where, 10,000 years ago, small groups of hunter-gatherers began to settle, clear the ground and grow crops, eventually developing into sizeable communities.

Towns grew into cities, and cities into kingdoms and mighty empires. In Mesopotamia the Babylonian and then Assyrian kings held sway, and the Persian Empire, founded in the sixth century BC, stretched from the Mediterranean to the Indus River.

Far to the east in China, in the third century BC, a new empire was established that would endure for more than 2,000 years and undertake the biggest construction job ever known—the Great Wall of China. The early 21st century world saw the completion of another Chinese wonder, the subject of intense controversy and widespread upheaval: the Three Gorges Dam. Whereas the Great Wall was a protection against hostile neighbors, the dam is

The Blue Mosque
Nemrut Dag
Pamukkale
Jerusalem
Dead Sea
Petra
Burj Khalifa
Red Fort
Taj Mahal
Himalayas
Potala Palace
Great Wall of China
Forbidden City
Mount Fuji
Beppu
Itsukushima Shrine
Three Gorges Dam
Guilin Hills
Ayutthaya
Wat Phra Keo
Angkor Wat
Borobudur

BELOW RIGHT An elaborate gateway at the Forbidden City in China (see pages 88–89).

designed to tame the Yangtze River as well as easing the passage of huge trading ships and providing a source of electricity.

Religion has left a visible mark all across Asia, in the form of churches, monasteries, shrines, mosques and pagodas, and Hindu and Buddhist temples replete with exuberant carvings. Islam flourished from the seventh century AD on, and its monuments range from the Dome of the Rock in Jerusalem—a city holy to three major faiths—to sites such as the Blue Mosque in Turkey and the evocative Taj Mahal in Agra, India.

Two religions exported from India inspired some of Asia's most impressive monuments. In Japan, the largest wooden building in the world was built at Nara to house an enormous image of the Buddha, and Borobudur in Java is the world's largest Buddhist temple. The immense temple complex, Angkor Wat in Cambodia, raised to celebrate the Hindu god Vishnu, has survived the ravages of time and modern war, and its scale is still capable of astonishing the visitor.

PAMUKKALE

■ **Pamukkale means 'cotton castle' in Turkish.**

■ **The tiers of tufa basins reach a height of around 91m (300ft).**

■ **There is some seismic activity in this area nearly every day.**

THE HOT SPRINGS AT PAMUKKALE, in a remote region of western Turkey, are a dazzling sight on a bright, sunny day. The effect is rather like looking at an ice fall on a glacier. People have come here to take advantage of the springs for centuries, but the extraordinary tufa basins and their cascades of water existed long before the first human visitors arrived.

The medicinal and therapeutic properties of some mineral waters have long been recognized, and the Romans built a thermal resort around the springs at Pamukkale. However, their structure was destined not to survive the ravages of time as successfully as the tufa. Some Roman ruins can still be seen, though, and there is now a modern spa resort built on the same site.

The hot springs of a geothermal area are invariably rich in mineral salts, but the composition of the waters varies from place to place, depending on the underlying rocks through which they flow. Hot water is able to dissolve any number of different salts, although some are more soluble than others. The water is usually saturated—as concentrated as it can be—by the time it reaches the

ABOVE The tiers of thermal pools are a unique geological phenomenon, constantly renewing themselves.

RIGHT Remains of the baths, tombs, temple and theater of the ancient thermal spa of Hieropolis, established in the second century BC, survive around the site.

BELOW The pools overlook an agricultural plain and supply a system of manmade canals that take water to the surrounding fields and villages.

MINERAL WATERS

Water is an essential ingredient of life in any form, but some waters with particular mineral contents are considered to be positively beneficial to health. Pamukkale has been a popular health spa for 2,000 years, since the Romans first came to bathe in the hot springs.

Tourists driven away by earthquakes in the 14th century returned in abundance in the 20th century to enjoy the site. Now, as then, the water runs through open channels, losing heat as it goes. However, by the time it reaches the open-air swimming pools and terraces it is still warm enough to bathe in for about half of the year.

Outside the Roman temple of Apollo nearby, the fountain once used water carried here by the aqueducts.

surface and once in the open air it starts to evaporate naturally. As the solution dries out, the salts contained in it crystallize, forming deposits on the ground. Although many salts are white, impurities can cause a range of different colors.

At Pamukkale the hot springs bubble out of the ground near the top of the hillside. This water, which is rich in calcium bicarbonate, emerges at a temperature of about 43°C (109°F). The water evaporates as it flows down the hillside, leaving a spectacular veneer of snowy-white salts encrusting the slopes, themselves formed of travertine, a calcium carbonate rock.

These salts have accumulated over thousands of years and now the deposits are quite thick. Such deposits, known as tufa, are not uncommon, but what makes those at Pamukkale so special is their unusual formation and scale. Tier upon tier of gleaming pools adorn the surface of the hill, like stacks of shallow porcelain basins. No other hot spring areas around the world exhibit quite the same shapes.

SEE ALSO
■ *Beppu* page 105
■ *Rotorua* page 228
■ *Volcanic Iceland* page 14

THE BLUE MOSQUE

■ The Blue Mosque's official name is the Mosque of Sultan Ahmet I.

■ Sultan Ahmet I died at the age of 27, shortly after the opening of his new mosque.

■ Around 20,000 tiles have been used to decorate the interior.

WORK ON THE BLUE MOSQUE, in what is now Istanbul, began in 1609 on the instructions of the 19-year-old Sultan Ahmet I. The architect of the mosque was Mehmet Aga, and his masterpiece took seven years to complete. All the standard features of mosque design can be seen, but the Blue Mosque is unusual in having six minarets—one at each of the four corners and another two, slightly shorter, at the outer edge of the courtyard. According to one story, the young sultan offended authorities at Mecca, the very heart of the Islamic religion, and was required to pay for the construction of a seventh minaret for the Haram mosque there, ensuring that it would have no rivals.

The temple courtyard can be approached from three gateways that lead into an outer colonnade of granite columns. Beyond the colonnade, which has a roof composed of 30 small domes, a hexagonal fountain stands in the middle of the courtyard. Such fountains are familiar features of mosques, and enable the faithful to wash before entering. To the east of the courtyard stands the *medressah*, or college.

ABOVE The name 'Blue Mosque' refers to its interior, lined with fine examples of blue-decorated Iznik tiles. Nothing on the exterior is blue.

BELOW The domes of the Blue Mosque (right) and Haghia Sophia appear to float above the modern city of Istanbul.

MUSEUMS

The Blue Mosque attracts large numbers of visitors, but many overlook the Carpet and Kilim Museum in the mosque's imperial pavilion. The museum houses a fine collection of Usak, Bergama and Konya carpets dating from the 16th to the 19th century. A range of restored Turkish carpets dating from the 13th to the 20th century is displayed along the ramp that forms the entrance to the pavilion, and in the rooms where the sultans used to rest.

The mosque itself presents a pleasing roofscape of domes—a large central one surrounded by four half-domes, and four more small domes beyond these. Inside, this arrangement of domes can be fully appreciated, with four huge elephant-foot columns supporting the whole structure. The dazzling effect of thousands of tiles might be overpowering if it were not for the spaciousness of the interior and the remarkable light that streams in through the 260 windows.

The *mihrab* (the niche facing toward Mecca) and the *nimber* (the pulpit) are carved from white marble, and the floor is covered in thick carpets, mostly deep red, but it is the complex of blue tiles that makes the greatest impact. There are numerous shades of blue, and many other colours can be seen on closer inspection. This elegant ceramic work is the product of the famous Iznik factories, which achieved tremendous success during the 16th century, exporting their ceramics far and wide. Insistent that this new mosque would have nothing but the best, Sultan Ahmet is said to have forbidden the potteries from producing tiles for any other building than his.

HAGHIA SOPHIA

Opposite the Blue Mosque is Haghia Sophia, the Church of Holy Wisdom. Built during the sixth century on the site of earlier churches, it is a vast domed basilica. It was the mother church of the Byzantine Empire until Constantinople (Istanbul) fell to the Turks in 1453. At this point it was transformed into a mosque. The mosaics inside, uncovered and restored since the building was declared a museum in the 1930s, are Christian. They depict Christ, flanked by the archangels Michael and Gabriel, with the inscription 'I am the light of the world'.

SEE ALSO
- *The Alhambra* page 58
- *Fez Medina* page 126
- *Jerusalem* page 76

NEMRUT DAG

- After centuries of obscurity, Nemrut Dag was rediscovered in 1881 by Karl Sester, a German engineer who also excavated the site.

- The statues' vast heads are an amalgam of Greek facial features with Persian headdresses and hairstyling.

- The tumulus (ancient burial mound) is 49m (160ft) tall and 152m (500ft) in diameter.

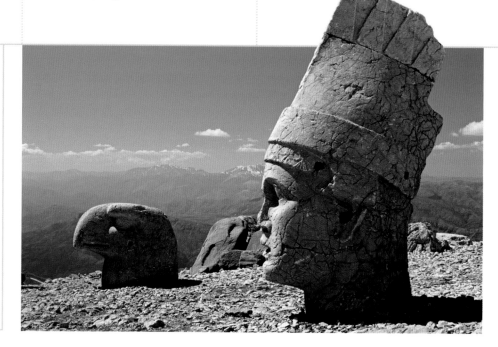

ARSAMEIA ON NYMPHAIOS

The arrangement of statues, altars, and tumulus on Nemrut Dag is known by the technical term *heirotheseion*. A similar complex, but with no surviving colossal statues, has been discovered nearby at Arsameia on Nymphaios—the *heirotheseion* of Antiochus's father, Mithridates I. Again, there are inscriptions and Antiochus is featured in a bas-relief, shaking hands with a god. Particularly intriguing is a long, manmade tunnel that descends 152m (500ft) into the rock before coming to a dead end.

A relief in the same area shows a Commagene king, presumably Mithridates, elaborately dressed and shaking hands with a naked god who carries a club and a lion skin, the hallmarks of Heracles.

ABOVE Antiochus I and the gods Zeus and Tyche amid melting snows on the west terrace.

ABOVE RIGHT The stone head of Antiochus I: he wanted his tomb to be in a high place, close to the gods.

ANTIOCHUS I, A KING OF mixed Persian and Greek descent, ruled the area known as the Commagene from 69 to 34 BC. On the 2,134m (7,000ft)-high summit of Nemrut Dag, in Anatolia (now part of Turkey), he built an extraordinary monument to his own glory and that of the gods.

A tumulus, formed of heaps of loose stones, crowns the mountain peak, guarded on the east and west sides by lions, eagles and 9m (30ft)-high statues of Heracles, Zeus-Oromasdes, Tyche, Apollo-Mithras and Antiochus himself. The seated figures have by now lost their heads, which lie nearby. Bas-relief figures, on stone slabs that once formed a long frieze, show Antiochus' ancestors, with incense-burning altars before them.

Antiochus had no doubt that he belonged with the gods, as he is shown shaking the hands of Apollo, Zeus, and Heracles in bas-reliefs on the west terrace. Another slab depicts a lion and the planets Jupiter, Mercury and Mars, arranged in an astronomical conjunction that occurred on July 7th 62 BC—possibly when building began.

THE DEAD SEA

■ The Dead Sea is the lowest point on the Earth's land surface, more than 400m (1,300ft) below sea level.

■ Its waters have been dropping by over 1m (3.3ft) a year.

■ A Jordanian plan to replenish water levels via a tunnel from the Red Sea was launched in 2009.

BELOW Mineral-rich mud is thought to benefit the skin.

THE DEAD SEA IS NOT really a sea at all, but a lake made up of two basins that together are around 72km (45 miles) long and 14km (9 miles) wide. Water flowing into them is evaporated by the Jordan Valley's intense heat, leaving a deposit of minerals and salts. While the high salinity ensures that buoyancy is no problem, actually swimming in the Dead Sea is tricky. It is simpler just to sit comfortably, supported by the water. No fish can survive the extreme saltiness, but the Dead Sea supports a number of salt-loving bacteria.

At the southern part of the lake there are hot springs and pools of rich black mud, which have long been held to have healing powers. Hotels here allow guests to enjoy their mudbaths in air-conditioned bathrooms, rather than face the searing heat of the Dead Sea's shimmering shores.

SEE ALSO
■ *The Camargue* page 22
■ *Lake Nakuru* page 132

LOOKING BACK

The shores of the Dead Sea are as remarkable as the lake itself. Great pancakes of salt have been left by the evaporating water, and pillars of salt stand at the southern extremes of the lake. One of these salt pillars is embedded in legend. A Biblical story recalls the cities of Sodom and Gomorrah, which were rife with sin. Lot, a righteous man, was warned that the cities would be destroyed as a punishment, and that he should flee with his family. Lot and his relations were warned that they should not look back. Unfortunately, Lot's wife took one last look, and she was turned into the large salt pillar near the modern town of Sedom.

SUPER SITE
JERUSALEM

- Jerusalem Old City covers 1 sq km (0.4 square mile).

- Its walls are about 12m (40ft) high and 4km (2.5 miles) long.

- Until the late 19th century the city gates were still locked every night.

- There are more than 300 holy buildings and monuments in Jerusalem.

For 5,000 years people have made their homes in this area between the Mount of Olives and the Judean Hills. Today Jerusalem is divided into the New City and the walled Old City, where seven gates lead into the historic heart, sacred to the Jewish, Christian and Islamic faiths. Among its cobbled streets, markets, houses and courtyards are three particularly significant monuments: the Wailing Wall, the Dome of the Rock and the Church of the Holy Sepulchre.

RIGHT The Islamic shrine of the Dome of the Rock marks the sacred summit of Mount Moriah. The site is also significant to Judaism and Christianity.

KING DAVID CAPTURED JERUSALEM at the beginning of the first century BC and built an altar on the summit of Mount Moriah, where Abraham had prepared to sacrifice his son Isaac. This rock was considered by many to be the center of the world. It was here that David's son Solomon later built the Great Temple, which housed the Ark of the Covenant, and a small part of the platform on which it stood still exists. The temple was rebuilt after the destruction of the city by Nebuchadnezzar, and both platform and temple were extended by King Herod during the first century BC. In the seventh century AD a mosque was built nearby, marking the spot where Muhammad ascended to receive the Islamic commandments from Allah. Pilgrims can still see his footprint and three hairs from his beard.

The Wailing Wall, properly known as the Western Wall (*Kotel Maaravi* in Hebrew), is one of Judaism's most poignant symbols. After the Roman army had destroyed Jerusalem in AD 70, killing or enslaving its inhabitants, survivors were forbidden to return to the site of the Temple of Solomon. Later, the faithful were permitted to return once a year to the scene of devastation to weep over the stones, and the tradition continues to this day. The wall, which remained in Jordanian hands from 1948 until the Six-Day War of 1967, is part of the platform of the enlarged temple dating from the time of King Herod.

LEFT The Tower of David citadel, originally constructed during King David's time. It has been destroyed and refortified several times.

RIGHT View over Jerusalem's Old City and the Dome of the Rock. The dome is said to have been gilded originally with melted-down coins.

RIGHT The Church of All Nations, which commemorates the Garden of Gethsemane.

THE HISTORY

- **3000–2000 BC** *Jerusalem founded by Canaanites.*
- **960 BC** *Solomon builds the First Temple.*
- **586 BC** *Nebuchadnezzar destroys Jerusalem and takes captives to Babylon.*
- **525 BC** *Jewish exiles return to build the Second Temple.*
- **AD 70** *Temple destroyed after Jewish revolt against Rome.*
- **AD 688–692** *Arab conqueror Umar ibn-Khatib uncovers temple rock and builds mosque nearby.*
- **AD 1228** *Christian Crusaders capture Jerusalem.*
- **AD 1517–1917** *Ottoman Empire rules the city.*
- **AD 1917** *British troops capture Jerusalem. British declare support for Jewish homeland in Palestine.*
- **AD 1948** *First Arab-Israeli war ends in partition of city between Israel and Jordan.*
- **AD 1967** *Israel takes control of whole city.*
- **AD 2003** *Scientists use carbon dating to show when Jerusalem's Siloam Tunnel, was excavated.*

BROAD WALL

Archeologists had to revise their ideas about the Old City after a team led by Professor Nahman Avigad discovered part of the city wall in the 1970s. Known as the Broad Wall, it indicated that, during the eighth century BC, Jerusalem had extended much farther than experts had previously believed, reaching as far as the slopes of Mount Zion.

The unearthed section, which is 7m (23ft) thick and up to 3m (10ft) high, dates from 701 BC when King Hezekiah of Judah built defenses against Assyrian invasion, having refused to pay tribute to the Assyrian king, Sennacherib. The Biblical account given by Isaiah—a contemporary of Hezekiah's—tells of Hezekiah noting 'the breaches of the city of David', numbering the houses of Jerusalem and breaking them down to fortify a new wall.

Excavations revealed that residences on the site had been demolished and that their stones had been reused. Isaiah goes on to describe a ditch being constructed between the two walls for the 'water of the old pool'—namely the Pools of Siloam. In the end, Sennacherib overran most of Judah but did not take the city of Jerusalem.

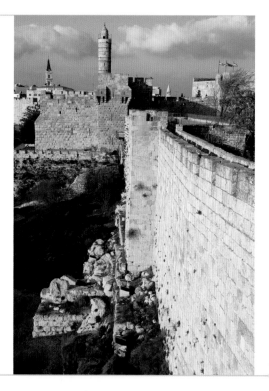

Built of huge dressed stone blocks more than 1.2m (4ft) high, it gives a memorable indication of the vast scale of the temple.

The Church of the Holy Sepulchre, in the northwestern quarter of the Old City, stands at the end of the Via Dolorosa, the route along which Christ carried his cross from the headquarters of the Roman procurator to the place of his crucifixion. The first church to stand here, built in AD 326 by Helena, mother of Emperor Constantine, was destroyed by the Persians in 614. A rebuilt version was razed by the Egyptian caliph El-Hakim in 1009 and a series of shrines was built in its place. When the Crusaders entered the city in the 12th century, they brought the shrines under one vast, cruciform roof, an arrangement that largely survives to this day.

SEE ALSO
- *The Blue Mosque* page 72
- *Carthage* page 124
- *Fez Medina* page 126

LEFT Blue-and-white tiles from the 16th century decorate the façade of the Dome of the Rock.

ABOVE The Church of the Holy Sepulchre is believed to mark the site of Christ's resurrection.

THE DOME OF THE ROCK

The Dome of the Rock is one of Islam's holiest shrines and is in the world's oldest Islamic building. The dome, said to have been made originally of gold, is an outward symbol of the sacred rock that it shelters and is 20m (65ft) in diameter and 34m (110ft) high.

An outer arcade has an octagonal plan echoed by the outer walls of the building. The rock sits at the center of the building and the arcades around it allow processions of pilgrims to move freely around the object of veneration. Inside there is sumptuous mosaic work showing clear Byzantine influence.

PETRA

- The façade of the Treasury measures 27m (90ft) in width and 40m (130ft) in height.

- Its design is classical rather than Nabataean.

- The urn that tops the Treasury's façade is believed to have contained treasure belonging to a pharaoh. Early visitors took pot shots at it in the hope of dislodging its riches.

MENTION PETRA AND CHANCES are that someone will respond with the familiar quotation: 'A rose-red city, half as old as time'. These words are from a poem by the 19th-century Englishman J.W. Burgon. Unfortunately, the description is not completely accurate, as Burgon himself conceded when he visited the place some years later. Petra is not so much rose-red as salmon-pink and is not really a city either. It's more of a monumental cemetery— any houses here were probably made of mud and have long since disappeared. Petra is a place that poses many unanswered questions, and this air of mystery makes an already spectacular site all the more fascinating.

In the sixth century BC a nomadic tribe, the Nabataeans, gained control of a rift valley area between Aqaba and the Dead Sea on the eastern side of Wadi Arabah in Jordan. (A wadi is a ravine or dry river valley that may flood at certain times of the year.) Gaining control over important existing trade routes, the Nabataeans became powerful and wealthy, and Petra is their legacy. It is a complex of monuments once believed to be houses but now recognized as tombs, cut into the rock in an inaccessible area 914m (3,000ft) above sea level. Some have remarkable classical detailing while others have a distinctive Nabataean 'crow-step' decoration and reveal the influence of Egyptian and Assyrian building styles. All the emphasis is on the façades; inside, the bare chambers are completely free of ornament.

Petra became part of the Roman Empire in AD 106, acquiring a forum, baths, a theater and all the usual elements associated with Roman civilization. Trade patterns changed with the rise of Palmyra and obscurity followed. For centuries Petra was known only to local tribesman, who had little difficulty in warding off inquisitive strangers until rediscovery came in 1812. A Swiss explorer, Johan Burckhardt, fluent in Arabic, persuaded a local

THE DEIR

A climb of about half an hour from Petra leads to the Deir, which has been described as a monastery or a temple. Here is another huge rock-cut façade similar to the Treasury, 40m (130ft) high and 46m (150ft) wide, with a doorway that, at 8m (26ft) high, dwarfs anyone standing in it.

Inside there is one large chamber and, approached by steps at the far end, a niche that may have held an image of god. According to one theory, the Deir was the scene of important religious festivals and the area in front of it was levelled to accommodate large groups of pilgrims or worshippers.

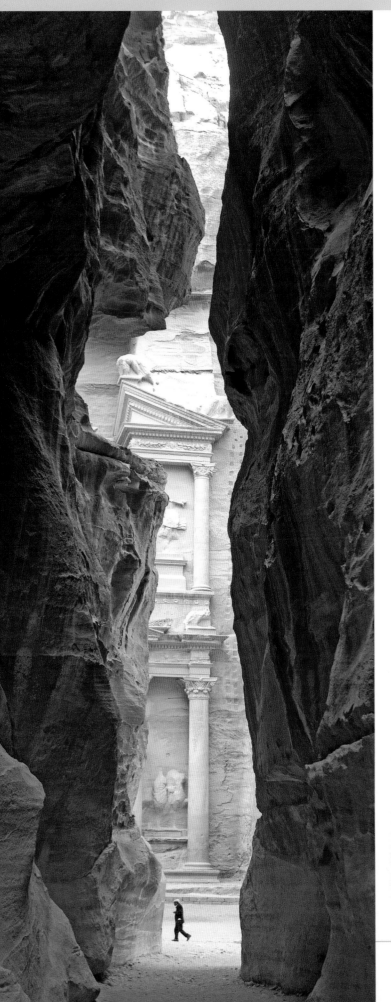

guide that he wished to sacrifice a goat at a tomb, near which there was said to be a buried city. Burckhardt was escorted along the Siq—the deep, narrow cleft in the rocks through which visitors approach the site today— and he came upon the dramatic view of the Treasury, or el-Kasneh, perhaps Petra's most famous monument.

Beyond the Treasury the valley opens out, revealing numerous rock-cut tombs in pink sandstone. The carving that has been exposed to the wind has eroded, although enough archeological evidence has been found to suggest that originally Petra was clad in stucco decoration.

SEE ALSO
- *Ayutthaya* page 112
- *Carthage* page 124
- *Jerusalem* page 76

LEFT AND OPPOSITE PAGE The towering walls of the Siq conceal Petra from the approaching visitor until the last moment, when the Treasury comes into view. Petra's Treasury resembles a Greek classical structure, but it was carved out of solid rock.

THE HIGH PLACE

A steep climb leads to the Attuf Ridge, where two obelisks sit, one on a manmade plateau and another, a little farther up, on a flattened area measuring around 61m by 18m (200ft by 60 ft).

This 'High Place' has been interpreted as a setting for ritual sacrifice with a high altar on which offerings were made, perhaps to the two gods that the Nabataeans are believed to have worshipped, Dusares and Al Uzza.

The altar is equipped with drainage channels, presumably for blood, and there is some evidence to suggest that some sacrifices performed by the Nabataeans were human.

BURJ KHALIFA

- **Standing 828m (2,717ft) Burj Khalifa, in Dubai, is the tallest building in the world and the tallest structure of any kind ever built.**

- **Construction began in 2004 during Dubai's great building boom and was completed in 2009 in the depths of an economic recession.**

- **Originally known as Burj Dubai, it was renamed in honour of President Khalifa of Dubai.**

SIGNIFICANTLY TALLER AT THE TIME of its completion than any other buildings on the planet, the silvery steel and glass tower of Burj Khalifa rises out of an artificial lake and appears to spiral its way to a dramatic point. It has been described as one of the world's most elegant skyscrapers, and like a plant whose upper stalks have been peeled away. The project was conceived as part of Dubai's strategy of using grand architectural statements to diversify from being solely an oil-based economy to becoming also a world-class center for business and tourism. A property boom in the first decade of the 21st century transformed the city's skyline: Dubai is now firmly identified with iconic modern buildings.

Burj Khalifa architect Adrian Smith had been involved in the design of many of the world's tallest structures, including the Trump Tower in Chicago and the Jin Mao Tower in Shanghai. His approach is to relate his designs to their time and cultural setting, and he has certainly played his part in reinforcing the new building culture of Dubai, inspired by local forms including sand dunes and minarets. The Y-shaped floorplan of the tower is based on a local desert flower, and aims to maximize natural light and views for those inside.

Smith is said to have argued successfully for increasing the planned height of the tower by some 20m (66ft) during construction—not to achieve more commercial floorspace, but simply to enhance the elegance of the design. At the time of completion it outstripped the world's next tallest structures, Toronto's CN Tower (553m/1,815ft) and Taiwan's

Taipei 101 skyscraper (509m/1,670ft), by wide margins. However, Smith describes Burj Khalifa as created primarily not to deliver a list of firsts, but to lift the spirits of the nation.

Built at a cost of US $1.5bn, the tower is nearly twice the height of the Empire State Building. As it stands in an area prone to high winds and earthquakes, this raised unprecedented technical challenges. Its resistance to wind pressure was tested by subjecting a scale model to the forces of a wind tunnel. Its double-decker lifts, running at 64 km/h (40mph), are among the fastest in the world.

Burj Khalifa is part of Downtown Dubai, a new district encompassing some of the city's major landmarks. As well as the tower and one of the world's largest shopping malls, it is home to the Dubai Fountain, a choreographed sound-and-light show extending over the lake and featuring 6,600 lights and 25 colored projectors. Its jets spout water as high as 150m (490ft) into the air. Daily performances, held in the evening, are accompanied by classical, contemporary Arabic and world music.

The tower's completion as the tallest structure on earth returned the Middle East to a position it has not held since the early 14th century, when Lincoln Cathedral in England overtook the Great Pyramid at Giza; the Pyramid had held the record for nearly 4,000 years. By 2010, around four out of five of the world's tallest buildings were in Asia or the Middle East, and many more have been proposed, although it remains to be seen when and whether they will be constructed—and for how long Burj Khalifa will retain its premier status.

PALM BEACHES

Dubai's development boom featured massive land reclamation projects. Most striking are the artificial island complexes, constructed largely of sand dredged from the shallow waters of the Arabian Gulf. The World, an archipelago roughly in the shape of the continents, lies 4km (2.5 miles) offshore, while The Palms, three schemes shaped like palm trees, are closer to land.

Palm Jumeirah, pictured here, consists of 16 'fronds' and a curving surrounding island that acts as a breakwater. The first monorail in the Middle East, opened in 2009, links it to the mainland. Still under construction at the time of writing, these planned developments will together increase Dubai's coastline by more than 640km (400 miles).

SEE ALSO

- *The Eiffel Tower* page 26
- *The Empire State Building* page 162
- *The Great Pyramid* page 118

SUPER SITE

THE GREAT WALL OF CHINA

- At the top, the wall was 5.5m (18ft) wide, enough to allow infantry to march along it ten abreast or cavalrymen to ride five abreast.

- Existing sections stand an at average of 9m (30ft) high.

- The watch towers rise to 12m (40ft).

- During the Ming dynasty (1368–1644) the wall was renovated 18 times.

The Great Wall of China is one of the most remarkable feats of engineering of all time, and one of the most brutal. It was constructed over about 10 years after 220 BC by the first man to rule a united China, the savagely formidable despot Qin Shihuangdi. The wall was a bulwark against the warlike nomadic horsemen of the Mongolian plains to the north, and probably also a titanic assertion of the Emperor's own power and glory.

BELOW The Great Wall crosses rugged country near Simitai, northeast of Beijing. This section has closely spaced towers and forms the highest part of the defenses.

OPPOSITE PAGE At Jinshanling (top), some of the watch towers have been restored to their original 16th-century appearance, while elsewhere (below) they remain semi-ruinous.

THE HISTORY

- **770–476 BC** *Ducal states extend existing defense works.*
- **220–210 BC** *Qin Shihuangdi, ruler of unified China, orders the building of the Wall.*
- **127–119 BC** *Wall extended westward into Hexi corridor and Xinjiang region by Emperor Wu of the Han dynasty.*
- **AD 607** *Reconstruction work begins under Sui dynasty.*
- **AD 1368–1644** *Further building takes place under Ming dynasty, using bricks and granite.*
- **AD 1987** *Listed as a World Heritage site by UNESCO.*

SECTIONS OF DEFENSIVE WALL had been built earlier by the various rival minor kingdoms of northern China, but nothing on the scale of the Great Wall. Qin Shihuangdi conscripted an army of peasants, soldiers, convicts and political prisoners, and put his most successful general, Meng Tian, in charge of rebuilding and connecting the earlier sections in a single barrier through the mountains on his northern frontier. The wall snaked its way up and down the mountains, through desert country and through marshes, and was built of earth faced with brick on stone foundations. From the watch towers, smoke signals during the day and bonfires at night sent information cross-country with unprecedented speed.

It is said that 300,000 people toiled to build the wall: the organization of such a workforce was itself an astonishing achievement. Legend says that a wizard told Qin Shihuangdi that the wall would not stand unless *wan* ('10,000') were buried in it. In an attempt to avoid the prophesied slaughter, the emperor had a man named Wan killed and interred in the wall instead. Despite this it seems that thousands who worked on the wall did die there, and were buried in its foundations. It has been called the world's longest graveyard: the Wall of Tears.

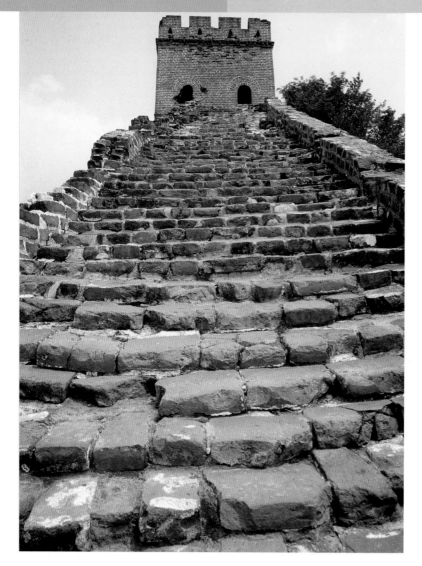

The Great Wall was an effective defense when properly manned, but over subsequent centuries it was neglected, abandoned and rebuilt many times over. When the Sui dynasty rulers ordered reconstruction in the seventh century, it is said that no fewer than a million people were forced to work on it and that half of them perished. The wall took its final shape under the Ming dynasty, and sections of it have been restored for tourists.

The wall runs from near Bo Hai Sea northeast of Beijing across China and into the Gobi Desert. Figures for its total length vary by hundreds of miles, because of the numerous rebuildings. The wall twists and turns on itself, with parallel walls in some places and numerous offshoots that may or may not be counted. A 2009 survey using the latest GPS and infra-red technologies found the total wall length was 6,259km (3,889 miles)—including 290km (180 miles) of previously unmapped wall that had been submerged by sandstorms.

SEE ALSO
■ *The Forbidden City* page 88
■ *The Three Gorges Dam* page 92

LEFT Steps lead up to a watch tower. Goats were used as beasts of burden in the construction, each carrying a single brick at a time.

LEFT BELOW A hiking route from Jinshanling to Simitai passes sections of the wall that survive from the Ming dynasty.

THE MING TOMBS

The Ming dynasty ruled China from 1368 to 1644, and 13 of their emperors rest in the Badaling Valley, near the Great Wall. Their tombs were positioned according to the principles of Chinese geomancy, which ensured that they would be surrounded by positive supernatural influences.

A succession of great gates marks the Spirit Way, which each emperor's funeral procession followed. At the Great Red Gate, everyone had to dismount and proceed on foot, as the central arch of the gate was to be used only by the emperor's coffin. Just beyond the arch is a stele (an upright slab of stone) 9m (30ft) high, which rests on the back of a huge stone tortoise, a symbol of the universe and immortality. The road passes between 15th-century statues of lions, horses, camels and other animals that are believed to bring good fortune, with human figures providing a guard of honor.

The Dragon and the Phoenix gates lead to the tombs. The largest and best-preserved one belongs to Emperor Yongle, who died in 1424. It is believed that 16 concubines were buried alive in his tomb.

QIN SHIHUANGDI

Qin Shihuangdi, of the Qin dynasty, was one of the most ruthless and effective tyrants in history, a Chinese version of Russia's Ivan the Terrible.

He was born in 259 BC and succeeded to his father's kingdom as a boy of 13, though it was rumored that his real father was a merchant. A terrifying autocrat, he mastered the various warring kingdoms along the Yellow River and to the south to create an empire in 221 BC.

He was a great builder and used forced labor to construct roads and canals as well as the Great Wall. He also standardized Chinese script and coins, weights and measures.

Qin Shihuangdi left his mark on China, as his imperial system lasted through recurrent changes of dynasty from 221 BC until 1911, when it was finally toppled after more than 2,000 years, the longest surviving political regime in history. A few years after his death in 210 BC, the Han dynasty took power.

BELOW The fortifications at Jiayuguan date from 1372. The pass here once marked the most westerly point in China and was part of the ancient Silk Road.

THE FORBIDDEN CITY

- The Forbidden City is square in shape, on an axis running north to south, and is surrounded by a broad moat and a 9m (30ft)-high wall.

- All the major buildings face south, turning away from hostile supernatural forces and the Siberian winds.

- There are nearly 10,000 rooms altogether.

CUT OFF BY ITS MOAT and purple wall, banned to all ordinary mortals, roofed in the yellow tiles allowed only to emperors, the Forbidden City was a city within a city at the heart of Beijing. The Ming and Qing dynasties lived and ruled here until the fall of the empire in 1911.

Beijing's history goes back much further, but the Forbidden City itself was created by Emperor Yongle of the Ming dynasty, who moved his capital here from Nanking in 1421. It was pillaged when the Manchus toppled the Ming dynasty in 1644, but the Manchu emperors, who installed themselves on the Dragon Throne as the Qing dynasty, restored it to its former majesty. New temples and palaces were built and lakes and gardens were laid out. By the 18th century the city had reached the height of its glory.

BELOW The Forbidden City, a UNESCO World Heritage Site, has the largest collection of preserved wooden buildings in the world.

OPPOSITE BELOW Golden lions guard the Gate of Heavenly Purity, which leads to a raised walkway to the emperor's official residence, the Palace of Heavenly Purity.

IMPERIAL CAPITAL

Beijing was given its present name, which simply means northern capital, by Emperor Yongle in the 15th century. He built the Forbidden City inside the Imperial City, which was also square in shape and surrounded by its own walls. It had been an important town long before that, but in the 13th century it was sacked by Genghis Khan's Mongol hordes.

The oldest buildings in Beijing today date from the subsequent rebuilding, from 1267, by Kublai Khan, the Mongol emperor who made it his winter capital.

In 1648 the new Qing emperor ordered the Chinese inhabitants to leave to make room for his Manchu and Mongol supporters. The Chinese inhabitants moved to the south, and this area was later named the Chinese City.

Inside, arranged symmetrically, are palaces, gates, courtyards, streams and gardens. The emperor, his mother, his wives and his concubines lived here, along with an army of eunuchs and servants. Life was regulated by an elaborate code of rules, etiquette and taboos.

The main gate is the massive southern Meridian (Wumen) Gate, from which the emperor formally reviewed his troops. Beyond it is a courtyard crossed by a stream, known as the River of Gold, which is itself crossed by five marble bridges, representing the five virtues and leading to the elegant Gate of the Supreme Harmony. Beyond this gate is a vast courtyard, said to have been designed to hold 90,000 people. At the far side, raised on a high marble terrace, is the largest building in the Forbidden City: the Hall of Supreme Harmony, where the emperor sat enthroned on great state occasions.

Beyond this lie two more grand ceremonial chambers, the Hall of Perfect Harmony and the Hall of Preserving Harmony. Farther north is the warren of rooms where the emperor and his family lived. In some of them are displays of the impressive and beautiful artifacts that the emperors accumulated, including a notable collection of clocks and automata. However, these are only a fraction of the original treasures: the Japanese looted the Forbidden City in the 1930s and the Nationalists took many items away with them to Taiwan in 1949. Landscaped imperial gardens surrounded the Forbidden City on three sides: two are now public parks.

SEE ALSO
■ *The Great Wall of China* page 84

OUTSIDE THE CITY

South of the Forbidden City is the vast expanse of Tiananmen Square. The name, which means 'Square of the Gate of Heavenly Peace', is inextricably linked with the violent repression of protests in 1989. Mao Zedong proclaimed the People's Republic of China here in 1949 and the People's Culture Palace occupies the former Temple of the Imperial Ancestors.

Not far away, in a spacious park, is the Temple of Heaven, where emperors carried out the rituals believed to preserve the order and harmony of the universe, offering sacrifices at the circular three-tiered Altar of Heaven.

In the northwest outskirts of Beijing is the Summer Palace. This was looted in 1860, but a new palace was built in 1888.

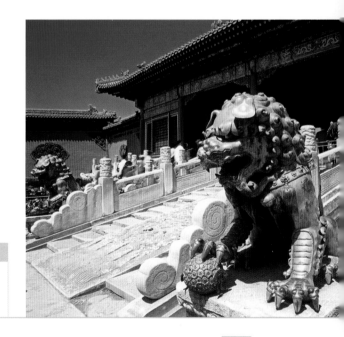

THE GUILIN HILLS

- The limestone region, of which the Guilin Hills are a part, stretches across south-central China to northern Vietnam.

- In Chinese, Guilin means 'forest of cassia trees'.

- The Guilin Hills reach average heights of 99m (325ft).

- Fubo Hill gives panoramic views of Guilin City.

PINNACLES OF ROCK CLUSTER together on the shores of the River Li, in the Guangxi Zhuang Autonomous Region of southern China. The thick layers of limestone that form the Guilin Hills were laid down under an ancient sea. Millions of years later the land was uplifted and acidic rain began to dissolve those rocks, which were already weakened by cracks and fractures. When the land was uplifted a second time, some weakened rocks collapsed, leaving free-standing conical towers made of a limestone more resistant to erosion. These towers are good examples of what is known as 'tower karst' scenery.

ABOVE Country roads curve around an isolated limestone peak. A popular Chinese saying has it that Guilin's scenery is the 'best among all under heaven'.

LAND AND WATER

Limestone consists almost entirely of calcium carbonate. Groundwater and rain can both contain carbon dioxide, forming a mild acid that is capable of dissolving limestone, especially where the rock is already weakened by cracks and crevices. Thus water that moves across the surface of harder rocks may suddenly disappear underground when it reaches the softer limestone, often into geological formations known as sinkholes, sometimes reappearing elsewhere as springs.

As the water flows underground, caves are eroded, and the dissolved minerals are deposited on the walls of caves or drip from the ceiling to form stalactites and stalagmites. Some of the best caves formed in this way include the Frasassi Caves in Italy and Réseau Jean-Bernard in the foothills of the French Alps, one of the deepest known caves in the world.

The steep-sided hills rise abruptly from bright-green valley floors and disappear into the distance as row upon row of jagged summits and peaks. Many are draped with vines and small trees that maintain a tenuous hold on their rocky sides. Others explode with color when orchids come into bloom. Sometimes shrouded in a soft mist and reflected in the sluggish waters of the River Li, these hills emanate a mystical quality that has been an inspiration for artists and poets for centuries.

This ageless landscape was for many years closed to Western visitors. The Ming court, which retreated to Guilin when the Manchus took over Beijing in 1664, included some Jesuit priests, who were attempting to convert the royal household to Christianity. Apart from a small group of imprisoned Portuguese seamen in 1550, these Jesuits were the first Westerners to see the Guilin Hills. When Communist forces took over Guilin in 1949, they closed the city to most foreigners; the city was reopened only in 1973.

The Guilin region contains rich agricultural land, and the underground water is often pumped to the surface for irrigation. Some of the underground rivers that flow through the tropical karst are used as sources of hydroelectric power. Karst landscapes get their name from an area of caves and sinkholes covering 80km (50 miles) in northwestern Slovenia. Formed of limestone, such landscapes usually have dry and arid surfaces, which are drained of water by underground channels and streams. This kind of landscape accounts for about 10 percent of the surface of the Earth.

SEE ALSO
■ *Table Mountain* page 146
■ *Tierra del Fuego* page 208

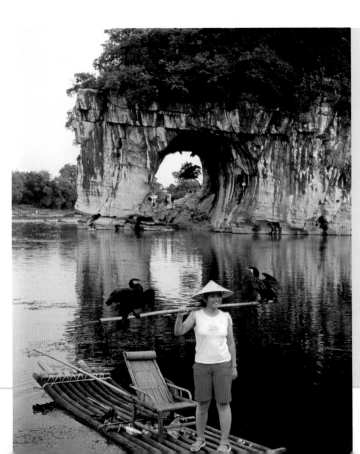

SECRET PLACES

The Guilin Hills are riddled with caves and passageways created by the erosive rain, and during World War II many people hid here to escape Japanese bombing. It was also the site of fierce fighting in the late 1960s when clashing Red Army factions turned the region into a battlefield. The people of Guilin once again fled to the caves in the hills to hide from the fighting.

One well-known cave is the Reed Flute Cave, one of a series of caverns and channels full of delicate stalactites and stalagmites. It is named for the reeds that grow outside it, which are used to make the flutes that produce the haunting melodies evocative of China.

ABOVE Tiers of painstakingly created rice terraces make use of the hilly terrain of the Guilin ridge known as the Dragon's Spine.

THE THREE GORGES DAM

- **Three Gorges is the collective name given to the Qutang, Wuxia, and Xiling gorges.**

- **The Three Gorges area begins at Baidicheng in Fengjie County, Sichuan Province and ends at Nanjinguan in Yichang County, Hubei province, 193km (120 miles) away.**

- **This is the world's biggest hydroelectric scheme.**

ABOVE Two new locks enable barges to bypass the dam. Six times more freight can now pass through the gorges than before the dam was built.

CHINA'S MASSIVE HYDROELECTRIC DAM project, begun in 1994 and largely completed in 2008, was a task of staggering proportions. The project was conceived to control calamitous floods and provide irrigation and electricity, but has been questioned by environmentalists and human rights groups across the world.

The Yangtze, Asia's longest river, has always been prone to flooding, often on a devastating scale. In the 20th century alone more than a million people were killed by floodwaters. Production of electricity, the dam's other main purpose, is also an urgent need in this vast country: the dam's hydroelectric system generates the equivalent of 12 nuclear power stations. Another aim was to enhance trade and industry by improving navigation for large ships, which could not previously pass into the upper reaches of the river. Ships of up to 3,000 tons (3,307 tons) will be lifted over the dam in the biggest ship-lift container ever built—120m (394ft) long and 18m (59ft) wide—scheduled for completion in 2014.

Opponents of the dam pointed to the submerging of hundreds of historical and cultural sites, the loss of around 1,500 villages and towns and 13 cities, and the displacement of well over a million people. They also fear that it will lead to the extinction of many endangered species and the destruction of commercial fish stocks, as pollutants and sediment become concentrated upstream of the dam. Whatever the pros and cons of the project, there is no denying its breathtaking ambition.

Proposals for a dam were first mooted in 1919, the first designs were planned in the 1950s and the go-ahead

BELOW Around a quarter of a million people worked on the Three Gorges project, with some 20,000 involved in constructing the dam itself.

was given in 1970. In order to make construction work possible engineers had to divert the Yangtze, using coffer dams to shift the river away from the site itself in the biggest such project ever undertaken.

At the center of the dam, 22 gates act as an overflow, a fail-safe element designed to deal with four times the Yangtze's average flow and cut the risk of a catastrophic flood downstream from once every 10 years to once every 100 years. But as demand for electricity has soared in China, the project now meets only a few percent of the country's requirements, rather than the 10 percent that was planned originally.

SEE ALSO
■ *The River Nile* page 122
■ *The Hoover Dam* page 168
■ *Feats of Engineering* page 224

ABOVE New landscaping at Yichang provides visitors with a view over the site. Tourism may help to provide an income for people displaced by the dam.

THREATENED SPECIES
Endangered wildlife species threatened by the Three Gorges Dam include the giant panda, the Chinese tiger, the Chinese alligator, the Chinese sturgeon and the Siberian crane. The World Wildlife Fund for Nature considers the rare Yangtze dolphin to be one of the most endangered creatures in the world.

Environmentalists and conservationists suggested that an alternative scheme involving a number of smaller dams would have a less devastating ecological impact. The government's argument was that although such a scheme would succeed in monitoring floodwaters and irrigating crops, it would be unable to generate the vast quantity of power that the Three Gorges project was intended to produce.

SUPER SITE
THE TAJ MAHAL

■ Arjumand Banu Begum, Shah Jehan's wife, was known as Mumtaz Mahal (Chosen One of the Palace). Taj Mahal is an abbreviation of her name.

■ The Taj Mahal was built by an estimated 20,000 workers and took 22 years to complete.

■ The dome is shaped like a pearl, an Islamic symbol representing both womanhood and paradise.

In 1631 the wife of the Moghul emperor of India died at the age of 36, giving birth to her 14th child. Her husband, Shah Jehan, had lost a beloved wife and a shrewd political advisor and, according to one account, his hair turned white with grief. He vowed to build a tomb worthy of his wife's memory, something utterly without equal anywhere in the world, and few would deny that in the Taj Mahal, he succeeded.

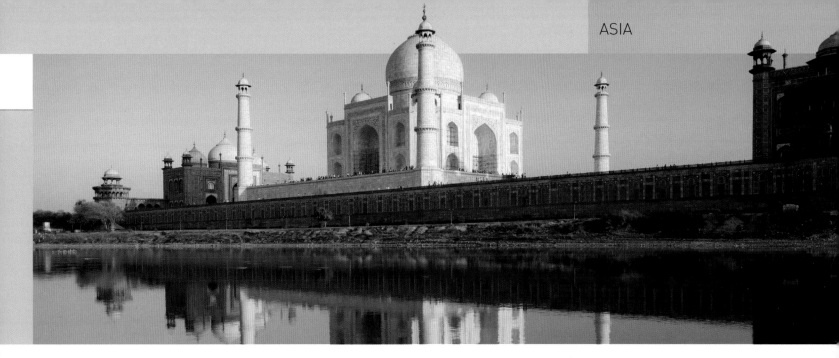

THE TAJ MAHAL HAS BEEN lauded so many times that many visitors approach it wondering if they will be disappointed. The silhouette, familiar from countless photographs, crops up whenever one instantly recognizable emblem of India is needed. And yet disappointment is rare. The Taj can be seen again and again and still surprise, such is its ability to take on a different character according to the time of day and the nature of the light. Although a tomb, the building lacks the cold monumentality one might expect; instead, it seems to float between heaven and Earth. The proportions, the remarkable symmetry, the surrounding gardens, and the reflections in the water all combine to create a place of indescribable beauty.

A Frenchman and a Venetian are said to have had some part in its construction, but no single architect's name is recorded with any certainty, as befits a building intended to be associated with the name of its occupant only. It is made of marble brought from quarries 322km (200 miles) away, but is by no means the pure white building that some photographs suggest. Thousands of precious stones are inlaid in the marble surfaces, and black marble is used for calligraphic decoration. There is also remarkable craftsmanship in the pierced marble screens, which cast dramatic shadows when struck by the sun. Once there were silver doors and, inside, a gold

ABOVE Flanking the central mausoleum are the symmetrical red sandstone mosque and rest house, each with four octagonal towers and three domes.

ABOVE Shah Jehan was one of the most powerful rulers of his time. His name can be translated as 'king of the world'.

OPPOSITE The Taj Mahal is enclosed by a geometrically patterned walled garden in the Persian style. The four minarets are shorter than usual to emphasize the height of the dome.

THE HISTORY

- **1612** Arjumand Banu Begum marries Prince Khurram.
- **1628** Prince Khurram becomes the fifth Moghul Emperor and is named Shah Jehan.
- **1631** Death of Arjuman Banu Begam.
- **1653** Taj Mahal completed.
- **1810** Cracks discovered in underground vaults.
- **1830s** Lord William Bentinck, the Governor General of Bengal, proposes to dismantle the Taj Mahal and sell off the marble.

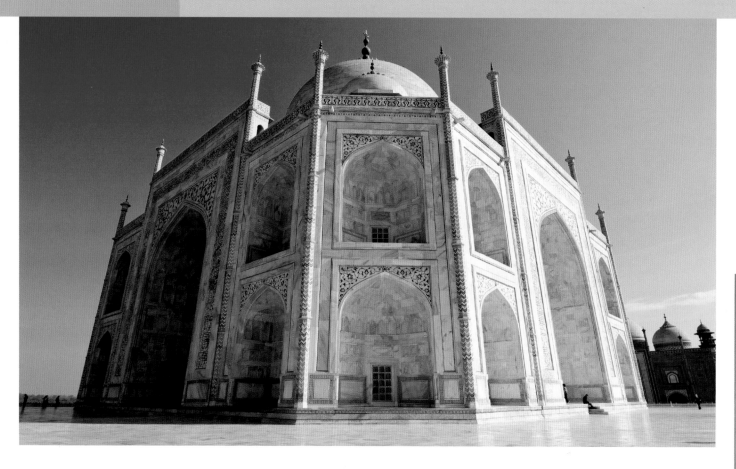

ROBBERS AND RESTORATION

The activities of the thieves who made off with the precious metals of the Taj look negligible compared with a scheme hatched by Lord William Bentinck, who was a governor general of Bengal in the 19th century. In the 1830s he put forward a money-making proposal to dismantle the Taj Mahal (which was neglected and overgrown) and ship the marble to London where it could be sold. The idea was abandoned when a similar plan for marble stripped from the Red Fort at Delhi failed due to a lack of buyers.

In the 20th century Lord Curzon, who became Viceroy of India in 1900, had the Taj Mahal restored to its former glory. He also retrieved some marble panels from the Red Fort that had previously found their way to London and had them restored to their original position. As well as the buildings he attended to the neglected ornamental gardens.

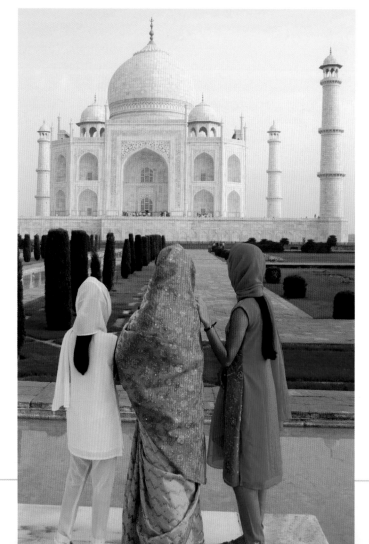

ABOVE The delicate floral patterns of inlay work adorning the marble walls feature dozens of different types of precious and semi-precious stone, such as lapis lazuli.

LEFT Lord Curzon considered the restoration of the Taj Mahal as his legacy to India: 'If I had never done anything else in India, I have written my name here...'.

railing and a cloth of pearls over the queen's cenotaph (which stands directly above the actual burial place). Thieves stole these precious items, and many have tried to extract inlaid jewels from their settings, but the magnificence still remains overwhelming.

The building is set in landscaped gardens and is approached through a massive and magnificent gateway, symbolically an entrance to paradise. Surmounted by domed pavilions, it originally had a door of solid silver studded with hundreds of silver nails. This was plundered, and the present door is of brass.

In 1658, Shah Jehan's son Aurangzeb proclaimed himself emperor and held his father under house arrest in the fort at Agra for nine years until his death. From the fort, Shah Jehan had a view of the Taj Mahal in the distance and later, he too was buried there.

SEE ALSO

■ *The Red Fort* page 98

MOGHUL ARCHITECTURE

The Taj Mahal represents the high point of Moghul architectural achievement. The style of the monumental tomb—standing on a plinth, furnished with minarets, and approached with the same reverence as a mosque—can be seen developing and declining in Northern India. Humayun's Tomb, begun in Delhi in 1564, is an ancestor of the Taj, solid and imposing rather than delicate and ethereal. In the late 1670s Aurangzeb built an imitation of the Taj Mahal for his wife at Aurangabad, but it lacks the grace and proportion of the original.

Another tomb in Delhi, that of Safdar Jang, begun in 1753, has been called 'the last flicker of the lamp of Moghul architecture'. There is a standard pattern for these monuments: a large, onion-shaped dome, water channels, a garden divided into four sections, a plinth and minarets. The builders of the Taj managed to combine these in a way that created something unique. Some say Shah Jehan intended to build himself a black marble monument across the Jumna River, but in the event the Taj Mahal remained in solitary splendor.

THE RED FORT

■ Shah Jehan ordered the 'peacock throne' to be built for the fort's private audience chamber. The throne took seven years to build and was studded with jewels.

■ The Diwan-i-khas was a chamber for private consultations between the emperor and foreign ambassadors. It had a spacious courtyard, marble pavement and silver ceiling.

LORD CURZON
Lord Curzon, Viceroy of India at the beginning of the 20th century, arranged for restoration work to take place at the Red Fort.

After the Indian army's uprising in 1857 the British removed some inlaid marble panels from the Diwan-i-am and sent them to London. One of the subjects depicted was the Greek myth of Orpheus, which suggested that this was the work of a European. These marble panels, which had suffered the indignity of being used as table tops, were eventually exhibited in the Victoria and Albert Museum, London. Lord Curzon retrieved them and put them back in their rightful position. He also found gardeners for the Red Fort's ornamental gardens, which had been neglected.

ABOVE Shah Jehan used the Diwan-i-am for daily public audiences. The columns were painted in gold.

THE RED FORT, OR Lal Qila, takes its name from the red sandstone used to build its vast walls. Its palaces and audience chambers were celebrated for their opulent marble, silver, gold and jewels, but inevitably much of this wealth has disappeared over the years, along with some of the buildings. The fort was built for the Moghul Emperor Shah Jehan between 1638 and 1648, when he transferred his capital from Agra to what is now Delhi, then a new city called Shahjehanabad. The fort's audience chambers—the public Diwan-i-am and the private Diwan-i-khas—still survive, as do some of the royal palaces (there were originally six), including the Mumtaz Mahal, which is now a museum, and the Rang Mahal ('painted palace'), but without its paintings and silver ceiling. The Khas Mahal is a set of three private imperial apartments designed for eating, sleeping and worship. An arcade of shops leads into the fort from the impressive Lahore Gate, and the royal baths also survive.

BELOW Standing at the heart of the planned city of Shahjehanabad (now Old Delhi), the fort complex at one time housed more than 3,000 people.

POTALA PALACE

- ■ Potala Palace is on a rocky outcrop called Marpori (The Red Hill), about 90m (295ft) above Lhasa.

- ■ The name of the palace derives from a Sanskrit word meaning 'Buddha's mountain'.

- ■ The solid-silver *stupa* (tomb chest) of the 13th Dalai Lama, who died in 1933, stands more than 21m (70ft) high.

THE PALACE OF THE DALAI LAMA dominates Tibet's holy city of Lhasa, towering 13 floors high, with white walls, regiments of windows, and serried roofs. Songsten Gampo, Buddhist king of Tibet in the seventh century AD, built a palace on this spot, and in 1645 the fifth Dalai Lama, ruler of Tibet, ordered work to begin on a new palace on the site. When he died in 1682 the building was not yet finished, so his death was kept secret until its completion in 1694. Now a museum, it was the winter residence of the Dalai Lamas until the 14th escaped into exile in India in 1959.

In the 1,000-plus rooms there are 10,000 shrines and 20,000 statues. In addition to government offices, staff living quarters and a monastic training school, there were meditation halls, libraries, armories, granaries, torture chambers and a dungeon called the Cave of Scorpions. The fifth Dalai Lama and seven successors are all laid to rest in the palace complex.

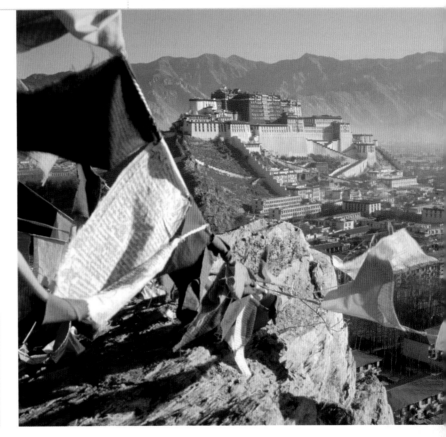

SEE ALSO
- ■ *Ayutthaya* page 112
- ■ *Metéora Monasteries* page 56
- ■ *Wat Phra Keo* page 110

ABOVE Prayer flags flutter on Chokpuri Hill, one of the three sacred hills of Lhasa. The palace, beyond, is on another holy site.

LEFT As they process around the walls of one of the palace shrines, pilgrims spin prayer wheels.

OCEAN OF WISDOM

Tibetan Buddhism developed from a combination of the Buddhism of northern India and Nepal and the native Tibetan religion, Bon. The Dalai Lama, the head of the sect that eventually came to power, means 'ocean of wisdom'. A feature of Tibetan Buddhism is succession by reincarnation: when a Dalai Lama dies, the search begins for the child in whom he is reborn. This may take several years, and the child is often revealed by his ability to pick out objects that were his as the previous Dalai Lama.

Once found, the new Dalai Lama was traditionally brought to Lhasa for training before taking up his duties at the age of 18.

HOUSES OF WORSHIP

The concept of sacred sites is probably as old as humanity itself, and almost as old is the practice of marking such sites with shrines, monuments or buildings. Over the centuries these houses of one god or many have ranged from simple places of meditation to vast, ornate spaces where the faithful can congregate.

■ The Hall of the Great Buddha at Nara, Japan, is the largest wooden building in the world. The Great Buddha here was cast from 444 tons (489 tons) of bronze and the ears are 2.4m (8ft) long.

■ The 14th-century Protestant minster in Ulm, Germany, has the tallest spire in the world. It was completed in 1890 and stands 161m (528ft) high.

MOSQUES

Mosque design flourished under Islamic dynasties between the 11th and 19th centuries. Ottoman buildings emphasize the large central dome, guarded by minarets, and during the Moghuls' reign, elements of Hindu architecture were introduced. Local influences were sometimes incorporated —as in west Africa's mud-built mosques—but most designs feature a courtyard, a fountain and a colonnaded hall housing the *minbar* (pulpit) and the *mihrab*, a prayer niche set into the wall facing Mecca. Abstract decoration (depiction of living beings is forbidden) includes mosaics, fretwork and calligraphy.

Each year, Muslims from more than 70 nations undertake the *hajj*, or pilgrimage, to Mecca, in present-day Saudi Arabia. Once there they must make seven circuits of the Ka'ba (Islam's holiest shrine) and touch the Black Stone.

Left Appearing to cling precariously, the 1,400-year-old Xuankong Si ('hanging monastery') near Datong in Inner Mongolia, China, is supported by beams driven into the cliff.

Below The Ka'ba, in Mecca's Haram Mosque. The stone structure is covered with brocade draperies embroidered with holy texts; the Black Stone is in its eastern corner.

CHURCHES AND SYNAGOGUES

Early synagogues and churches were based on Roman basilicas, with a recess at the eastern end for the holy scriptures or altar. Later churches developed a cruciform structure, with four equal arms (in Eastern Europe) or one long western arm housing the nave (in the West). From the 12th century the western Gothic style introduced pointed arches and spires.

The Renaissance brought a revival of classical architecture, and decoration became increasingly lavish. More recent buildings combine several styles—as in Gaudí's Sagrada Família church in Barcelona, which mixes Gothic with swirling Art Nouveau.

TEMPLES

Hindu temples are approached through a series of towered gates. A complex of halls surrounds the square shrine, marked by a tower, and walls are exuberantly carved.

In Buddhist shrines the *stupa* (covering the Buddha's relics or form) is the ultimate goal. The Chinese equivalent—brought to Japan with Chinese Buddhism—is the tiered pagoda. Japan's indigenous religion, Shinto, is observed in plain, temple halls on stilts with steep, over-hanging roofs, approached via a *torii* or gate.

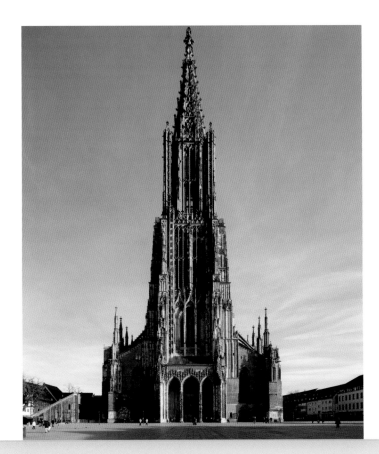

Left Ulm Minster took more than half a millennium to build. Construction began in 1377, but was not completed until 1890.

Right The Great Buddha of Kamakura was cast in 1292. More than 13m (43ft) high, it is the second-largest Buddha statue in Japan.

THE HIMALAYAS

■ The Himalayas contain 96 of the 109 peaks in the world that are over 7,315m (24,000ft) high.

■ The highest mountain in the world is Chomolungma (Mount Everest), which is 8,848m (29,029ft) high.

■ The longest glacier outside the polar regions is Siachen in the Himalayas, measuring 76km (47 miles).

EVOLVING MOUNTAINS

More than 200 million years ago the former single land mass known to geographers as Pangaea broke into two super-continents, Laurasia and Gondwana. Laurasia was made up of present-day North America, Greenland, Europe and Asia, while Gondwana comprised South America, Africa, India, Australia and Antarctica.

When Gondwana began to fragment, South America and Australia started to move toward their present positions, but Africa and India continued their northward drift until they finally collided with Eurasia. Over millions of years, and still continuing today, these collisions buckled the rocks of southern Eurasia and produced the mountains we know as the Alps and the Himalayas.

THE HIMALAYAS ARE THE GREATEST mountain range on Earth. The South American Andes form a longer chain, but are not as high. Facts and figures are one thing, but the awesome sight of the Himalayas is quite another. Although the highest mountain in the world is known across the world as Mount Everest, perhaps its Nepalese name conveys an image that might be applied to the whole range: Chomolungma, Goddess Mother of the Snows.

The Himalayan mountain range, including the Karakoram Mountains, stretches for more than 1,500 miles (2,400km) across the northern edge of the Indian subcontinent, separating it from Asia to the north. From the northwest, in northernmost Pakistan, the Karakorams extend to the southeast through Kashmir in northern India. The Himalayas sweep round to the east, taking in the mountain kingdoms of Nepal, Sikkim and Bhutan and continue into the Arunachal Pradesh province of northeastern Assam. The northern boundaries of these countries lie along the watershed of the mountains. To the north lie the Chinese regions of Tibet and Chinese Turkestan. To the west of the Karakoram the mountains divide into the Pamirs and the Hindu Kush. To the east there is a sharp swing to the south into the smaller mountains of northern Burma.

Though the native peoples of the Himalayas are expert at mountain survival, climbing as a recreation was largely developed by European sportsmen. In the 19th century, while pioneering climbers were conquering peaks in the Alps, the Department of Survey of the Government of India had triangulated the position of

BELOW Gangapurna, part of the Annapurna massif, towers above the Manang valley in Nepal. Manang village is a popular starting point for trekking and climbing expeditions.

a peak that seemed higher than the others. In 1856, the final calculations showed that the height of Peak XV on the Tibet-Nepal border was 8,840m (29,002ft), the highest in the world. (This height was revised upward in 2005.) The peak was named after Colonel Sir George Everest, the former Surveyor-General of India. Now there was a new target for the mountaineers. Not until May 29, 1953, was the summit conquered by the New Zealander Edmund Hillary and the Nepalese Sherpa, Tenzing Norgay.

In 2004, a 26-year-old Nepalese Sherpa, Pemba Dorje, set a new world record by repeating the journey to the top that had taken Hillary a total of seven weeks. It took Dorje just eight hours and ten minutes.

SEE ALSO
■ *Mount Fuji* page 106
■ *The Andes* page 209
■ *The Matterhorn* page 40

ABOVE Lamayuru is perched at 3,510m (11,515ft). This *gompa*, or Tibetan Buddhist monastery, is one of the largest and oldest in Ladakh, northern India.

HIMALAYAN MOUNTAINEERING

W. W. Graham was the first European to tackle the Himalayan mountains, in 1883. Ten years later the Royal Society and the Royal Geographical Society sent an expedition from England, under Martin Conway, to explore and climb the Karakoram Mountains. Then, in 1895, A. F. Mummery set out to climb Nanga Parbat, a peak in the Karakoram Mountains that is 8,126m (26,660ft). Many expeditions followed, often climbing subsidiary peaks while reconnoitering routes on major peaks. Between the two World Wars, the major effort focused on Mount Everest, approaching it from Tibet because Nepal was closed to expeditions.

After World War II, Nepal opened its borders to Everest expeditions and explorations from the south side began. Mountaineers now seek greater challenges, for example, by making solo ascents or ascents without oxygen tanks.

ITSUKUSHIMA SHRINE

■ Dogs are not allowed on the island of Miyajima where the shrine stands, lest they disturb the resident deer.

■ Mount Misen, the island's highest point at 530m (1,740ft), has wonderful views.

■ Offshore on a separate platform is the oldest Noh theater in Japan, built in 1568 and later restored.

JAPAN'S MOST FAMOUS GATEWAY is the red wooden *torii*, or portal, of the Itsukushima Shrine on Miyajima island, near Hiroshima. Reconstructed in 1875 on the site where a gate has stood since 1168, it stands in a small bay, its two main pillars rising 16m (53ft) and supporting a curved lintel 23m (76ft) long. Beyond it are the shrine buildings, constructed on wooden piles so that at high tide they seem to float on the water. The principal shrine is dedicated to three Shinto goddesses,

daughters of the storm god Susano, one of the major native Japanese deities. Other buildings include halls of prayer, purification and offerings, a stage for traditional Shinto dances and shrines for the god Okinonushi, a son of Susano, and another for the god Tenjin. The buildings in the bay are linked to each other by covered gangways and to the shore by a red wooden bridge.

Miyajima island is so sacred that for centuries no one could be born or die there, and pregnant women and the elderly or ill had to cross to the mainland. The dead are still buried on the mainland and their relatives are ritually cleansed before they can return to the island.

ABOVE The present shrine was rebuilt in the 16th century to a design first drawn up in 1168.

BELOW At high tide, the *torii* appears to float, but at low tide visitors can walk out to it.

PHOENIX FROM THE ASHES

At 8.15am on August 6th 1945, an area of Hiroshima, 6.5km (4 miles) in diameter was laid flat by the first atom bomb. Estimates of the numbers killed start at 100,000 and go up from there.

Since 1949 Hiroshima, which is near Miyajima island, has been rebuilt and is now a thriving city with a population of about a million. Only the skeleton of a domed exhibition hall that somehow remained standing at the heart of the destruction has been left as it was. It is now known as the A-Bomb Dome, and stands in the city's Park of Peace.

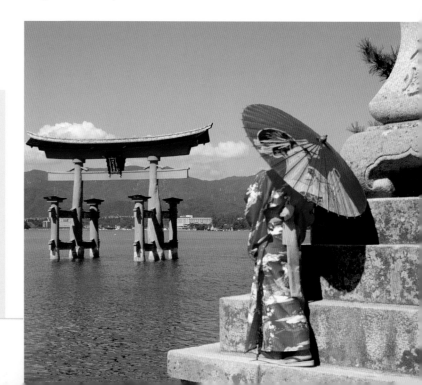

BEPPU

- ■ Beppu is one of the world's largest thermal regions.

- ■ Its hot springs and geysers emit more than 57,000 cu m (2 million cu ft) of water each day.

- ■ There are about 3,500 fumeroles (vents that allow gases to escape), hot springs and geysers in the Beppu area.

IN THE BITTER COLD OF WINTER in Beppu, in southern Japan, small monkeys head for the warmth of volcanically heated waters, occasionally sitting up to their necks in warm water while the snow settles on their heads. They even have a rota system, sending one or two delegates to fetch food while the others wait in the warm water.

The city of Beppu is at the bottom of a slope of volcanic debris hurled from one of several nearby volcanoes in the recent past. Its hot springs and geysers emit huge quantities of water each day, and the area is a major tourist attraction, with visitors immersing themselves in hot sand baths and the healing, mineral-laden waters.

For those who don't want to get into the water there is plenty to admire, including nine boiling ponds, called *jigoku* ('hells'), which occur in a fantastic range of sizes and shades. Chinoike Jigoku, for example, is rust red because the water has oxidized some of the underlying rocks, whereas the larger Umi Jigoku is deep blue, reflecting the color of the sky. The geyser Tatsu-maki Jigoku erupts every 20 minutes or so and a great spray of steam is forced high into the air with an ear-splitting hiss.

ABOVE Chinoike Jigoku owes its striking color to natural oxides.

SEE ALSO
- ■ *Pamukkale* page 70
- ■ *Rotorua* page 228
- ■ *Volcanic Iceland* page 14

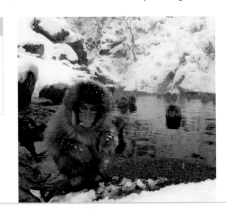

RIGHT Macaque monkeys keeping warm in Beppu's natural hot springs.

VOLCANOES AND THERMAL SPRINGS

Japan has been described as sitting on 'Mother Earth's Cradle', and with more than 500 volcanoes on the main islands, the description is apt. Many volcanoes are extinct but some remain active, including Fuji, Asama and Aso. As well as volcanoes there are hundreds of areas of thermal activity, the best known being Noboribetsu, Beppu and Kusatsu.

Noboribetsu, on Hokkaido, Japan's largest island, is home to the Jigokudani Hot Springs. Geysers, boiling springs and bubbling mud, as well as vents that give off rather unpleasant sulfurous gas, occupy a volcanic crater 2km (1.25 miles) across.

MOUNT FUJI

- Mount Fuji rises to 3,776m (12,388ft) at its peak.

- Japan is part of a string of volcanic islands on the Pacific rim, known together as 'The Ring of Fire'.

- Of Japan's 65 volcanoes, 60 are classified as active.

ALL ALONG THE PACIFIC MARGIN of Japan there is evidence of the country's dramatic volcanic history: long-dead lava fields, hot spring areas and volcanoes, several of which are still active. Many Japanese volcanoes exhibit the classic cone shape, and the most famous of these is Mount Fuji.

ABOVE Symbols of Japan: carp streamers flown for Children's Day in May, with cherry blossoms and Mount Fuji in the background.

Fuji-san (the Japanese name may be translated as Fuji-mountain or simply as a respectful form of address) lies on the main Japanese island of Honshu, about 100km (60 miles) southwest of the capital, Tokyo. It is the highest mountain in Japan and has for centuries provided an important focus in Japanese culture. Seen from the south, the mountain stands majestic and isolated, its symmetrical sides leading steeply to the truncated summit, which hides the central crater. On the southeastern flank is the explosion crater of Hoei-zan that was formed during the volcano's last eruption, in 1707. The oldest lavas on Mount Fuji have been dated as only 8,000 years old, making it a very young volcano.

Careful geological survey and the examination of drill cores from the mountain have shown that Mount Fuji is based on two much older volcanoes. Kofuji was active from about 50,000 to 9,000 years ago and is now completely hidden beneath the lava and ashes of Fuji. Kofuji itself covered an even older volcano, Komitake.

VOLCANIC SOURCES

As the crust of the Pacific Ocean floor expands from the centre, it causes volcanic activity around the margins of the ocean, where the oceanic crust slides beneath the adjacent continental crust. The oceanic crust is heated by friction against the overlying rocks, causing melting and expansion. The resulting forces lead to eruptions and earthquakes.

The younger rocks of Japan are largely volcanic in origin and earthquakes are common. Japan is not unique in this respect, as all the lands and islands surrounding the Pacific Ocean experience some form of volcanic activity. Geologists call the Pacific Rim 'The Ring of Fire'.

The popular image of Japan as a volcanic island chain is only partly true. Ancient Precambrian rocks and the sedimentary rocks that lie over them have been folded over during a slow sequence of mountain-building events. These upheavals of the Earth have given rise to Alpine-style ranges of mountains. Japan's volcanic activity—known to geologists as island-arc type volcanism—has been predominant only during the past 60 million years, which in geological terms makes this a new kid on the block.

The beauty of Mount Fuji lies in its near-perfect shape, with the top of the cone permanently covered in snow. On a fine day it is a magnificent sight, and at sunrise and sunset the mountain assumes an ethereal quality, suffused with a rose-pink light. Fuji is regarded by the Japanese as an icon of peace and serenity, the home of the gods. Followers of the Shinto religion worship the beauty of nature, so for them the sight of Mount Fuji in spring—with flowering cherry trees in front—is a moving and spiritual experience.

SEE ALSO
■ *Mount Erebus*
page 232
■ *Mount Kilimanjaro*
page 136

TOP In clear winter weather the snowy cone can be seen from central Tokyo.

LEFT With many nearby residents, seismic activity is carefully monitored.

RIGHT Climbing Fuji is a summer activity: lakes freeze there in winter.

BOROBUDUR

■ The name Borobudur means 'many Buddhas'.

■ The monument has 1,500 panels carved in relief with scenes of the Buddha's life. Hundreds of other panels depict scenes of everyday life.

■ The monument is said to contain more than 57,000 cu m (2 million cu ft) of stone.

ANCIENT KINGDOMS

Central Java is historically and culturally the island's heartland, and is rich in archeological remains. There are Buddhist and Hindu temples, ancient mosques, Portuguese castles and the palaces of Muslim sultans. With Indian influences powerful in Indonesia from the eighth century on, there were Buddhist and Hindu kingdoms whose rulers claimed to be earthly incarnations of Indian gods.

The temple complex of Prambanan was built in the ninth and tenth centuries and, like Borobudur, is covered with bas-reliefs in stone. These vividly depict mythical beasts, frolicking monkeys and the cosmic dance of the Hindu god Shiva.

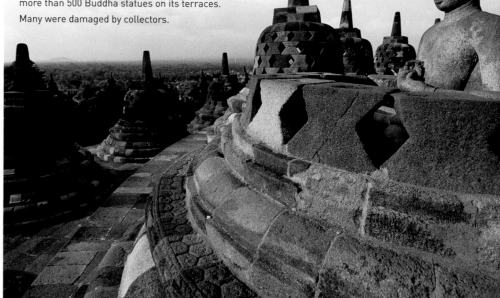

BELOW AND BOTTOM LEFT Borobudur originally had more than 500 Buddha statues on its terraces. Many were damaged by collectors.

BOROBUDUR, THE LARGEST MONUMENT in the southern hemisphere, is Java's version of Mount Meru, the giant golden peak of Indian mythology on which the universe rests. Built on and over a hill, Borobudur is a step pyramid of receding terraces, rising to about 400m (1,300ft). The five lower, square terraces represent the material world, while above them, three circular terraces represent the spiritual realm. On the upper terraces are 72 openwork *stupas* (bell-shaped shrines), each of which contains a statue of the Buddha. At the top, at the center of the highest terrace and commanding a wonderful view of the surrounding mountains, is a single shrine 15m (50ft) in diameter, which represents nirvana (spiritual freedom or heaven).

Borobudur was built by the Sailendra dynasty of kings around the year AD 800. It probably took an enormous workforce several decades to construct. The site was abandoned 200 years later and was rediscovered by an English army officer in the 19th century.

ANGKOR WAT

■ There may be as many as 200 temples on the site, an area of 260 sq km (100 square miles).

■ The whole temple complex was virtually lost in the jungle for 600 years.

■ In 1973 the complex of temples became a Khmer Rouge hideout.

THE WORLD'S MOST STUNNING EXAMPLE of Hindu architecture is in Cambodia, where the 12th-century god-king Suryavarman II built the huge temple of Angkor Wat. Dedicated to the Hindu god Vishnu, it doubled as a sanctuary and funeral monument for Suryavarman himself. Cambodia's Khmer rulers (10th–13th century AD), considered themselves to be earthly incarnations of Vishnu, and Angkor Wat was seen as a heavenly palace where the spirit of the king might roam.

The temple is surrounded by a moat, and large reservoirs lie outside the walls. The scale of the moat, some 190m (620 ft) wide, helped prevent the site becoming covered in jungle. The plan is similarly enormous. An outer wall encloses an area of 83,600sq m (100,000 square yards), and visitors approaching through a gate in the outer wall see the whole building rising up on a succession of platforms.

The temple has vivid stone carvings depicting scenes from Hindu epics, exuberant gods and goddesses cavorting in erotic poses and real figures from Khmer history marching in friezes that stretch for hundreds of meters.

SEE ALSO
■ *The Parthenon* page 54
■ *The Temple of Karnak* page 116
■ *Wat Phra Keo* page 110

ANGKOR THOM
Khmer art shows both Hindu and Buddhist influences, and both religions appear to have been treated with equal respect. Angkor Thom, a Khmer city built for Jayavarman VII at the beginning of the 13th century near Angkor Wat, has at its heart a Buddhist monument, the Bayon. Again, the king was honored in conjunction with a god and there were towers, rectangular galleries and a central, elevated shrine.

Bas-reliefs depict rulers riding on elephants surrounded by crowds of people. The deity here is Lokesvara, the Buddha who has attained the state of nirvana. The towers of the city are crowned with massive, smiling faces, which represent this state of blissful serenity.

BELOW Angkor Wat's towers are shaped like lotus buds, and would have been decorated with gilded stucco.

WAT PHRA KEO

■ The Grand Palace covers an area of 218,400 sq m (2,350,838 square feet) and has more than 100 buildings, including the Temple of the Emerald Buddha.

■ The palace walls are 1,900m (6,233ft) long.

■ The stone used to build the palace is believed to be inhabited by a guardian spirit that protects Bangkok.

BELOW Built in the 'old Bangkok' style, the 18th-century temple has polished orange and green tiles, gilded roof ornaments and pillars richly inlaid with mosaic.

WHEN RAMA I ASCENDED to the Thai throne in 1782 he moved the center of administration from the west to the east bank of the Chao Phraya River. Here, on the site of present-day Bangkok, he had fortifications and monasteries built and established his residence and offices in a huge complex of buildings now known as the Grand Palace. In 1784 the Wat Phra Keo, or Temple of the Emerald Buddha, was completed and consecrated on the upper terrace of the Grand Palace, connected to the royal residence by a gate. This most sacred of Thai temples houses the country's most revered image: a small statue of Buddha, carved from a block of jade and

TEMPLE MURALS

Above the window frames of the Wat Phra Keo are murals depicting the life of Buddha. The series starts in the southwest corner to the right of the high altar, with illustrations of Buddha's birth, childhood and youth, and his renunciation of wealth and material gain in favor of the search for Truth. On the east wall facing the high altar, more paintings show the temptation of Buddha and his subsequent enlightenment. Underneath his seat is a figure representing Mother Earth.

From here the story progresses along the northern wall with depictions of Buddha's mission and his death. The cycle ends in the northwest corner of the wall. Painted at the back of the temple is a representation of the universe.

seated high on a golden altar that represents the flying chariot of the Hindu gods. From outside, the temple is a dazzling visual and aural experience with the sun glinting on its gilded walls and bells tinkling along the roof-line. The interior is decorated with statues and murals illustrating the lives of Buddha, and door panels inlaid with mother-of-pearl depict scenes from the Indian epic Ramayana (known in Thailand as the Ramakien). A private chapel, designed for the monarch's own use, is partitioned off from the main shrine.

The 79cm (31in)-high Emerald Buddha has had an eventful life. Its origin is unknown, but it is first recorded in 1434, when it was covered in stucco, which subsequently crumbled away. King Tilok of Lannathai acquired the figure and took it to his capital, Chiang Mai, to be enshrined. When a new capital, Viang Chan, was built,

the Buddha was moved there, where it stayed until its eventual seizure by the king of Thonburi. When King Rama I built Bangkok, he had the Emerald Buddha installed with great ceremony.

Rama III had two standing images of Buddha cast and set in front of the high altar, dedicating them to his royal predecessors. One more statue of Buddha—the Samphutthapanni Buddha—was added before the altar by King Mongkut, Rama IV (all kings were known as Rama); this too is held in high veneration.

The Wat Phra Keo Museum in the palace compound contains the seasonal costumes worn by the Emerald Buddha, offerings made to him by those attending the temple, and architectural fragments from the temple picked up during restoration work.

ABOVE The Kinaree, legendary creatures that are half human and half bird, symbolize love in Thai mythology.

LEFT One of the 5m (16ft)-high statues of giant mythical demons that guard the temple entrance.

OTHER PALACE BUILDINGS

There are other sacred buildings near the Wat Phra Keo on the upper terrace. The Royal Pantheon is surrounded by gilded Kinaree, half-human figures, holding Buddhist sculptures, and the golden Phra si Rattana Chedi contains the Buddha's ashes. North of the terrace, at ground level, are the Scripture Library, which has a fine western façade, the gabled Wiharn, which is adorned with tiles and porcelain, and the Royal Mausoleum, the last resting place of several members of the royal family.

Two small chapels behind the Assembly Hall to the west contain effigies of Buddha, one of which is decorated with murals attributed to a well-known Thai painter, Khrua In Khong. He was renowned for the mural work he produced during the reign of Rama IV (1851–68).

SEE ALSO

■ *Ayutthaya* page 112
■ *Potala Palace* page 99

AYUTTHAYA

■ **During Ayutthaya's ascendancy as the Thai capital, 33 kings of different dynasties ruled the kingdom.**

■ **Ayutthaya historical park was declared a UNESCO World Heritage Site in 1991.**

■ **Ayutthaya's Elephant Kraal, an enclosure made of teak logs, was used to pen wild elephants.**

BETWEEN 1350 AND 1767, Ayutthaya was the capital of the Thai—then the Siamese—kingdom. Founded by King U-Thong, it replaced Sukhothai, which had served as the capital until northern forces pushed the Thai people southward. For 417 years the city flourished, until its destruction by the Burmese in 1767. Today its ruins are a tranquil tourist sight, a daytrip from Bangkok, and the *prang* (pagodas or reliquary towers) and 400-plus Buddhist monasteries only hint at the glory of its heyday.

At the heart of the city is the Ancient Palace, originally built by King U-Thong but extended during later reigns. Among the new additions were Wat Phra Si Sanphet, the most significant temple within the complex, of equivalent status to the Wat Phra Keo (Temple of the Emerald Buddha) in Bangkok's Grand Palace (see page 110). This housed a 16m (52ft)-high gilded Buddha cast by King Ramathipodi II in 1500, which weighed about 170kg (375lb). When the Burmese sacked Ayutthaya, they set fire to the image to melt off the gold, destroying both the image and its temple in the process.

ABOVE A long line of robed Buddha statues at Wat Yai Chai Mongkhon. The temple, constructed in 1357, was restored in the 1980s.

ANCIENT RIVALRIES
Chedi Phu Khao Thong, a temple usually known as Golden Mount Pagoda, soars 80m (263ft) high on the northern outskirts of Ayutthaya. It was originally built in Burmese style by King Burengnong of Burma to mark his successful invasion of Ayutthaya in 1569. However, after the city's independence had been restored by King Naresuan in 1584, the pagoda was reworked in a more obviously Thai style.

A short distance outside the city is Wat Yai Chai Mongkhon, built for King U-Thong in 1357. In 1592 King Naresuan killed the Burmese Crown Prince in combat on elephant-back. He promptly had the temple's pagoda added to match the high pagoda at Chedi Phu Khao Thong. Though it is in a dilapidated state, this pagoda can still be seen from miles away.

Other buildings that suffered during the assault of 1767 included several pavilions, which were reduced to their brick foundations, porticoes and walls. Further monuments and buildings that fell victim to the Burmese have since been renovated in their original style. The Tri Muk Building, a wooden structure with a brick foundation, was rebuilt during the reign of King Chulalongkorn in 1907, and in 1956 the Thai government undertook to rebuild all of the historic city's ruins. In that year various buildings were restored, including three 15th-century *chedis* (bell-shaped towers), which were constructed to house the ashes of Ayutthayan kings, and the Wihan Phra Mongkhon Bophit, which contains one of Thailand's largest bronze images of Buddha.

Chankasem Palace was added to the city during the reign of King Maha Thammaraja, the 17th Ayutthayan monarch, and served as the residence of his son, King Naresuan. After lying in ruins for many years it was reconstructed for King Mongkut of the present Chakri dynasty, who used it as a residence for his visits to Ayutthaya. Chao Sam Phraya National Museum, on Rochana Road, opposite the city wall, has displays of ancient bronze Buddha images and carved panels, along with relics associated with the Buddha and works of art dating back more than 500 years.

SEE ALSO
■ *Wat Phra Keo* page 110

TWIN TEMPLES

Wat Phra Mahathat, on the corner of Chi Kun Road and Naresuan Road, was built by King Ramesuan in 1384 and had a high pagoda, or *prang*, which was destroyed by the Burmese. When major restoration work was begun in 1956, the pagoda was excavated and a treasure chest was unearthed, it contained valuables, including a relic of Buddha inside a golden casket, several golden Buddha images and other objects in gold, ruby and crystal. All are now housed in Bangkok's National Museum.

Opposite the temple is its twin, the Wat Ratburana, built by King Boromraja II, the seventh Ayutthayan king, at the site of his brother's cremation. Items unearthed during its restoration in 1958 include royal regalia, exquisitely worked gold pieces and images of Buddha.

ABOVE At Wat Phra Mahathat, the roots of a banyan tree have grown around the sandstone head of a damaged Buddha statue to create a surreal image.

BELOW Wat Chai Watthanaram was built in 1630 in the Khmer style, which originated in Cambodia. Its central tower, or *prang*, is 35m (115ft) high.

AFRICA

The Temple of Karnak 116

The Great Pyramid 118

The River Nile 122

Carthage 124

Fez Medina 126

The Great Sahara 128

The East African Rift Valley 130

Lake Nakuru 132

Great Landscapes 134

Mount Kilimanjaro 136

The Congo River 138

Madagascar 140

Victoria Falls 142

The Okavango Delta 144

Table Mountain 146

BELOW The Great Pyramid of Giza was constructed using more than 2.25 million blocks of limestone (see pages 118–121).

AFRICA IS THE SECOND-LARGEST OF THE CONTINENTS, occupying about a fifth of the world's land surface; it is also the probable cradle of the human species. The earliest known ancestors of modern humans lived here between seven and four million years ago, later venturing out to settle other parts of the Earth. By 5000 BC there were farming communities in the fertile valley of the Nile. To the west the Sahara was not yet a desert, and there is evidence of cattle-breeding in what is now a great wilderness. By about 3000 BC there was a unified kingdom of Egypt, from which a major empire developed. It survived for 2,000 years and more, until the land of the pharaohs was conquered by Assyrians in the seventh century BC and Persians in the sixth. Meanwhile, the Phoenicians established a colony at Carthage, in modern Tunisia, which would become a formidable power in its own right until its destruction by Rome in 146 BC.

The Arabs conquered Egypt in AD641 and swept in a torrent across North Africa. Mosques were raised in walled cities such as Fez in Morocco, which was the seat of a university founded as far back

Carthage

Fez Medina

Great Sahara

Great Pyramid

River Nile

Temple of Karnak

East African
Rift Valley

Zaire River

Lake Nakuru

Mount Kilimanjaro

BELOW The Sahara Desert features some of the hottest and driest places in the world (see pages 128–129).

Victoria Falls

Okavango Delta

Madagascar

Table Mountain

as 859. To this day Fez retains its ancient battlements, its venerable mosque and its narrow, crowded, clamorous streets. From the 15th century on, Africa was a magnet for European powers, who exploited its mineral wealth and its people. In the 19th century the continent was carved up between them, and not until the 20th century did most African states win their independence one by one.

Today the continent is home to a rich diversity of peoples—a population of more than a billion, who speak over 1,000 languages. Landscapes range from desert to great lakes and from rainforest and swamps to snow-covered mountains. In Madagascar, the island that broke away from the mainland about 165 million years ago, there is a staggering array of plants and animals that were left to evolve in a unique habitat, free from outside interference.

THE TEMPLE OF KARNAK

- The New Kingdom in Egypt dates from about 1560 to 1085 BC.

- In Egyptian mythology the pillars symbolized palm trees from the island where life began.

- The Great Pillared Hall covers an area one third the size of St Peter's in Rome.

ABOVE Detail from the relief carvings in the tomb of Pharaoh Seti I, depicting him in the presence of various deities.

THE CITY THAT THE GREEKS called Thebes, the capital of Egypt for some 1,500 years, stood approximately where the town of Luxor is today, on the east bank of the Nile. Nothing is left of the city itself, but the mighty ruins of the Temple of Karnak still overawe today's visitors. With its imposing gates, its courts and halls, its forests of pillars, its carvings and statues and obelisks, it was the largest temple complex in ancient Egypt.

The principal temple here was sacred to Amun, god of the winds and the air. He was represented as a human figure with a double feather crown and his special animal was the ram. Originally a minor local god, he was made Egypt's national god by the New Kingdom pharaohs, from the 16th century BC on, and he was identified with Ra, the sun god. He was worshipped here with his consort, the goddess Mut, and their son the moon god Khons.

RIGHT A colossal statue of Rameses II guards the entrance to the Second Pylon at the Temple of Amun. His daughter is represented by the small figure at his feet.

BELOW The gardens in which the buildings were set vanished long ago, but there is a fine view of the complex from across the sacred lake.

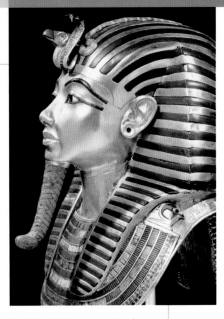

THE VALLEY OF THE KINGS

With their capital at Thebes, most of the New Kingdom pharaohs were buried in the desert to the west of the Nile, in the Valley of the Kings, where more than 60 tombs have so far been discovered. By far the most famous is the tomb of Tutankhamun, which was opened in 1923, revealing a coffin of solid gold, golden diadems and masks, jewels, statues, chariots, weapons, ornaments and paintings. There was such a profusion of treasures that it took three years to clear.

The pharaoh, who died when he was only 18 in 1327 BC, still rests inside his sarcophagus in the tomb, but the treasures are in the Egyptian Museum in Cairo. The tombs are particularly interesting for their murals with scenes of the afterlife.

The little temple to Amun at Karnak was enlarged by Thutmose I at the beginning of the New Kingdom, and expanded by his successors. Different areas are entered through huge portals known as pylons, each consisting of a doorway flanked by massive towers. There are ten of these at Karnak. As the worshipper penetrated the temple, he passed from the bright sunlight of the outside world into the deepening darkness of the great halls toward the mystery of the innermost shrine, which contained the image of the god. This shrine was barred to all except the king and the priests.

The complex was approached along two avenues of ram-headed sphinxes, one leading from the Nile and the other from Luxor. The vast front pylon of the main temple still stands; beyond it is the Great Court, surrounded by a colonnade with subsidiary temples opening off it. The second pylon opens into the Great Pillared Hall and a third leads to the central court. Beyond, there are three more pylons that lead to the inner sanctuary, where the golden statue of the god stood in his sacred boat. To the south lies the Temple of Mut, surrounded on three sides by the sacred lake. The complex also contains temples of Khons and other gods.

SEE ALSO

■ *The Great Pyramid* page 118

THE COLOSSI OF MEMNON

Not far from Luxor, on the west side of the Nile, two enormous seated figures of Pharaoh Amenohotep III stand alone in a field. These are the Colossi of Memnon, made from carved blocks of quartzite, which tower more than 15m (50ft) high and that once stood at the entrance to the pharaoh's temple. The northern statue depicts the pharaoh with his mother, Mutemwia, and the southern statue shows him with his wife, Tiy, and one of his daughters.

After an earthquake in 27 BC a strange bell-like ringing was sometimes heard from the statues. The Roman Emperor Septimius Severus tried to repair the statues in AD 199 and somehow put an end to their magical song.

SUPER SITE

THE GREAT PYRAMID

- The Great Pyramid stands at a height of 137m (450ft).

- It is constructed of more than 2.25 million blocks of limestone, which each weigh more than 2.5 metric tons (2.75 tons).

- The granite roof slabs over the King's Chamber weigh up to 50.75 metric tons (56 tons).

- The largest blocks weigh more than 15 metric ton (16.5 tons).

The Great Pyramid at Giza has stood at the edge of the desert, to the west of the River Nile, since the 26th century BC, when it was built for Pharaoh Khufu (Cheops). Two later kings of the fourth dynasty—Khafre (Chefren) and Menkaure (Mycerinus)—built pyramids of their own close by, and together these form one of the world's most familiar groups of monuments, regarded for centuries with fascination and awe.

ONE FASCINATING ASPECT of the Great Pyramid, which weighs over six million metric tons (nearly seven million tons), is that its massive stone blocks were moved without the use of modern machinery. An estimated 20,000 to 30,000 people worked here over 80 years, using ramps, levers, rollers, ox-drawn sledges and brute force. Despite the difficulties involved, the pyramid was constructed with uncanny accuracy. For example, it stands on an artificially flattened site that deviates from a level plane by less than 2cm (0.5in). The base of the pyramid is remarkably close to being a perfect square, which means that the four corners are almost perfect right angles. The building was carefully aligned with the cardinal points of the compass, with the four sides facing due north, east, south and west, again with only a tiny deviation from achieving pinpoint accuracy.

Mysterious origins

No one knows for certain why the Great Pyramid was built. The generally accepted theory is that it was the Pharaoh's tomb, which may well be true, but no corpse was ever found. When an official party broke into the pyramid in the ninth century AD and, with great difficulty, forced their way into the King's Chamber, they found the great stone coffin empty, but with no obvious sign of previous disturbance by robbers.

ABOVE The Great Pyramid (right) was one of the Seven Wonders of the Ancient World.

BELOW Climbing to the top of the pyramid is hazardous, and officially forbidden.

THE HISTORY

- **2589–2566 BC** *Great Pyramid is built for Pharaoh Khufu.*

- **2558–2532 BC** *Khufu's son Khafre has a second pyramid built.*

- **2490–2472 BC** *Menkaure, possibly Khafre's son, rules as pharaoh and adds the third, and smallest, of the pyramids.*

- **AD 820** *Abdullah Al Mamun has a tunnel bored into the pyramid to search for treasure.*

- **AD 1954** *Khufu's 'sun boat' is excavated on the south side of pyramid.*

- **AD 1982** *Five more boat pits are discovered at the base of the south face.*

RIDDLE OF THE SPHINX

The Sphinx depicts a recumbent lion with a human head, and was built by Pharaoh Khafre (the head was apparently a portrait of him). Although it can seem a mere kitten with the vast bulk of the pyramids looming behind, it is 20m (66ft) high and 73m (240ft) long, made out of a knoll of rock left in place when the stone was quarried for the Great Pyramid.

Presumably the Sphinx is a guardian of the necropolis behind it, but no one knows for sure. It wears a royal headdress and has the symbol of a cobra on its forehead. Its nose is partly missing and the beard has gone completely. It was once plastered over and painted red.

In front of the Sphinx there is a stela, an upright slab of granite on which is recorded the curious experience of a pharaoh of the 15th century BC, Thutmose IV. He sat down to rest in the shade of the Sphinx during a hunt and dreamed that he would win Egypt's throne if he cleared the sand from the monument. He did, and the prediction was fulfilled.

ABOVE Khufu's 'sun boat', reassembled in the museum, is the world's oldest intact ship, found sealed in a pit cut into the bedrock.

BELOW Symbols of Egypt now, camels were not widely used in Ancient Egypt. Many were brought in by later invaders.

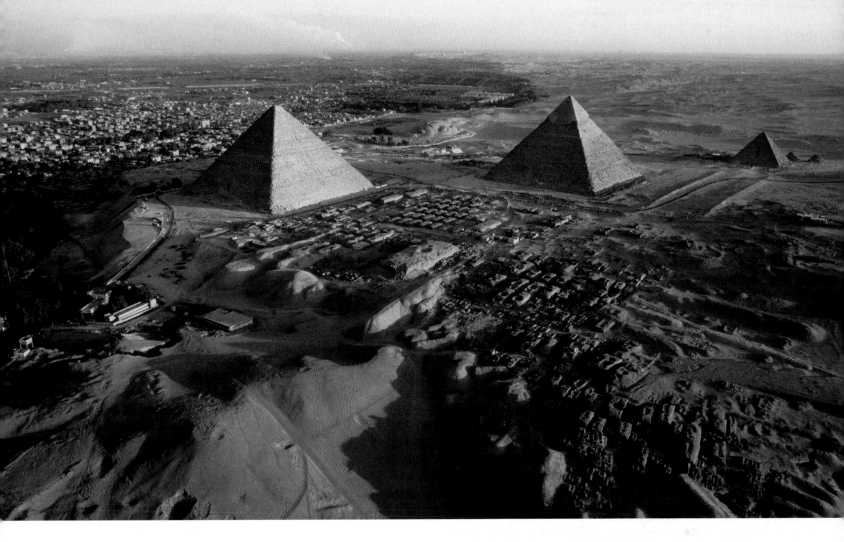

There is an entrance to the north side from which a narrow passage leads the cramped and crouching visitor to a long passage called the Grand Gallery, 46.6m (153ft) long. This leads to what is usually called the King's Chamber, 42.7m (140ft) above ground level, containing an empty granite sarcophagus. The two other chambers inside the pyramid are both empty. In 1954 a cedar boat was found in a long pit just outside the pyramid. Partly dismantled, it was 43.6m (143ft) long and it can be seen today in the Khufu Boat Museum on the site. Other boats were buried close by, perhaps for the dead ruler's voyages in the afterlife.

The three pyramids are part of a complex that includes temples, miniature pyramids thought to have been provided for the pharaoh's wives, and the tombs of priests and officials. This city of the dead is guarded by the watchful Sphinx, which gazes out over the desert sands.

SEE ALSO
■ *Borobudur* page 108
■ *Teotihuacán* page 186
■ *Tikal* page 192

TOP Today the outskirts of Cairo almost reach the pyramids. The monuments can be clearly seen from the center of the city.

ABOVE Inside the Grand Gallery, the largest of the sloping passages that run through the pyramid. Its purpose is now unknown.

THE RIVER NILE

■ **The Nile is the longest river in the world, at 6,695km (4,160 miles) long.**

■ **The Nile Delta is one of the most fertile places on earth.**

■ **Over the 1,600km (1,000 miles) between Juba and Khartoum the White Nile falls only about 73m (240ft).**

THE WORLD'S LONGEST RIVER originates in the great lakes of Africa and winds its way for thousands of miles through deserts and swamps, sometimes meandering gently and sometimes plunging down cataracts and rapids. South and east of Khartoum, two rivers—the White Nile to the south and the Blue Nile to the east—converge to become the Nile.

ABOVE Transporting animal feed, near Aswan.
BELOW Feluccas, traditional wooden sailing boats are still in use around Aswan and Luxor.

The Blue Nile rises in Lake Tana in the Ethiopian highlands. From here the river flows southeast over the magnificent Tisisat Falls, and then for more than 640km (400 miles) in a grand arc, cutting through the Ethiopian plateau, before pouring down into the hot plains of southern Sudan. On its way, the river slashes a huge gorge through the middle of the plateau, reaching 1.6km (1 mile) deep and 24km (15 miles) wide in some places.

The difficulty of crossing the desert southeast of Khartoum and following the river through the untamed gorge prevented an exact mapping of the Blue Nile until Colonel R.E. Cheesman's efforts in the 1920s and 1930s, although Europeans had reached its sources hundreds of years before. The first to make the discovery was Pedro Paez, a Portuguese priest who journeyed to Tisisat Falls in 1618, but the best known was a Scotsman, James 'Abyssinian' Bruce, who reached them in 1770.

In contrast to the fast-paced Blue Nile between Juba in the southern Sudan and Khartoum, the White Nile is slow and sluggish. In the Sudd, a region of seasonal swamp, the river degenerates into a series of constantly shifting channels choked with underwater reeds and roots. Until 1899, when a permanent channel was finally carved out of it, the Sudd halted almost all boats trying to sail up river.

At the north end of the river the Nile Delta is still vital to Egypt's economy. The building in 1970 of the Aswan High Dam, 970km (600 miles) from Cairo, has threatened the delta area, preventing the deposit of valuable silt. The flood control, however, has allowed for year-round irrigation, and as many as three crops a year can be harvested. Sub-Saharan countries, which suffer from periods of severe drought, are eager to exploit the Nile's waters themselves, and are in dispute with Egypt and Sudan about the control and use of this great river.

THE NILE CROCODILE

The ancient Egyptians revered the Nile crocodile. The god Sebek had the head of a crocodile, and crocodiles were kept in temples and given gold bracelets to wear. Even a city, Crocodilopolis, was named after the creature. Archaeologists have discovered thousands of crocodile graves, where the animals were buried with great care and sometimes with expensive jewels.

The Nile crocodile no longer abounds on the shores of the Egyptian Nile and is in fact quite rare in Africa today. There are some conservation initiatives, and small populations are being monitored and protected in places such as Lake Turkana in northern Kenya.

LEFT Winter winds blow up river, so the feluccas can travel in that direction easily with a sail, returning down river using the flow of the water. The boats each contain around ten passengers.

SEARCH FOR THE SOURCE

By the 1850s the discovery of the White Nile's sources had become the world's greatest geographical challenge.

In 1858 John Hanning Speke, on a diversionary journey from an expedition led by Richard Francis Burton, became the first European to reach Lake Victoria, which he proclaimed as the source of the Nile. Burton, meanwhile, insisted that it was in fact Lake Tanganyika. Other explorers, including the Scottish missionary David Livingstone, attempted to resolve the question.

In the 1870s Henry Morton Stanley circumnavigated Lake Victoria, proving that it had no major river running into it and only one major outlet, Ripon Falls, where the Nile actually starts. Speke was right all along.

CARTHAGE

- ◾ The name *Carthage* is derived from the Phoenician words for 'new city'.

- ◾ Carthage appears to have been based around the Byrsa Hill, which means 'ox hide'.

- ◾ According to the Greek historian Appian, an island in the city's naval dock had dry-dock space for 220 vessels.

DIDO WAS THE SISTER of the king of the ancient capital of Phoenicia, Tyre. When the king murdered her husband for his money, Dido gathered a band of supporters and set sail in search of a new kingdom. She built a magnificent city on the coast of North Africa and it was here that the Trojan prince Aeneas arrived with his fleet during his long journey to Italy after fleeing from defeated Troy.

Dido's city was Carthage, and the story of her love for Aeneas and her suicide when he left her, poignantly told by the Roman poet Virgil in his epic poem *The Aeneid*, inspired many later writers, artists and composers to rework this universal tragedy of love conflicting with duty.

Where Carthage is concerned, it is almost impossible to separate legend from fact; despite much archaeological work, clues remain elusive. Even the date of the city's founding is uncertain. Roman legend suggests the end of the ninth century BC, but there is no archaeological evidence to indicate occupation before the eighth century BC.

During the sixth century BC Carthage grew increasingly powerful, building up a fleet and acquiring a number of colonies. Signs of her naval power can be seen in two manmade ports near Topheth. One was a circular naval dock connected to a large merchant port, whose silted-up entrance has been traced.

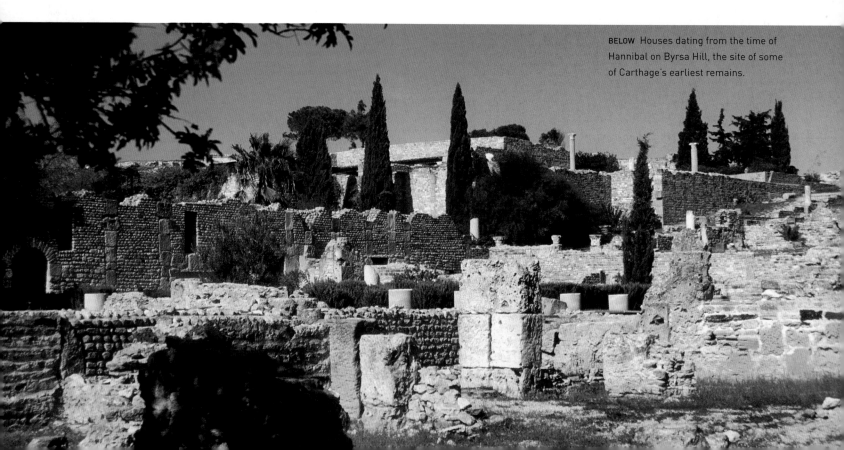

BELOW Houses dating from the time of Hannibal on Byrsa Hill, the site of some of Carthage's earliest remains.

HANNIBAL AND THE PUNIC WARS

Hannibal, the young Carthaginian general who led an army of 38,000 foot soldiers, 8,000 cavalry and 37 elephants over the Alps to take Rome totally by surprise, has captured the imagination of generations.

Between 264 and 241BC the Romans and the Carthaginians fought the First Punic War—the inevitable consequence of increasing rivalry between the two powers. Carthage was ultimately forced to surrender her hold on Sicily and made to pay a huge indemnity.

In 218BC Hannibal seized the initiative by overrunning Etruria. Then in 216 he defeated the Roman army at the battle of Cannae. Hannibal fought on until recalled to Carthage in 203. The Second Punic War finally ended in 201 when Rome invaded Carthage.

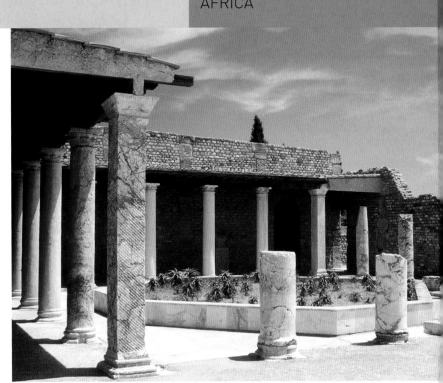

ABOVE Roman townhouses often had gardens with colonnades, similar to the later medieval cloisters of cathedrals and monasteries.

BELOW The Antonine Baths, built by the Romans in AD 162, included an indoor pool about the size of a modern Olympic swimming pool.

If Carthage is a prominent feature in European artistic tradition, it is less prominent on the ground. In the middle of the second century BC the Roman senate resounded with the words of Cato the Elder, who repeatedly declared that Carthage must be destroyed. In 149BC, after a long period of intermittent conflict, Rome declared war again. Carthage, the one-time ally of Rome, was besieged and reduced to ruins in a fire that was said to have raged for 10 days.

The heart of the city appears to have been on the Byrsa Hill and there is now an archaeological museum here. Excavations on the side of the hill have revealed some houses and shops belonging to the late third or early second century BC. However, most of the remaining ruins that can be seen today—an amphitheater, the ground plans of the Antonine Baths and a number of villas—bear the stamp of the city's triumphant rival Rome, whose force Carthage was unable to withstand.

SEE ALSO
- *The Colosseum* page 42
- *The Pont du Gard* page 30

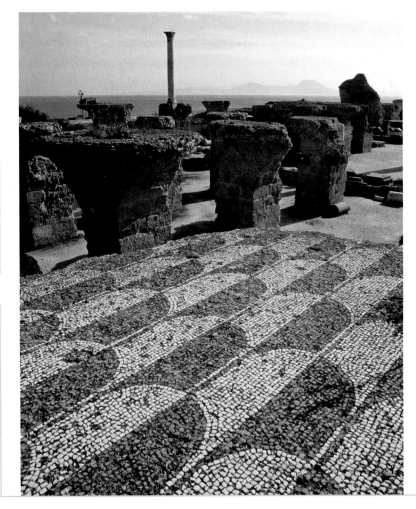

THE DARK SIDE OF CARTHAGE

The oldest finds in Carthage are sinister ones. An area known as the Topheth, apparently a sanctuary of the goddess Tanit, has produced evidence of infant cremation on a large scale. The theory is that young children were sacrificed to the city's main god, Baal Hammon, in moonlit ceremonies.

There seems to have been a tradition of sacrificing members of prominent and ruling families, whose bodies were laid to rest along with goods for the afterlife. The story of Dido's death may be connected with a primitive idea that the death of a monarch could benefit the country.

FEZ MEDINA

- ■ The old city at Fez, Fez el Bali, was divided into almost 200 different districts, each one a community with its own mosque, *hammam* (Turkish bath) and bakery.

- ■ The city is the home of one of the oldest universities in the world and was a focus of academic debate in the Middle Ages.

VOLUBILIS

Fez was founded by a descendant of Muhammad called Moulay Idriss, who chose to create his new city rather than expand the existing Moroccan metropolis at Volubilis.

Volubilis was originally a Roman city and the ruins that can be seen today give a good idea of Roman civilization in Africa during the third century AD. The remains of a basilica, a capitoline temple (dedicated to three deities—Jupiter, Juno and Minerva), and a forum are at the heart of the site, and there are also a triumphal arch, the remains of some public baths and a number of houses.

This region supplied Rome with large quantities of olive oil and you can still see ancient oil presses here. Some of the treasures found at Volubilis are housed in the Museum of Antiquities at Rabat.

FEZ IS A LARGE, modern city with more than half a million inhabitants, where it is possible to leave behind cars, wide streets and high-rise buildings and enter a medieval metropolis. Medina was the city to which the Prophet Muhammad escaped in AD 622 when he came under threat in Mecca, and the name has since been applied to the old quarter of any Islamic city. The Medina at Fez is the old city (Fez el Bali) established in the ninth century, where narrow, winding streets, fountains in elegant courtyards, traditional houses and the noise and bustle of the bazaar combine to offer a window onto a different world. Many of the goods on sale may be modern and much may be aimed specifically at tourists, but the atmosphere and the scale of the old city survive.

With nearly 800 mosques (most with schools attached), thousands of shops and enough houses for a population of around 125,000, by the 13th century Fez had become one of the world's most important cities. The principal mosque, the Karaouyine, was founded in the ninth century and rebuilt in the 12th. It is the largest mosque in North Africa (it can accommodate 20,000 people), and connected with it are Fez's ancient university and an outstanding library.

Fez also has a large number of *medressahs* (Koran schools), which usually consist of three rooms—school, prayer hall and library—arranged around a courtyard with a central fountain. The Bou Inania Medressah is particularly impressive, with decoration that manages to be lavish without being overpowering and that has similarities to the Moorish architecture of Spain. A curious arrangement of windows, wooden blocks and brass bowls has been

ABOVE View over the Karaouyine University and mosque. Founded in AD 859, the university is a center of Islamic scholarship and the oldest continuously functioning academic institution in the world.

RIGHT Tanning and dyeing leather is carried out in stone vats at the world's oldest surviving tannery. The processes here have scarcely changed since the 11th century.

described as a water clock dating from the 13th century; a reconstruction started in 2004 to restore it to working order. The brass bowls here may have been shaped by distant ancestors of the men who can be seen today beating various metals into shape in the Place Seffarine.

Dyeing and tanning are two other traditional activities, unchanged for hundreds of years, that can be seen at Fez. At the dyers' *soukh* (marketplace) by the river, a watermill is used to crush the seeds that provide vegetable dyes. Farther down river there are tanners hard at work.

TOP LEFT The public fountain, decorated with mosaic tiles in geometric patterns, in Nejjarine Square. This is the heart of the carpenters' quarter of the medina.

TOP RIGHT Ceramic tiles also provide coolness underfoot at a courtyard at the Karaouyine Mosque, the largest mosque in northern Africa.

SEE ALSO

■ *The Alhambra* page 58
■ *The Blue Mosque* page 72

THE GREAT SAHARA

■ The Sahara is the largest hot desert in the world, covering an area of around 9,270,000sq km (3,580,000 square miles).

■ Dunes in parts of the Sahara roll forward at a rate of 11m (36ft) per year.

■ One of the hottest places is Kebili, where temperatures can reach 55°C (131°F).

THE SAHARA DESERT sprawls over the northern part of Africa, stretching 5,149km (3,200 miles) from Egypt and the Sudan to the west coasts of Mauritania and Spanish Sahara. Its name invokes images of great baking yellow sand dunes, interrupted all too infrequently by jewel-like oases of green. The immense area of the Sahara contains just about every kind of desert terrain, including barren rocky plateaux littered with broken rocks, strange geological formations and parched scrubland.

The bulk of the desert is far inland, and the prevailing winds dry any moisture from the air before it can reach the interior. Mountain ranges between the desert and the sea cause clouds to drop their rain long before they reach the interior. With few clouds in the sky, days in the desert are ferociously hot. Cloudless skies also allow the heat to escape easily into the atmosphere once the sun has gone down, and temperatures at night can drop below freezing. One of the hottest places in the

ABOVE Nomadic Tuareg herdsmen still live a traditional desert life. Their indigo-blue head coverings are worn to protect them from evil spirits.

LEFT The Sahara's largest areas of sand dunes contain little or no vegetation. Some of the dunes can reach 180m (590 ft) in height.

OASES: GREEN EYES IN THE SAND

Oases are fertile areas in the desert—sometimes just a few trees around a small spring, sometimes the banks of a river, such as the River Abiod, which flows through Algeria toward the Sahara. Seen from the air, the river is a ribbon of dark green palms, with groves of date palms, apricots, pomegranates and figs.

A different kind of oasis is found at Nefta in Tunisia. This is an important watering station for caravans crossing the northern fringes of the Sahara, and was known and used in Roman times. Each year the water table under the Nefta area rises, saturating the porous rocks and forming underground wells. Water is forced out of the wells as springs, nourishing fruit trees and palms.

desert is Kebili, where high temperatures are due not only to the burning hot sun, but also to the Sirocco. This wind originates in the scorching interior of the desert and blows hot air northward like a blast from a furnace.

The best-known areas of the Sahara are the sand dunes associated with the battles in North Africa during World War II. These tracts of rolling waves of sand cover a vast area of around 100,000 sq km (39,000 square miles). In places, these great dunes are highly mobile, driven by the wind, and oases such as Faja are under constant threat from this ever-advancing tide of smothering sand. In other areas the dunes appear not to have moved for thousands of years. This has resulted in the formation of trenches between them, which have become permanent paths for caravans crossing the desert.

Because the Sahara is arid it cannot be cultivated, and nomadic tribes still wander with their small herds of animals. There is mixed farming around a few oases, but most of the desert is economically unproductive.

Concern has grown recently about a process known as desertification, which has been taking place around the edges of the Sahara Desert. Inappropriate agricultural methods combined with natural factors such as drought and wind storms have resulted in the advance of the desert across what was once productive arable land. Countries to the south have proposed planting a 'Great Green Wall' of trees along its entire southern edge, aiming to slow the rate of damage caused by wind erosion.

SEE ALSO
■ *The Elements* page 234

DISCOVERY OF LAKE CHAD

Before the 19th century, Europeans had very little knowledge of the interior of the Sahara. Their first accurate information came from attempts to solve the mysteries surrounding the source of the River Niger. The first significant exploration was by an expedition involving three British explorers: Dixon Denham, Hugh Clapperton and Walter Oudney.

The small party left Tripoli in 1822, spent 68 days going through the uncharted desert and on February 4th, 1823, they became the first Europeans to see Lake Chad. Denham went on to explore the area to the south, while Clapperton and Oudney turned west toward the Niger. Not long afterward Oudney died, but Clapperton reached the great walled towns of Kano and Sokoto, both of which are in Nigeria.

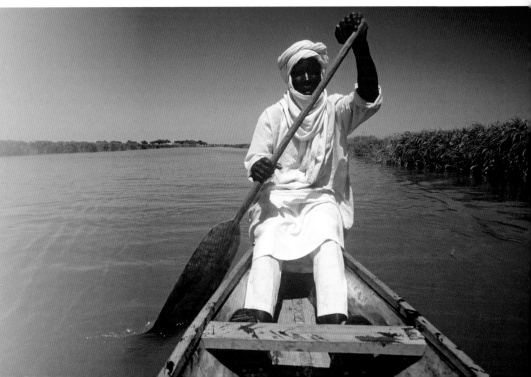

THE EAST AFRICAN RIFT VALLEY

■ Lake Tanganyika is the second deepest lake in the world.

■ The Ngorongoro crater measures 20km (12.5 miles) across.

■ Where the Rift Valley widens, the earth's crust thins from about 40km (25 miles) to about 6km (4 miles).

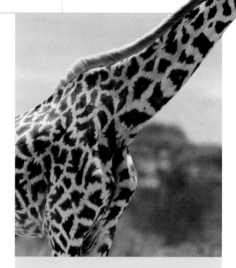

LIFE IN THE VALLEY

The sheer scale of the Rift Valley is difficult to grasp. Most visitors to the area concentrate on seeing the abundant wildlife that typifies this part of Africa.

The crater of Ngorongoro is volcanic in origin; it formed in a titanic explosion about three million years ago. It is the site of Africa's finest wildlife reserve, where elephants, Cape buffalo, lions and hyenas are among the inhabitants.

North of Lengai is Lake Natron, a very shallow lake partly fed by soda-rich hot springs that support a rich growth of algae. The springs provide ideal breeding grounds for thousands of pink flamingoes.

Near Ngorongoro is Olduvai Gorge, where hominid fossils were discovered; it is regarded by some as the birthplace of the human race.

THE EAST AFRICAN RIFT VALLEY is a vast split in the Earth's crust and is one of the great geological features of the planet. The view from the top of the steep slope on one side is of a sweeping panorama across a deep, flat-bottomed valley, in places too wide to see the opposite side. The western arm of the rift extends for about 3,060km (1,900 miles) from Lake Malawi in the south, close to the Mozambique coast, then northward along the line of the great African lakes to the west of Lake Victoria.

The eastern arm starts to the east of Lake Victoria and continues northward for about 2,570km (1,600 miles). It goes from Tanzania through Kenya and into Ethiopia and the complex area known as the Afar Triangle, an area of volcanic rocks and frequent earthquakes. Here the rift divides, with one part continuing north toward the Red Sea, while the other strikes eastward into the Gulf of Aden.

The German meteorologist Alfred Wegener, who first proposed the theory of continental drift in 1912, noticed that the opposing shores of the Red Sea formed a perfect match, and that the sea could be closed by sliding Africa against Arabia—except that the Yemen would overlap the Afar Triangle. Geologists now recognize that the volcanic rocks in both these areas are younger than the Red Sea, and so could not have existed before the Red Sea opened; thus the match would have been perfect.

Active rifts are characterized by earthquakes and volcanic activity, and in the African rift, the Afar Triangle is currently the most active part. Earthquakes are

BELOW Losiolo, in Kenya, has some of the most spectacular rift landscapes. The rugged country here is the territory of nomadic peoples who live by herding animals.

frequent here, but the shape of the rift is less spectacular because volcanic activity, with huge outpourings of lava over thousands of years, has tended to fill the valley. Volcanism currently occurs around Lake Victoria, in the Virunga Mountains of southwestern Uganda to the west and in northern Tanzania to the east. Lengai, in Tanzania, is the only active carbonatite volcano in the world, where the lava is like a volcanic limestone that turns to the color of dirty snow within 24 hours of erupting.

The other main feature of the African rift is the intermittent line of lakes along the valley floor. Lake Tanganyika has 5,000m (16,500ft) of sediment beneath it, indicating a long or very fast history of rifting.

SEE ALSO
■ *The Grand Canyon* page 176
■ *Zion National Park* page 166

ABOVE The gnu and the zebra are among the many grazing mammals that thrive on the rich grasslands of the rift valley.

FORMATION OF A RIFT VALLEY
A rift valley is formed by tension in the Earth's crust where the opposite sides of the valley are slowly moving apart. As the valley widens, the floor of the valley drops between two roughly parallel escarpments.

The fault systems along the valley margins are complex, but generally result in wedge-shaped slices of crust that slip downward to jam in the widening gap.

Over millions of years the valley gradually widens and deepens, but continued erosion blurs the sharp lines of the escarpments and sediments accumulate on the valley floor. When the crust grows too thin, a new crust is formed by magma erupting from the underlying mantle. The bed of the Atlantic Ocean was formed in this way.

LAKE NAKURU

■ **Lake Nakuru lies south of the equator at an altitude of 1,759m (5,770ft).**

■ **It has a catchment area of about 1,800sq km (700 square miles).**

■ **Most of the lake's water flows into it from two main rivers, the Njoro and the Nderit.**

LAKE NAKURU FORMS THE HEART of the national park that bears its name, and is truly one of the great wildlife spectacles of the world. It is, however, only one of a series of important bodies of water that lie in a string down the east side of Africa in the Rift Valley from Lebanon to Mozambique. These lakes are found at different altitudes, and vary in saltiness from fresh water through those of moderate salinity to others that are hypersaline or soda lakes.

There is no major outflow from Lake Nakuru, but its surface area varies with the level of inflow (dependent on rainfall), the amount of water taken for human use, the input from other intermittent springs and the rate of loss by evaporation.

This is a hypersaline lake, the result of very high levels of carbonates and bicarbonates—not chlorides, as is the case with sea water. Such an alkaline environment is very harsh. Living things require a very high level of specialization to be able to survive these conditions, and so the diversity of aquatic species is very low. The waters do not support any large plants, but six species of phytoplankton have been recorded. By far the most numerous of these is the tiny blue-green alga *Spirulina platensis*, which occurs in such vast numbers that it turns the water dark green with a thick, slimy

LAKE OF MANY BIRDS

As well as the lesser flamingo there are also extensive numbers of the greater flamingo, a bigger bird that feeds on the midge larvae and the copepod.

More than 100 other bird species are represented at Nakuru, including the fish-eating cormorants, anhingas, several types of heron, great white pelicans, yellow-billed storks, spoonbills and African fish eagles.

Most birds use the lake for feeding on the way to their nest sites. The great white pelicans have a relatively short journey to their nests on nearby Lake Elementeita. The lesser flamingoes, however, breed on Lake Natron, across the border in Tanzania, which involves marathon flights of 193km (120 miles) or more.

RIGHT AND TOP Best known for its flamingo population, the national park is also home to species such as the Bohor reedbuck (right) and the hyena (above), and to predators such as lions, cheetahs and leopards.

FILTERING MACHINES

Lesser flamingoes feed on the protein-rich, blue-green alga *Spirulina platensis*, and on some lakes more than 60 metric tons (59 tons) of algae can be consumed per day.

A floating bill helps the lesser flamingo concentrate its feeding effort in the surface waters. Its close relative, the greater flamingo, has a heavier bill to enable it to feed on the copepods and midge larvae in the lake's depths.

Lesser flamingoes feed with their head upside down, filtering food from the water with their tongue, which pumps the water through fine filters in the bill and traps most of the *Spirulina*. The greater flamingo has a coarser filter that allows most of the *Spirulina* to pass through.

consistency. This tiny species forms the basis of the entire food web in the lake. It is unusually high in protein and contains large amounts of beta-carotene, which give the flamingoes their pink hue. The alga is the main prey of the five species of zooplankton, four species of water boatmen, two midge larvae and a calanoid copepod, which together make up the entire natural aquatic invertebrate fauna. There is also one fish species, introduced to the lake in 1953 and again in 1962 after the lake had entirely dried up and then reflooded.

The combination of these different species make Lake Nakuru a wildlife spectacle, providing a vast food resource for countless birds. Most notable are the flamingoes, which come to the lake to feed, forming a brilliant pink carpet around its margins. More species of bird have appeared on the lake since fish were introduced.

SEE ALSO

- *The Camargue* page 22
- *The Dead Sea* page 75
- *The East African Rift Valley* page 130

GREAT LANDSCAPES

Our planet is constantly in flux. Land rises, folds in on itself, cracks open, then melts away in the rain and the winds. Rivers alter their course, sculpt gorges and caves. Glaciers become lakes, lakes become valleys, oceans become deserts. Every change leaves its mark on landscapes that, to the human eye, seem permanent.

■ Mount Etna, the biggest volcano in Europe, is 600,000 years old and emerges from the sea bed to tower 3,322m (10,900ft) above Sicily's eastern coast.

■ Siberia, the largest of the former Soviet regions, covers 10.4 million sq km (4 million square miles) of coniferous forest, mountains and plains.

Above The isolated rocky formations of Monument Valley, Arizona, are the last remnants of the sandstone layers that once covered the entire region.

Below In Patagonia, Argentina, the Perito Moreno glacier is still advancing. It forms an ice dam across a lake until the water tunnels underneath.

THE LIVING LAND

There are many places where the Earth can be seen in the course of change. The eastern Hawaiian Islands spew magma from their mountain vents as the crust of the Pacific moves westward.

Iceland's spouting geysers, bubbling mud and volcanic eruptions are evidence of mid-Atlantic forces pulling the land apart. The island forms one of the world's newest land masses.

In New Zealand recent eruptions have created new lakes and geysers, and even in the icy Antarctic volcanoes continue to steam and blow, often unseen by human eyes.

AT THE EXTREMES

Some landscapes are almost beyond comprehension. It is hard to imagine the vast complexity of the Grand Canyon, the way that the Great Sahara spreads across most of northern Africa, or the long journeys of the Amazon and the Nile, which confounded explorers for so many years. We feel dwarfed by the stupendous power of Niagara Falls or the soaring Himalayan peaks.

But other distinctive landscapes, such as the world's wildlife-rich wetlands and its farming landscapes shaped by grazing or terracing, are on a more human scale.

USING THE LANDSCAPE

People have exploited some of the most bizarre landscapes. The Göreme Valley in Turkey is a region of weirdly eroded rock fingers and cliffs, where hundreds of churches and living spaces have been carved. Also in Turkey, Pamukkale's rock basins of mineral water have made bathing pools for 2,000 years.

Above Rice terraces in Bali represent the vast achievement of cultivating mountainous country.

Above right Mount Etna, Sicily, is one of the most active volcanoes in the world.

Right In Cappadocia, Turkey, people have for centuries cut into rock faces to make houses and churches.

SEE ALSO

■ *The East African Rift Valley* page 130
■ *The Grand Canyon* page 176
■ *The Great Sahara* page 128

MOUNT KILIMANJARO

- Kilimanjaro covers an area 97km (60 miles) long and 64km (40 miles) wide.

- In Swahili its name means 'The Mountain that Glitters'.

- Tropical rainforest grows on its slopes.

- It is 5,899m (19,350ft) high.

THIS TOWERING VOLCANO with its spectacular snow-covered cap looms over the semi-desert of northern Tanzania. It is the tallest mountain in Africa, and it can be seen for many miles across the plains of Tanzania and Kenya. Its profile is very distinctive: gently rising slopes lead to an elongated, flattened summit—really a volcanic caldera. On very hot days and from great distances the blue mountain base is sometimes indistinguishable from the savannah.

Kilimanjaro is so large that it can influence its own weather. As moisture-laden winds blow in from the Indian Ocean they are forced upward when they meet Kilimanjaro, and drop their water as rain or snow. The increased rainfall makes the slopes of the mountain more fertile than the scrub land that surrounds it.

At the very peak of the mountain are Kilimanjaro's permanent glaciers—an unusual feature since the mountain lies only three degrees south of the equator. Recent evidence suggests that these glaciers are retreating. The rainfall on top of the mountain is only 20cm (8in) a year, and this is insufficient to keep pace with the amount of water lost through melting.

Some scientists believe that the volcano is warming up, speeding up the melting process; others blame global warming or deforestation. Whatever the cause, it is clear that Kilimanjaro's glaciers are smaller than they were in the 19th century. If the situation remains constant, Kilimanjaro's icy cap will be gone by the year 2200.

BELOW The record time for climbing and descending Kilimanjaro is less than nine hours, but most trekkers take between five and seven days.

ABOVE Elephants in the grazing lands surrounding Kilimanjaro, with the vast mountain looming behind them.

RIGHT The white cap of Kilimanjaro (right) is visible from a great distance, but the peak of Mawenzi (left) is rarely covered in snow.

Kilimanjaro is really three volcanoes linked together by a complex history of eruptions. The oldest volcano, Shira, lies to the west of the main mountain. It was once much taller, and is thought to have collapsed following a violent eruption, which left only a plateau of 3,810m (12,500ft).

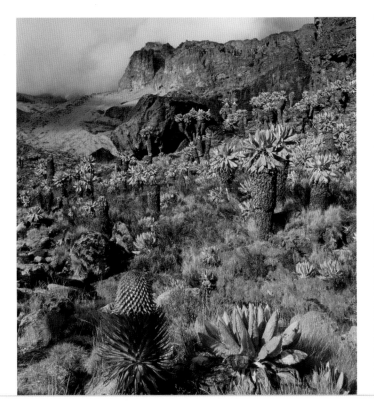

The second oldest volcano is Mawenzi, a distinct peak attached to the east side of the largest mountain. Even though it appears insignificant next to Kilimanjaro's summit, it rises to a height of 5,334m (17,500ft).

The youngest and largest of the three volcanoes, Kibo, was formed during a series of eruptions, and is topped by a caldera about 2km (1.25 miles) across. A second volcanic cone with a crater developed inside the caldera during a subsequent eruption and a cinder cone formed during a third eruption. The caldera of Kibo forms the distinctive flattened summit of the mountain.

SEE ALSO
■ *Mount Erebus* page 232
■ *Mount Everest* page 102
■ *Mount Fuji* page 106

LEFT Unique mountain vegetation is well adapted to the harsh alpine conditions.

OL DOINYO LENGAI VOLCANO

Erupting frequently and spewing ash and sodium carbonate dust into the air, Ol Doinyo Lengai volcano is in a state of high activity. The volcano lies in a region of the Rift Valley in Tanzania called Sykes Grid, where the Earth's crust is thought to be particularly thin.

This volcano is unusual because its contents are rich in sodium but low in silica. From a distance, Lengai appears snow-capped, like Mount Kenya and Mount Kilimanjaro. On closer inspection, however, it becomes apparent that the whitish substance on its peak is not snow, but the alkaline sodium carbonates deposited from its recent eruptions.

THE CONGO RIVER

■ **The Congo River rises more than 1,524m (5,000ft) above sea level.**

■ **It is the second-longest river in Africa.**

■ **The Stanley Falls drop the river by 457m (1,500ft) over a course of 97km (60 miles).**

THE SECOND LONGEST RIVER in Africa after the Nile, the Congo has a forbidding image inextricably tied to its immense natural power. Between 1971 and 1997 it was known as the Zaire, a name deriving from the Portuguese interpretation of a west-African word meaning 'the river that swallows all rivers'. Indeed, it is an awe-inspiring natural force: more than 4,300km (2,700 miles) long, with a basin that is 3.9 million sq km (1.5 million square miles), and a flow that is second only to the mighty Amazon of South America, pouring a volume of water equivalent to nearly 20 Olympic-size swimming pools into the Atlantic every second.

STANLEY AND THE CONGO

By the 1870s the Congo was still shrouded in mystery to Westerners. Was it connected to the Nile, the Niger, the mysterious Lualaba in the heart of Africa, or was it a totally separate river? No one knew for sure—not even the Arab slavers who went to places in central Africa where no Europeans had ever been.

All the major questions about the African watershed were resolved by the Welsh journalist and explorer Henry Morton Stanley (1841–1904) between 1874 and 1877. With the backing of *The New York Herald* and *The Daily Telegraph* of London, he made a remarkable trans-African expedition from Zanzibar to the mouth of the Congo, sailing along the river to reach the Atlantic after 999 days.

The river rises in the highland savannah of northern Zambia and meanders through Zambia into the Democratic Republic of Congo (formerly Zaire), where it joins the Lualaba. Under that name, it begins its slow descent toward the tropical rainforests of West Africa, which it reaches some 800km (500 miles) later. The river flows north more than 1,600km (1,000 miles) before crossing the equator, becoming the Congo and then turning westward in a magnificent arc that recrosses the equator going south.

In the northeast of the great arc are the Stanley (or Boyoma) Falls, a series of cataracts and rapids. This is followed by a 1,600km (1,000-mile) stretch of navigable river, culminating in Malebo Pool (once called Stanley Pool), a 24-km (15 mile) wide expanse that separates Kinshasa, the capital of the Democratic Republic of Congo, from Brazzaville, the capital of the Congo. In the 19th century the explorer Henry Morton Stanley built a road around the cataracts and falls up to Malebo Pool.

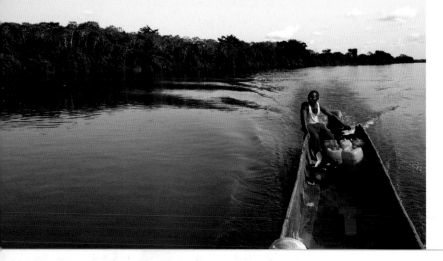

BELOW Dugout boats, hollowed out from a single tree trunk, are common on the Congo. The oldest boats ever found are of this type.

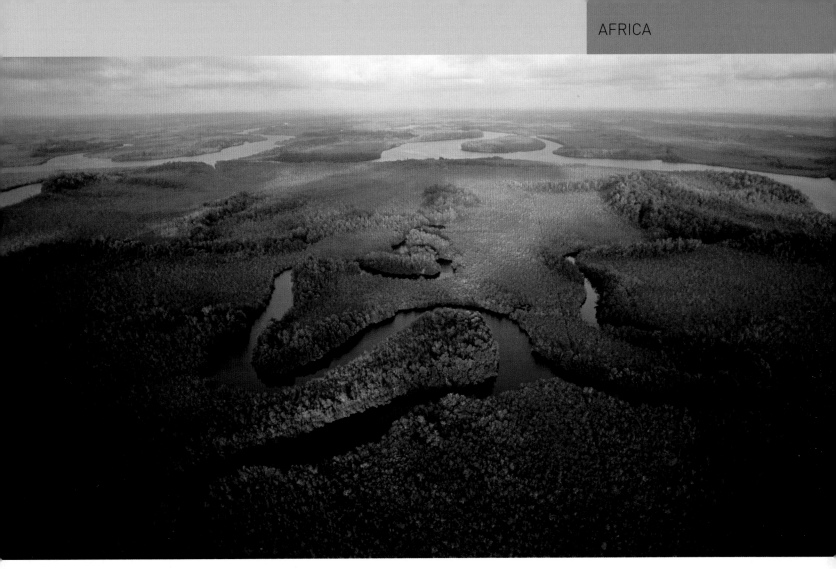

THE RIVER IN THE RAINFOREST

The Congo flows through equatorial rainforest that is home to some of the densest growth on earth. Oak, mahogany, rubber, ebony and walnut trees grow higher than 60m (200ft), forming a canopy that creates a perpetual gloom beneath.

Below this colossal ceiling is a nether world of intensely thick undergrowth, oppressive heat and humidity, deadly animals—crocodiles, pythons, cobras, hairy forest pigs and poisonous spiders—and debilitating and even fatal diseases such as malaria, bilharzia and blackwater fever. And nowhere is it more a maze of mystery than between the river and the fabled Mountains of the Moon—the Rwenzori range that serves as the Congo's easternmost watershed.

ABOVE The Congo and its tributaries run through the second largest rainforest in the world after the Amazon. The river remains a communications lifeline in territory without roads or railways.

Beyond Malebo Pool are the Livingstone Falls, a 350-km (220 mile) stretch that includes an entire series of rapids and 32 cataracts. The last of these, the Cauldron of Hell, takes the river out from the Crystal Mountains and down to sea level. Even after rushing the final 160km (100 miles) down to the Atlantic, the Congo is not drained of power. Moving with a current of 9 knots (10mph) it sweeps its huge volume of water through a submarine canyon 1,200m (4,000ft) deep for another 160km (100 miles) out to sea. There, in the waves of the Atlantic Ocean, it is still possible to see both the muddy red-brown stain of the rainforest and the bits of lighter vegetation that have been carried all the way down from the plains.

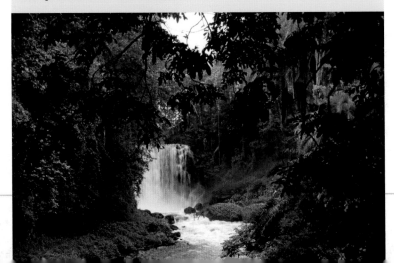

SEE ALSO

- *The Colorado River* page 176
- *The River Nile* page 122
- *Victoria Falls* page 142
- *The Yangtze River* page 92

MADAGASCAR

■ Madagascar is 1,600km (1,000 miles) long.

■ About 10,000 species of plant exist only in Madagascar, along with half of the world's chameleons.

■ The brookesia, a species of chameleon so tiny that it sits easily on the tip of a human thumb (see image below), lives only in Madagascar. Islanders believe it brings bad luck.

RARE WILDLIFE

Lemurs are the best known of Madagascar's primates, and species include the ring-tailed, sifaka, black, sportive, ruffed and gentle lemurs.

Primates are characterized by large brains, slender limbs, and hands and feet adapted for climbing. Lemurs are lower primates, and are less well adapted for walking on two legs.

Like apes and monkeys, lemurs have manual dexterity, and they have developed certain monkeylike traits, although there is considerable variation between the different species. For example, the rare and elusive Coquerel's lemur is monogamous, small and golden-brown in color, while the more common ring-tailed lemur tends to live in groups.

MADAGASCAR IS AN ISLAND of staggering biological diversity. When the island ripped away from Africa 165 million years ago, animals and plants continued to evolve without interference from outside. Madagascar became, in effect, a huge natural laboratory, and the plants and animals there are often unlike any others on Earth.

On the west of the island lies the forbidding Tsingy National Reserve of Bemaraha, where sharp fingers of limestone point 30m (100ft) into the air over an area of 155sq km (60 square miles). The local people say that there is barely enough flat land in the area on which to place a foot. This factor helps to protect at least some of Madagascar's plants and animals from human destruction.

South of Tsingy is Morondava, where rain falls for only four months of the year. Six species of baobab trees grow in this unique habitat—that is, five more than survive today on mainland Africa. The trees are specially adapted to Madagascar's climate: they gorge themselves on water during the rainy season and then survive on the reserves for eight months until the rains come again. Like other areas in Madagascar, the baobab forests are under threat from human expansion, but baobab forests are particularly difficult to repair once the damage has been done. The trees live for hundreds of years, and often do not fruit annually; an extended period of drought might kill an entire year's seedlings. Animals also pose problems: the giant jumping rat, for example, lives exclusively in a very small area in west Madagascar and eats baobab seedlings.

BELOW Rock climbers scale a granite face in the Andringitra National Park, southern Madagascar. Ring-tailed lemurs have adapted to the mountain landscape, surviving on the rocky outcrops.

LEFT The Avenue of the Baobabs in Morondava is a protected site, consisting of about a dozen trees around 30m (100ft) tall.

SEE ALSO
■ *Galapagos Islands*
page 204
■ *The Great Barrier Reef*
page 220

The small Berenty Reserve lies in the south of the island, where some of the largest fruit bats in the world roost in the giant tamarind trees. The colony, numbering several thousand, is believed to be one of the largest to coexist so near human habitation. Ring-tailed lemurs also thrive at Berenty, strutting confidently in front of visitors and regarding them with curious orange eyes.

Many of Madagascar's 1,000 unique species of orchid grow in the Montagne d'Ambre National Park on the northern tip of the island, but not all of Madagascar is rich and green, and years of deforestation, burning and illegal logging have taken their toll. On the island's east coast in particular, rivers run red with the clay that is being swept off hills once richly carpeted with vegetation.

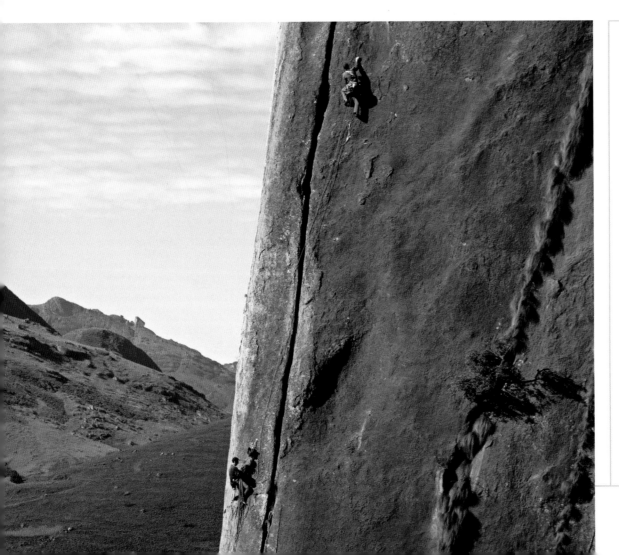

MADAGASCAR'S PRIMATES
Primates are a biologically similar animal group that includes apes—gorillas, chimpanzees, orangutans and humans, as well as gibbons and siamangs—and monkeys.

Fifty million years ago a squirrel-sized ancestor of all primates inhabited the subtropical forests of Africa. Over time, different species evolved from this creature: some became the ancestors of humans, apes, and monkeys, and others became lemurs, pottos, lorises and bushbabies. Lorises can be found in Asia, and pottos and bushbabies in Africa, while lemurs live exclusively in Madagascar and the nearby Comoros Islands.

Another primate unique to Madagascar is the aye-aye, a small, dark-brown animal that lives in a nest of leaves, emerging only at night to feed.

VICTORIA FALLS

■ When the Zambezi River is in full flood, 7,560 cu m (270,000 cu ft) of water surge over the falls every second.

■ The resulting spume of spray can be seen up to 40km (25 miles) away.

■ The local name for the Victoria Falls is *Mosi-oa-tunya*, which translates as 'the smoke that thunders'.

SOUTHERN AFRICA'S WATERFALLS

In South Africa, the Orange River takes a 146m (480ft) plunge over the edge of a plateau at the Aughrabies Falls, before ripping its way through a gorge of granite. In the dry season the Orange River is little more than a stream but, swollen with spring rain, the waterfalls are appropriately known as *Aughrabies*, a term that comes from the Hottentot word meaning 'the place of great noise'.

South Africa also has the Tugela Falls, Africa's highest falls, really a series of five cascades, where the water thunders down a staggering 945m (3,100ft).

Other falls that vary seasonally are the Lofoi Falls in the Democratic Republic of Congo. The 335m (1,000ft) drop is always impressive.

THE MIGHTY VICTORIA FALLS are on the Zambezi River, forming part of the Zambia–Zimbabwe border. The spray can rise to a height of more than 300m (1,000ft), and rainbows often shimmer above the water, adding to the beauty and drama of the scene.

The waterfall is only the start of an impressive water course, for the spray-shrouded river immediately churns its way through a narrow chasm, which zig-zags back and forth for almost 72km (45 miles). These hairpin bends were caused by faults in the rock that have been eroded by the sheer force of the water over thousands of years. The Zambezi River roams across a plateau formed of layers of sandstone and basalt, and it is at the points where these different rocks meet that the faults occur.

In November 1855, the Scottish missionary and explorer David Livingstone (1813-73) was the first European to reach Victoria Falls. He had first heard about the waterfall four years earlier when, with his companion William Cotton Oswell, he reached the banks of the Zambezi River 129km (80 miles) to the west. Between 1853 and 1856 Livingstone crossed Africa. Hoping to open the heart of the continent to Christian missionaries, he journeyed north from southern Africa, through Bechuanaland (modern Botswana) to the Zambezi. He then headed west to the coast at Luanda in Angola. Deciding that this route to the interior was too difficult, he headed back east, following the Zambezi most of the way, and reached Quelimane on the Mozambique coast in May 1856.

Surprisingly, the explorer was not happy with his discovery of the spectacular falls. To Livingstone this virtually unbroken wall of water some 1,680m (5,500ft) long and plunging 107m (350ft) was simply an impediment to Christian missionaries attempting to reach the people of the interior. To him the highlight of his journey was the discovery of the Batoka Plateau, a place he saw as a potential settlement site if the Zambezi proved to be fully navigable (which it did not). Even so, Livingstone stated that such a magnificent natural wonder as the falls should be named after the British queen, Victoria.

SEE ALSO
■ *Angel Falls* page 194
■ *Iguaçu Falls* page 202
■ *Niagara Falls* page 152

WATERFALLS OF WEST AFRICA

Dr David Livingstone described the Victoria Falls as providing 'scenes so lovely [they] must have been gazed upon by angels in their flight'. But West Africa also has its share of stunning waterfalls. The Tagbaladougou Falls in Burkina Faso are really three separate falls, including an elongated curtain of water flowing over a hard ridge, and a slender plume.

The picturesque Tannogou Falls in Benin pour off a plateau into a large pool. In Guinea, the Tinkisso River tumbles across erosion-resistant rocks in a series of rapids, culminating in the Tinkisso Falls.

ABOVE Although not the highest or the widest waterfall, Victoria Falls has the world's largest sheet of falling water.

LEFT The falls as viewed from Zambia. A steel bridge across the gorge was completed in 1905.

THE OKAVANGO DELTA

- The Okavango Delta covers a core area of 15,993sq km (6,175 square miles).

- During periods of flood after the rains this can increase to 22,000sq km (8,500 square miles).

- The Delta is home to the largest remaining number of red lechwe antelope. At least 20,000 live on the grasslands.

BELOW It takes almost nine months for the waters of the Okavango River to meander from their source to the delta. They drop only about 60m (200ft) over a distance of 450km (280 miles).

THE OKAVANGO RIVER RISES in the highlands of Angola and flows to the southeast. Before it can reach the sea it disappears in the arid wastes of the Kalahari Desert in Botswana, one of the driest countries in southern Africa. The slow-moving water passes through an intricate maze of channels where more than 95 percent of it evaporates. The remainder travels either farther south by way of the Boteti River for another 160km (100 miles) before reaching the Makgadikgadi Pans, or to the southwest, where it finally enters Lake Ngami.

The Okavango Delta represents not only one of the largest inland delta systems in the world, but also an area of unique character because of the juxtaposition of the highly productive wetlands and the extremely arid land of the Kalahari Desert. Even in this vast continent the Okavango Delta is one of the largest remaining wilderness areas.

The delta is a haven for a wide variety of both plants and animals. The upper reaches of the delta are covered by extensive dense reed beds dominated by papyrus. These are interspersed with areas of permanent water that support large stands of water lilies—popular with the pygmy goose, which feeds almost exclusively on lily fruit.

This wetland habitat is ideal for the hippopotamus, the crocodile and a number of species of antelope. Most notable is the sitatunga, which is very specifically adapted to an aquatic lifestyle and is largely confined to the most impenetrable areas of the delta and other similar areas in Africa. The kobs, which include the waterbuck, the puku

CHANGE AND MANAGEMENT
The delta's grassy plains are inhabited by the cattle-herding Tswana and Herero tribes. In the past their livestock were confined to the margins of the delta because of attacks by tsetse flies, carriers of sleeping sickness. Aerial spraying has all but eradicated the fly, allowing cattle and herdsmen to penetrate into the swamps. The unfortunate side effect of this success has been to reduce the range available to the antelope, by disturbing its habitats and making it compete with cattle for grazing. The numbers of antelope are thus in decline and the fragile integrity of this wilderness is threatened.

This threat has been recognized by the local people and the Moremi Wildlife Reserve, covering 3,900sq km (1,500 square miles), is the first wildlife sanctuary in southern Africa to be created and managed by the local people.

and the lechwe, are antelope species adapted for this aquatic lifestyle, and found only in southern Africa.

The reed beds and open water areas are also home to a large number of different birds, including some of Africa's rarest species. The spectacular African fish eagle with its evocative, piercing cry hunts in these areas, along with other species such as the little bee-eater, malacite kingfisher, a number of species of heron and egret, and the African fishing owl.

In the lower reaches of the delta the reed beds give way to acacia thorn scrub and grassy flood plains, which act as a magnet to the migrating herds of plains animals, including zebra, buffalo, elephant and antelope. The predators that follow these herds into the area include lions, leopards and hyenas.

SEE ALSO

■ *The Camargue* page 22

■ *The Danube Delta* page 36

■ *The Waddenzee* page 21

BELOW Visitors to the delta can take a safari in a local boat known as a *makoro*. The original vessels were carved from a single tree, but today many are made of fiberglass.

BOTTOM The delta has an ever-changing landscape of thousands of small islands. The white patches consist of salt deposits that are too barren to support plant life.

TABLE MOUNTAIN

- Table Mountain's apparently flat top stretches 3.2km (2 miles) from one end to the other.

- Its cliffs rise 1,070m (3,500ft) from sea level.

- Cape Town's annual rainfall is 65cm (25.5in), while precipitation on Table Mountain's summit averages 183cm (72in) per year.

TOWERING OVER the bustling city of Cape Town, Table Mountain is often shrouded in white clouds. When the clouds do lift, or resettle so that only the 'tablecloth' of mist remains draped over one end, a splendid sight is revealed. Viewed from the bay below, Table Mountain appears to have a perfectly flat top, and its cliffsides rise abruptly.

From Cape Town's bay the mountain is a great, blue-green monolith shimmering slightly in the heat, and doubtless a welcome sight to many sailors braving the stormy Atlantic seas around the Cape of Good Hope.

Table Mountain forms the northern end of a range of hills that lie between Cape Town and the Cape of Good Hope.

The range is made up of sandstone and quartzite resting on shale and older rocks of granite. The broken skyline of the escarpment is known as the Twelve Apostles. East of Table Mountain is Devils' Peak, 975m (3,200ft) high, while to the west are the smaller hills of Lion's Head and Signal Hill, which reach altitudes of 640m (2,100ft) and 335m (1,100ft) respectively.

The tablecloth drapes itself over the summit of Table Mountain but never reaches the lower slopes. The clouds that form are blown in by southeast winds, constantly forced northward down the slopes toward Cape Town, but they tend not to stay. On the summit, clouds can form very suddenly, and therefore make the weather there unpredictable.

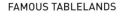

FAMOUS TABLELANDS

Tablelands are formed in several different ways. The Jugurtha Tableland in Tunisia is an example of inverted relief. It developed when softer rocks formed hills (upfold), and harder rocks formed the valley bottom (downfold). As the softer rocks eroded, the hard rocks of the valley floor became a tableland. In the case of Jugurtha, the table is a natural fortress, with steep-sided cliffs of 610m (2,000ft) to protect it.

Mesa Verde, in Colorado, is formed of sandstone, with layers of shale and coal. Successive uplifting of the land, combined with erosion of softer rocks by rivers, formed the tableland, which is now covered with forests of juniper and pine.

ABOVE The clouds of the 'tablecloth' result from warm, moist air being blown up the steep sides of the mountain to condense where it meets colder air at the top.

FAR LEFT Nelson Mandela, later president of South Africa, could see Table Mountain during his long imprisonment on Robben Island. He viewed it as 'a beacon of hope'.

SETTLING CAPE TOWN

The first European to reach the Cape Town area was the Portuguese explorer Bartholomew Diaz in 1488. He named this the Cape of Storms, and its turbulent reputation was not due only to the rough sailing conditions. Two decades after Diaz's visit, Portuguese sailors were massacred by the native Hottentots, and for many years afterward ships avoided the area altogether.

It was not until 1652 that a settlement was established by the Dutch beside Table Bay, which they used to supply passing East India Company ships with fresh vegetables. These early settlers built the Castle of Good Hope, South Africa's oldest surviving colonial building. Still operational as a military base, this fortress in the form of a five-pointed star also houses artifacts dating back to the 17th century, and troops dressed in historic uniform parade on its cobbled grounds.

Heavy rainfall on the summit has eroded a number of deep ravines running down the cliff face. The deepest of these, the Gorge, is also the shortest route to the top. Today visitors have a range of options for climbing to the top of Table Mountain. The easiest way up is on the cableway, but there are also hundreds of tracks of varying difficulty leading to the summit. The mountain is a popular venue for those who enjoy adventurous pursuits, and it's now possible to abseil off the top or to go paragliding from Lion's Head.

On clear days the views from Table Mountain are breathtaking. Three great oceans meet at the tip of southern Africa—the Atlantic, the Indian and the Southern. Cold currents from the south meeting the warmer waters of the Indian Ocean are responsible for some of the violent storms that pummel the region around the Cape of Good Hope.

SEE ALSO

■ *The Guilin Hills*
pages 90

NORTH AMERICA

The Canadian Pacific Railway 150

Niagara Falls 152

The Statue of Liberty 154

The Lincoln Memorial 158

Mount Rushmore 160

The Empire State Building 162

Great Architecture 164

Zion National Park 166

The Hoover Dam 168

The Golden Gate Bridge 170

The Devil's Tower 172

Yosemite National Park 174

The Grand Canyon 176

Redwoods and Giant Sequoias 178

Meteor Crater 179

The Everglades 180

The Hawaiian Islands 182

BELOW LEFT The Grand Canyon from the South Rim, eroded millions of years ago by the Colorado River (pages 176–177).

BELOW RIGHT The Golden Gate Bridge in San Francisco first opened in 1937 (see pages 170–171).

NORTH AMERICA'S FIRST HUMAN INHABITANTS ARE GENERALLY thought to have arrived from Siberia over 20,000 years ago, journeying on foot across the Bering Strait (which at that time was dry land), moving into Alaska and then onward south. Early Americans learned how to grow crops, how to make pottery and how to work copper and gold, and they developed a way of life tied intimately to their natural surroundings.

By the early 16th century European explorers were sailing along the eastern and southern shores of the continent and venturing into the interior. They were amazed by the diversity and immensity of the landscapes that greeted them, and charting the land became a vital part of the race for power. The French explored the St Lawrence River and the Great Lakes, headed south to present-day New York, and sailed the length of the Mississippi River. The Spanish made it into the central Rockies and the British pushed inland from New England and Virginia and laid trails across the Appalachian mountains. Control of territories and trade led to bitter conflicts, particularly between

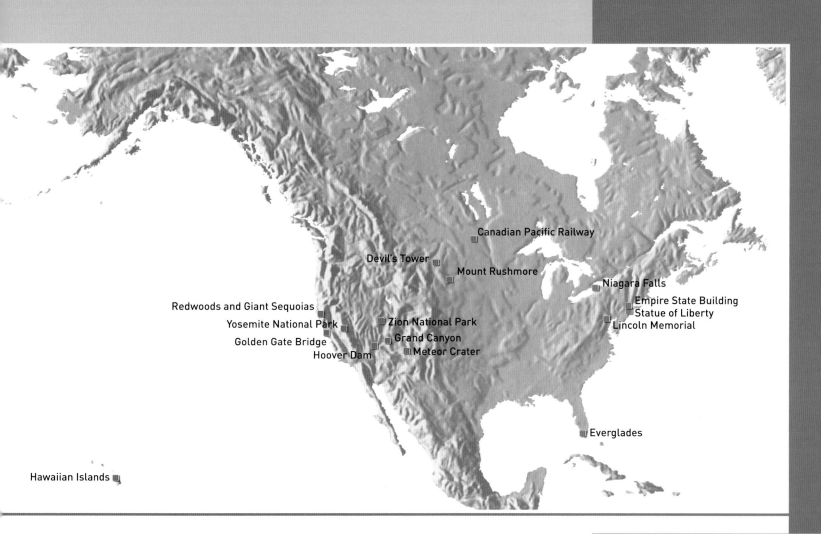

Canadian Pacific Railway

Devil's Tower

Mount Rushmore

Niagara Falls

Empire State Building
Statue of Liberty
Lincoln Memorial

Redwoods and Giant Sequoias

Yosemite National Park

Zion National Park

Golden Gate Bridge

Grand Canyon

Hoover Dam

Meteor Crater

Everglades

Hawaiian Islands

British and French colonists, which the British won. Native Americans were overwhelmed and driven from their homelands.

In the 18th century, thirteen American colonies threw off the yoke of British rule and declared their independence. The following century saw a frenzied drive to settle the West, and the building of the Canadian Pacific Railway brought the east and west coasts of North America closer together.

Immigrants poured into both Canada and the United States, lands of opportunity, to be greeted in the USA by the Statue of Liberty at the entrance to New York Harbor. North American architects and engineers invented the high-rise building, establishing a tradition symbolized by New York's Empire State Building. The continent's rich natural resources and pioneering spirit encouraged industrial growth, expressed in such engineering wonders as the Golden Gate Bridge across the entrance to San Francisco Bay and the Hoover Dam, which spans the Colorado River.

THE CANADIAN PACIFIC RAILWAY

■ On one stretch of the line beyond Calgary, a length of 183m (600ft) was laid in a record time of 4 minutes 45 seconds.

■ The line's original 1885 trestle bridge at Stoney Creek, British Columbia, was the highest timber bridge ever built.

■ Engineer William Van Horne began as a telegraph operator with the Illinois Central Railroad and was later knighted.

THE SINGLE TRACK between Montreal and Vancouver, 4,696km (2,918 miles) long, was one of the most heroic feats of engineering history and a vital factor in the development of modern Canada.

In 1867 the country's eastern provinces formed the Canadian Confederation, to the west of which lay a vast emptiness of prairies and mountains. On the Pacific coast was British Columbia, uncertain whether or not to link up with the United States. In 1871 British Columbia joined the Canadian Confederation, on condition that a railway crossing the continent be built within ten years.

In the event, work did not begin until 1881, with a formidable American of Dutch descent, William Van Horne, in charge. The line across the prairies was built rapidly in 15 months. From the supply base in Winnipeg construction trains moved west with clockwork regularity, each one carrying exactly the quantity of material needed for 1.6km (1 mile) of track: rail and ties, telegraph poles, bridging material. Getting the track through the Rocky Mountains presented a particular challenge. Beyond the little settlement at Calgary, the line had moved swiftly along the Bow River, but an army of 12,000 men was needed to drive over Kicking Horse Pass, 1,628m (5,340ft) up among the towering peaks, and down a dizzying descent on the other side.

The original plan was to follow the Columbia River, but a surveyor named A. B. Rogers discovered a pass, now named after him, through the Selkirk Mountains, saving 240km (150 miles). Because of avalanches the line had to be protected with miles of snowsheds; later a tunnel was driven through the worst section.

CHANGING FORTUNES

The completion of North America's oldest transcontinental rail line marked a spectacular engineering feat, and trains continued to run between Montréal and Vancouver for over 100 years. The service was discontinued in 1990, and the line given over to commercial traffic.

However, since 2000 the CPR-owned Royal Canadian Pacific has run tours along sections of the route every year between May and November, using cars from the vintage fleet that date from between 1916 and 1931. The Canadian Railway Museum at St Constant, in the southern suburbs of Montréal, has a collection of items relevant to the line.

BELOW The line running through Banff National Park, Canada's oldest national park, proposed by Van Horne and set up in 1885.

Beyond Shuswap Lake the track threaded through the Coast Mountains by way of the wild Fraser Canyon, which Van Horne described as one of the worst places in the world. The line was intended to end at Port Moody on Burrard Inlet, but Van Horne pushed it down the inlet to the site of what is now Vancouver.

The railway line opened central and western Canada to settlers, who came in their thousands. Winnipeg thrived on its railyards and the tide of immigrants pouring through to the prairies. Regina was created by the railroad and named in tribute to Queen Victoria when the first train arrived in 1882. Banff, the first major Rocky Mountain tourist resort, was named by the president of the Canadian Pacific Railway, a Scotsman originally from Banffshire.

SEE ALSO

■ *The Trans-Siberian Railway* page 66

ALL ABOARD

The last spike of the Canadian Pacific Railway was driven in a simple ceremony amid the mountains at Eagle Pass on November 7, 1885, at a spot that William Van Horne named Craigellachie. In his book *The Impossible Railway*, Pierre Berton describes how the line's directors arrived at the scene, drawn by locomotive No. 148, with its

diamond-shaped smokestack and gleaming brass boiler. The oldest of the directors, Donald A. Smith, drove the final spike in total silence, followed by a tremendous cheer as it went home, and the shrill whistling of the locomotive. Van Horne, not given to great speeches, simply remarked that the work had been well done, and a voice cried, 'All aboard for the Pacific!'

NIAGARA FALLS

■ The Horseshoe Falls in Canada form an arc about 790m (2,600ft) long.

BELOW A view of Niagara Falls from the nearby Skylon Tower.

■ The American Falls in the USA form a straight line about 300m (1,000ft) long.

■ Lake Erie's outflow pours into Lake Ontario via the 56km (35 mile) Niagara River down a drop of 100m (330ft).

A SPUME OF SPRAY lifts high into the air as the dark green waters of the Niagara River thunder into the frothing cauldron at the base of the falls. There are two main parts to this waterfall: the American Falls and the Horseshoe Falls. Between them is Goat Island, a tree-covered islet that sits in the middle of the river.

The Horseshoe Falls, on the Canadian side of the border, are perhaps the better known of the two. A road beside the river gives a good view of the falls at very close range, where the surface of the water has the appearance of dark green glass, turning to foaming white as it slides over the cliffs. The American Falls are smaller and have piles of broken rocks at their base, as opposed to the sheer plunge of the Horseshoe Falls. Both waterfalls are about 50m (165ft) high.

The Niagara Falls have been in existence only for around 10,000 years—a relatively short time in geological terms.

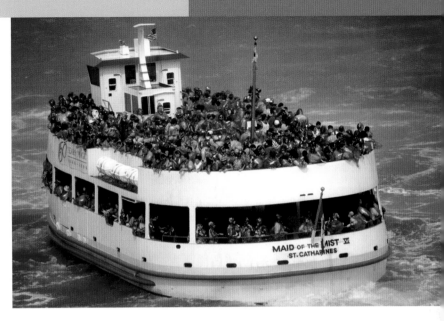

CANADA'S OTHER WATERFALLS

Canada is the world's second-largest country, so it is no surprise that it has many other spectacular waterfalls. At Virginia Falls in the Northwest Territories the South Nahanni River thunders over a precipice almost twice the height of Niagara. This little-known river descends 915m (3,000ft) over a distance of 595km (370 miles) in a series of tumbling rapids and deep gorges.

The Hunlen Falls and the Helmcken Falls are both in British Columbia. At the Helmcken Falls, the Murtle River cascades over a cliff of ancient rock to a spray-filled basin 137m (450ft) below. The Hunlen Falls are seven times the height of Niagara, and drop in a curtain of spray 366m (1,200ft) to the rocks below.

Above the falls the river bedrock is hard dolomite, but underneath the dolomite are layers of softer rocks such as shale and sandstone. Originally the river dropped over an escarpment about 11km (7 miles) north of the present falls, but as the softer rocks underneath the dolomite were eroded by the fast-flowing water, the dolomite collapsed. Bit by bit the waterfall retreated, so that the falls today are a long way from where they were 10,000 years ago, and in their retreat they have left behind a deep gorge. The falls moved back at a rate of about 1m (3ft) per year, and are about 300m (1,000ft) farther upstream than they were when Louis Hennepin, the French explorer, saw

them in 1678. However, Goat Island has divided the river in two, and this, coupled with the fact that at least half the water of the Niagara is diverted away from the waterfalls to generate electricity, means that the falls are much more stable now than they were in the past.

Bridges and parks on both sides of the river provide good vantage points. One of the most popular is Rainbow Bridge, named after the rainbows that shimmer in the spray above the falls. The sheer power and size of Niagara is best seen from the boats that brave the churning waters beneath the falls.

ABOVE One of the *Maid of the Mist* boats, taking visitors for an exhilarating trip close to the base of the falls. The service began in 1846.

OVER THE FALLS

Some people have taken the sheer power and size of the Niagara Falls as an irresistible personal challenge. Several adventurers have gone over the falls, in a variety of different vessels including barrels, boats and sealed capsules.

One of the most famous death-defying escapades took place on 30 June 1859, when Jean-François Gravelet, better known as Charles Blondin, crossed the falls on a tightrope. The rope was 335m (1,100ft) long, and suspended 49m (160ft) above the falls. Evidently Blondin found the whole experience a little too tame. A year later he made the crossing again, but this time with his agent on his back.

SEE ALSO
- *Angel Falls* page 194
- *Iguaçu Falls* page 202
- *Victoria Falls* page 142

SUPER SITE
THE STATUE OF LIBERTY

■ **Marking the entrance to New York Harbor, the Statue of Liberty is seen as the symbol of freedom.**

■ **Liberty's star-shaped pedestal was designed by American architect Richard Morris Hunt.**

The best known statue in North America—perhaps in the world—was dedicated by President Grover Cleveland on October 28, 1886 to the roar of a 21-gun salute, the blasts of ships' foghorns and a din of fireworks. Ever since that day, the towering figure holding Liberty's torch has been the first sight of America for passengers entering New York Harbor, and for millions of immigrants it has represented a promise of freedom from oppression and poverty.

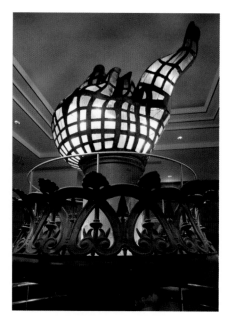

ABOVE The statue's original torch, now on display in the site museum, was unsuccessfully adapted to act as a light for shipping.

THE STATUE had its origins in French politics. In 1865, when Emperor Napoleon III was on the throne, an academic, Edouard de Laboulaye and his circle hatched the idea of a 'Statue of Liberty', to express approval of the great republic across the Atlantic and underline their own hopes for an end to the monarchy and the establishment of a new French Republic. A sculptor, Frédéric-Auguste Bartholdi (1834–1904), was encouraged to consider the project. He was helped in his task by the engineer Gustave Eiffel, creator of the Eiffel Tower, and Eiffel's head of research, Maurice Koechlin.

The mother of invention
Bartholdi had planned to build a lighthouse for the Suez Canal in the form of a colossal female figure holding a torch aloft to symbolize the light of progress coming to Asia. He adapted this idea to the new project with enthusiasm, inspired in his crafting of Liberty by Delacroix's famous painting *Liberty Guiding the People*, and basing her stern features on his own mother's face.

ABOVE Liberty Island, with Ellis Island to the right. The star-shaped base of the statue was part of a granite fort of 1811.

BELOW In her left hand the statue holds the US Declaration of Independence, to symbolize freedom and democracy.

BELOW AND RIGHT Images from the construction process. The statue parts were shipped from France in 1885, packed in more than 200 crates.

THE HISTORY

- **1884** *Frédéric-Auguste Bartholdi completes his sculpture of Liberty.*

- **1886** *Pedestal construction is completed in the US.*

- **1901** *Statue is placed in care of the War Department.*

- **1924** *Fort Wood's star-shaped walls and the statue within it are declared a National Monument.*

- **1956** *Bedloe's Island is renamed Liberty Island.*

- **1984** *The statue is designated a World Heritage Site.*

The huge size of the statue and its exposure to wind and weather posed severe technical problems for Bartholdi and the engineering team. Eiffel built an ingenious iron framework supported by a central pylon, and onto this flexible interior skeleton was attached the statue's visible

outer layer of copper, just 2.4mm (0.09in) thick. Starting with a model 1.2m (4ft) tall, Bartholdi then made three more, each bigger than the last, until the full magnificent size was reached. The final statue was constructed in Paris, where it was formally presented to the American ambassador on July 4, 1884 as a gift from the French to the American people. It was then taken to pieces and shipped in crates to New York, where it was reassembled on the massive pedestal built for it at American expense on Bedloe's Island (now Liberty Island).

THE GOLDEN DOOR

The Statue of Liberty inspired Emma Lazarus to write her poem *The New Colossus* (1903), describing the 'huddled masses' and 'wretched refuse' of the Old World coming to be welcomed by Liberty's lamp, lifted 'beside the golden door'.

From 1892 onwards the huddled masses actually arrived at nearby Ellis Island, where boatloads of immigrants were processed through a succession of bureaucratic and health checks in an intense atmosphere of nervous apprehension mingled with hope and excitement. An average of 2,000 new arrivals a day passed through the great hall in the busiest period in the early 1900s. In its peak year of 1907 Ellis Island handled more than a million people.

Not everyone had a chance of becoming an American citizen, however. In 1790 a law was passed stating that only white immigrants could be naturalized, and this law was not overturned until 1952. The Ellis Island immigration station closed in 1954, and the complex has been restored as a national monument.

The figure has the broken shackles of tyranny at her feet. In her left hand she holds a tablet that represents the Declaration of Independence. She wears a crown of seven rays, with the rays standing for freedom spreading across the seven continents. A spiral staircase inside the statue leads to the crown (a climb equivalent to walking up a 12-story building), a visit restricted to a few hundred people a day.

SEE ALSO
■ *The Eiffel Tower* page 26
■ *The Lincoln Memorial* page 158

VITAL STATISTICS

The Statue of Liberty is 46m (151ft) high and stands on Richard Morris Hunt's pedestal which is 47m (154ft) high. The tip of the torch is 93m (305ft) above the ground. The statue weighs a huge 204 metric tons (225 tons) and is 10.6m (35ft) around the waist.

The mouth is 91cm (3ft) wide and the right arm (the one holding the torch), is 12.8m (42ft) long. The index finger alone is 2.4m (8ft) long—far taller than the average man. The tablet in the statue's left hand is 7.2m (23ft) long, 4.1m (13ft) wide and 61cm (2ft) thick.

LEFT More than 120,000 people contributed money to pay for the completion of the pedestal. Their average gift was less than one US dollar.

THE LINCOLN MEMORIAL

- Lincoln's statue is 5.8m (19ft) high and equally wide.

- The memorial colonnade is 57m (188ft) long by 36m (118ft) wide.

- There are 38 columns. Each is 13.4m (44ft) high with a diameter of 2.26m (7ft 5in) at the base.

- The inner chamber is 18m (60ft) high.

ABOVE Lincoln's statue is flanked by carved symbols of the Roman republic.

ABRAHAM LINCOLN'S MONUMENT in Washington D.C. is a dignified, restrained and moving tribute to the man and to the virtues of tolerance, honesty and constancy that he represented. Within two years of the American president's death in 1865 there were proposals for a memorial in Washington, but not until 1915 was the foundation stone laid. The memorial was dedicated on May 30 1922. Its designer was the architect Henry Bacon, a specialist in monuments who was also responsible for a memorial to Lincoln in the city of Lincoln, Nebraska.

Washington's Lincoln Memorial is in the form of a classical Greek temple, echoing the design of the Parthenon in Athens. The rectangular building is flanked by 38 doric columns of white Colorado marble, two of which are set back slightly and mark the entrance. The remaining 36 stand for the 36 states of the Union at the time the memorial was dedicated.

THE LAST ACT

On the evening of April 14, 1865, five days after the surrender of the Confederate Army under General Robert E. Lee at Appomattox Court House, President Lincoln and his wife attended Ford's Theater in Washington to see a comedy called *Our American Cousin*. At 10.15pm a deranged actor called John Wilkes Booth shot and wounded the president. Lincoln was carried to the house across the street, where he remained unconscious in one of the bedrooms. Mrs Lincoln, who was in a hysterical state, waited as members of the Cabinet gathered at the house. At 7.22am Edwin M. Stanton, Secretary of War, emerged from the bedroom to announce the president's death with the words: 'Now he belongs to the ages'. Lincoln was 56. Ford's Theater has been restored, with a museum of Lincoln relics and objects. The house where Lincoln died is also open to the public.

DANIEL CHESTER FRENCH

French (1850–1931) was one of the most popular and successful sculptors of his day. Born in Exeter, New Hampshire, he started on his career path as a boy, carving comical figures out of turnips. He studied in Boston and New York and at the age of 24 received his first commission—a statue of *The Minute Man*, which stands on the Green in Concord, Massachusetts, commemorating the Battle of Lexington and Concord (1775) during the American Revolution.

After spending a year in Italy, French returned to Washington, where he opened a studio and forged his reputation as America's foremost monumental sculptor, making him a natural choice for this important memorial.

ABOVE The Lincoln Memorial and the US Capitol stand at each end of the monumental park of Washington's National Mall.

Inside, a colossal statue by Daniel Chester French shows the president seated in a massive chair, in a mood of contemplation that visitors can interpret as they will. The whole statue seems to be carved from one immense block of marble, but is in fact made of pieces so smoothly fitted together that the joints are invisible.

Beyond the president's head is an inscription: 'In this temple, as in the hearts of the people for whom he saved the Union, the memory of Abraham Lincoln is enshrined forever'. Also cut into the walls are the words of two of his great speeches, the Gettysburg Address of 1863 and the Second Inaugural Address of 1865. There are murals by Jules Guérin on the themes of the reconciliation of North and South after the American Civil War, and the freeing of the slaves.

The monument is floodlit at night to spectacular effect, and a wreath is placed every year on February 12, Lincoln's birthday. There are guided tours of the caves underneath the building, with their stalagmites and stalactites. The Lincoln Memorial is close to the Potomac River, aligned with the Capitol and the Washington Monument, toward which stretches the beautiful Reflecting Pool. To the west, crossing the Potomac, is the Arlington Memorial Bridge, itself a symbol of the reconciliation of North and South on which President Lincoln set his heart.

ABOVE Larger than life: the scale of Lincoln's figure is such that if it was standing up, it would be 8.5m (28ft) tall.

LEFT The obelisk of the Washington Monument, with the US Capitol in the distance, seen from the Lincoln memorial.

SEE ALSO

■ *Mount Rushmore*
page 160
■ *The Statue of Liberty*
page 154

MOUNT RUSHMORE

■ The monument cost almost $1m to create.

■ The presidents' faces are carved 18m (60ft) high on the rockface.

■ Sculptor Gutzon Borglum was determined to include Roosevelt in the group because of the sculptural challenge posed by his glasses.

CARVED IN THE GRANITE of Mount Rushmore in South Dakota, four huge faces of American presidents gaze out upon the world: George Washington, Thomas Jefferson, Theodore Roosevelt and Abraham Lincoln.

The idea of the monument was originally conceived by the local historian and publicist Doane Robinson as a spectacular project to draw tourists to the beautiful Black Hills. In 1924 he interested the sculptor Gutzon Borglum in this mammoth project, and it was decided to create a 'shrine to democracy'.

Borglum was 60 when work began at Mount Rushmore in 1927 and it occupied him for the rest of his life. He designed the monument and directed the sizeable workforce of local masons and miners, who blasted the mountain face with dynamite and shaped the great heads with hammer and chisel, while dangling precariously on swaying platforms. Borglum intended the presidents to be shown down to waist level. As the project was never finished, it has been remarked that it was just as well that he started with the heads.

At Mount Rushmore, Borglum had fierce arguments with the National Park Service, and his work was constantly interrupted by shortage of funds and bad weather. All the same, Washington's head was formally unveiled in 1930, Jefferson's in 1936, Lincoln's in 1937 and Roosevelt's

BELOW Left to right: Washington, Jefferson, Roosevelt and Lincoln, presidents who were key to US history.

The Black Hills were sacred territory to the Sioux, and the United States government confirmed this in a treaty of 1868 for 'as long as rivers run and grass grows and trees bear leaves'. This proved not to be as long as expected, because in 1874 gold was discovered in the hills at French Creek.

Prospectors swarmed in and the Native Americans went to war. They won a famous victory at the Battle of Little Bighorn (1876), where General George Armstrong Custer and his force of cavalry were wiped out to the last man. However, the Native Americans eventually lost the war and white settlers took over.

in 1939. After Borglum died in 1941, his son, Lincoln, worked on it for a while until the money ran out.

Borglum had ideas as grandiose as his name, which in full was John Gutzon de la Mothe Borglum. He was born in 1867 near Bear Creek, Idaho, of Danish Mormon immigrants. At his Roman Catholic boarding school in Xavier, Kansas, Borglum impressed his Jesuit teachers with his drawing skills and later he studied art in Paris, where he met the great sculptor Auguste Rodin. After returning to the US he was invited, in 1915, to carve a giant head of General Robert E. Lee at Stone Mountain, near Atlanta, Georgia. Borglum transformed this project into a parade 0.5km (0.25 mile) long of Confederate infantry and cavalry to be carved out of the mountain, with heroic figures of Stonewall Jackson and Jefferson Davis as well as Lee himself, all on horseback. However, Borglum and the committee could not agree on terms, and the project never came to fruition.

SEE ALSO

■ *The Lincoln Memorial* page 158
■ *The Statue of Liberty* page 154

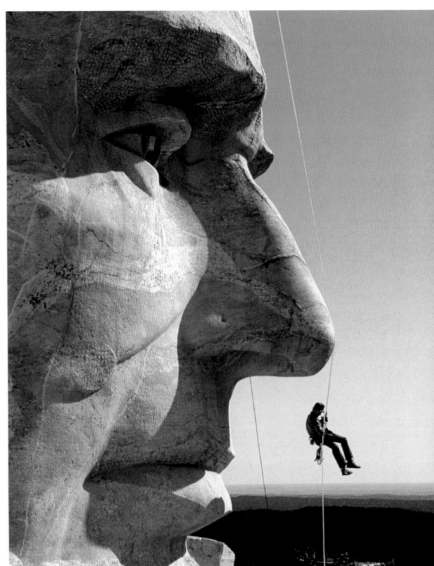

ABOVE Under the nose of Abraham Lincoln: climbers inspect the monument annually to monitor and seal cracks.

NATIVE AMERICAN SHRINE

Not far from this site, another enormous figure is being carved in the living rock of a mountain. Designed by the late Korczak Ziolkowski, who worked on Mount Rushmore, it is to depict the great Native American leader Crazy Horse (1849–77), bare-chested and on horseback, in a carving 172m (563ft) high and 195m (640ft) long. The sculptor was commissioned in 1939 by Sioux chiefs, who wanted to show that 'the red men had great heroes too'.

Since Ziolkowski's death in 1982 at the age of 74, the project has continued, as the great sculptor left detailed instructions for its completion.

THE EMPIRE STATE BUILDING

■ **The Empire State Building was the world's tallest building between 1931 and 1971, and is currently the tallest building in New York City.**

■ **On a clear day, you can see as far as 130km (80 miles) away from the top.**

■ **The TV antenna on the top of the building, installed in 1985, is 22 floors high.**

REACH FOR THE SKIES

Named to celebrate the state of New York (nicknamed the Empire State) and designed by Shreve, Harmon and Lamb, the building cost $41 million—well below estimate—and was erected at a speed that has never been surpassed. It rose at the rate of more than four floors a week, and in one hectic period, more than 14 floors were added in 10 days.

The building was opened in May 1931, but with the United States in the grip of the Depression the space proved hard to rent. For a while it was sardonically known as the Empty State Building. In fact it took 10 years for the office space—which can accommodate 15,000 people—to be fully occupied.

THIS TOWERING EDIFICE is a potent symbol of the excitement, glamor and sheer exuberant excessiveness of New York City. For more than 40 years it lodged itself firmly in everyone's mind as the world's tallest building, and although it has been overtaken by younger rivals, it is still for many people the skyscraper of skyscrapers. To make way for the building, the most select hotel in town, the Waldorf-Astoria, was demolished.

The building's statistics are appropriately awesome. Its 102 floors rise to a height of 381m (1,250ft) and the television tower on top makes the total height 449m (1,473ft). It was originally planned to moor airships to the building, but the idea was abandoned. The building occupies a site of some 0.8ha (2 acres) on Fifth Avenue. Although it weighs a mammoth 331,000 metric tons (364,865 tons), the foundations are only two floors deep, but it is held upright by steel beams weighing 54,400 metric tons (43,530 tons). The staircase from the ground level to the top (the 102nd floor) has 1,860 steps; once a year there is a race up the 1,576 steps to the 86th-floor observatory (the record time is less than 10 minutes).

With so many other tall office blocks all around it, it is difficult to get a good view of the great building at ground level. It was designed in a simple and elegant Art Deco

ABOVE The base of what is now the TV tower was designed for mooring airships, but high winds made this unfeasible.

LEFT A $20m refit started in 2009 aims to cut the building's energy use by 40 percent, saving emissions equivalent to those of 20,000 cars.

ABOVE The Observatory was featured as a meeting place in the movies *An Affair to Remember* (1957) and *Sleepless in Seattle* (1993).

style. The stone façade has strips of stainless steel running up it, and the higher levels are neatly set back. Inside, the marble-lined lobby is 27m (90ft) long and rises three levels, with panels depicting the seven classical wonders of the world, plus an eighth—the Empire State Building itself. The New York Skyride offers visitors a simulated helicopter ride and virtual-reality movie. Elevators rise to the 86th floor, where the views of the city are magnificent.

The classic movie *King Kong*, released in 1933, planted the building's image firmly in audiences' minds by showing the monster gorilla clinging to it while beating off attacking planes; 1933 was also the year of the building's first suicide. Catastrophe followed in 1945 when a plane crashed into the 79th floor, causing 14 deaths and $1 million worth of damage.

SEE ALSO
- *Burj Khalifa* page 82
- *The Petronas Towers* page 225
- *Taipei 101 Tower* page 225

GREAT ARCHITECTURE

Architectural design, whether to represent power or wealth, or to provide refuge or space for contemplation, is a statement of its era and creates an emotional response. Even functional structures such as bridges and railway stations can inspire affection, and few disciplines provoke as much debate as modern architecture.

■ In 2010 Dubai's Burj Khalifa, standing at 828m (2,717 feet), overtook Taiwan's Taipei 101 tower as the world's tallest building.

■ The 1997 Guggenheim Museum in Bilbao is coated in 30,000 glittering titanium sheets.

■ The Winter Palace in St Petersburg is made of five million bricks and has more than 700 rooms.

Left Norman Foster's cupola at the Reichstag building, Berlin, home to the German parliament. Its design embodies transparency and democracy.

Right The Temple of the Golden Pavilion, Kyoto. Traditional Japanese wooden structures such as these have been taken down and rebuilt many times to the original pattern.

Below Dubai's sail-shaped Burj Al Arab hotel was intended to become a symbol of the city, much like the Eiffel Tower in Paris.

GRAND PLANS

Before the modern age of great state-funded commissions, secular architecture represented the personal projects of monarchs and merchants. Louis XIV created the Palace of Versailles in the 17th century to convey his status and symbolize his harmonious reign, inspiring rulers across Europe to do likewise. More than 1,500 years earlier Emperor Vespasian had used the construction of the Colosseum in a similar way, displaying his wealth and power through the scale of the entertainments he provided.

It was personal enthusiasm that inspired Bavarian King Ludwig II's extravagant mock-medieval castle at Neuschwanstein near Munich, and it was newspaper magnate William Randolph Hearst's private wealth that enabled him to build copies of the world's great architecture for his 1919 Californian mansion Hearst Castle.

TEST OF TIME

Novel architecture can be controversial. Richard Rogers' Pompidou Center in Paris wears its innards—pipes, vents and ducts—on the outside, and provoked as much outrage as admiration when it was completed in 1977. Jørn Utzon's Sydney Opera House, now a much-loved symbol of the city, was not universally applauded at first, and Antoni Gaudí's exuberant Sagrada Família Church in Barcelona is still taking shape over a century after work began.

SPIRITUAL SPACES

The design of great religious buildings reflects the traditions and practices of the faith they were created to celebrate. Whether a tranquil place for prayer and contemplation, or a grand space reinforcing the insignificance of the individual compared to the power of the deity, they incorporate some of the most brilliant art and architecture of their time.

In Istanbul, Turkey, the Blue Mosque's interior tile decoration creates an impression of overwhelming complexity, while Chartres Cathedral in France uses rich blues to sublime effect in its stained-glass windows, adding to the overall sensation of soaring height created by the Gothic architecture. The graceful spaces of buildings such as the Alhambra in Granada in southern Spain and the Taj Mahal in India also create an almost religious sense of peace.

Above Revolutionary architecture at the Pompidou Centre made the building's exterior an instant new attraction for central Paris, eclipsing the exhibitions inside.

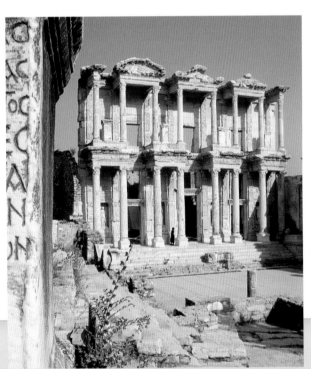

Left Ruined buildings evoke a past that can only be imagined. The façade of the Library of Celsius in Roman Ephesus has been re-erected, but its architect is unknown.

SEE ALSO

■ *The Sagrada Família* page 60
■ *Sydney Opera House* page 214
■ *Versailles* page 24

ZION NATIONAL PARK

■ Zion Canyon in Utah is only 24km (15 miles) long, but in places it reaches a depth of 762m (2,500ft).

■ At its northern end, in a section known as the Narrows, only 6m (20ft) separates the cliffs.

■ It is possible to hike along the Narrows in the dry season, although there is a danger from flash floods.

THOUSANDS OF YEARS AGO, a small stream meandered its way across the soft young rocks of a plateau on its way southward. As the land rose, the stream began to cut itself a path, scouring the underlying rock with particles of grit and sand eroded from farther upstream. The result of this was Zion Canyon, a winding gorge slicing through the Navajo sandstone to the older, underlying Kaibab limestone.

The Mormons discovered and named Zion Canyon in the 1860s, though it was not surveyed until 1872. In 1919, 383sq km (148 square miles) of the wilderness surrounding the canyon was designated as a national park. In 1956 this was enlarged to include an area of 596sq km (230 square miles). Zion National Park is a fascinating array of rock formations, mainly carved out of the predominant Navajo sandstone. The overwhelming image of the park is of towering cliffs, forbidding domes

and deep chasms, ranging from deep glowing red to a delicate rose-pink.

Zion has many extraordinary natural features. Checkerboard Mesa is a great slab of sandstone looming over the road, its surface intricately carved into squares by the effects of wind and water. In Verkin Canyon, a natural arch spans between two cliff faces, while Great White Throne stands flat-topped and massive among towering red cliffs. The highest point in the park is the West Temple, towering 1,158m (3,800ft) above the canyon base. The Towers of the Virgin are a group of jagged sandstone peaks ranging along the west wall of the canyon, and the natural amphitheater of the Temple of Sinawava provides splendid views of the surrounding cliffs and domes.

Another well-known feature is the Weeping Rock, where water from springs higher up the rock trickles across its surface, dropping like tears from its overhangs. A similar phenomenon occurs at Hanging Gardens, but instead of

AMERICA'S NATIONAL BEAUTY

About 310,000sq km (120,000 square miles) of the US in about 320 different sites come under the care of the National Park Service, which covers historical sites as well as sites of natural wonder. These include battlefields (such as Saratoga and Gettysburg), early trading posts and archaeological sites where evidence of Native American settlement has been discovered.

The first national park, founded in 1872—and which remains one of the most popular in America—was Yellowstone. Since then many other sites have been considered important parts of America's heritage, and their protection has been assured by their designation as national parks or national monuments.

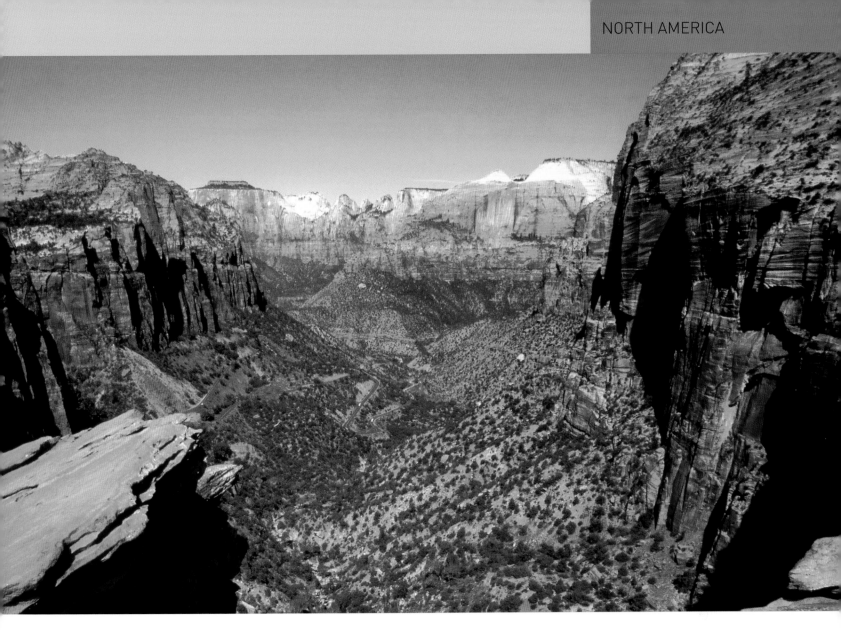

LEFT Millions of years of erosion have scored deep lines between the layers of red Navajo sandstone on this hillside.

ABOVE Canyon Overlook: a short hiking trail leads to a panoramic viewpoint over the National Park's characteristic cliffs and overhangs.

dripping away, the water is absorbed by the plants that cling precariously to its slopes.

The pale sides of Zion Canyon's west rim show clear lines where the Navajo sandstone has been formed in neat, regular layers. Fast-running water has scoured out caves, which provide shelter for a variety of birds, small mammals and insects. In some of the larger caves, archaeologists have discovered items from the ancient settlements of the Pueblo people.

SEE ALSO
■ *Redwood National Park* page 178
■ *Sequoia National Park* page 178
■ *Yosemite National Park* page 174

BRYCE CANYON

Bryce Canyon National Park lies only a short distance from Zion. Water has raged across the sedimentary rocks, eroding them into a complex system of ravines and gullies, a process that is continuing today as flash floods cause walls to split and columns to collapse. Metallic minerals mixed in with the sediments have produced rocks of rich reds and oranges, and even pale mauve in places.

The Pink Cliffs escarpment is perhaps the best-known area, containing a fantastic jumble of pinnacles, ravines and oddly shaped pillars. The first European pioneer to explore the area, Ebenezer Bryce, remarked that this is 'one heck of a place to lose a cow'.

THE HOOVER DAM

■ There is as much steel in the Hoover Dam as in the Empire State Building.

■ When formally dedicating the dam in 1936, President Roosevelt called it the Boulder Dam, which it remained until 1947, when Congress restored the original name.

■ The dam drains an area covering 7.7 percent of the US.

FROM ITS HEADWATERS in the Rocky Mountains the mighty Colorado River flows southwest across the states of Colorado and Utah and through the Grand Canyon, to form the border between Arizona and Nevada and then between Arizona and California, before crossing into Mexico and finally reaching the sea in the Gulf of California. In 1905 this unpredictable river abruptly changed course, creating the 780sq km (300 square miles) of the Salton Sea and threatening to inundate the entire Imperial Valley in California. To bring the river under control and improve irrigation, and at the same time generate electricity, it was decided to build a vast dam on the river along the Arizona-Nevada border. Congress provided the money in 1928, and construction work began in 1931. As Herbert Hoover was president at the time and had taken a vigorous interest in the project, the dam was given his name.

The dam, at that time the biggest ever built, is a huge mass of 2.5 million cu m (3.25 million cubic yards) of concrete. More than 8 million metric tons (8.8 million tons) of rock had to be excavated to build it. It is 201m (660ft) thick at the base and stands 221m (726ft) high—about the height of a 70-storey skyscraper. It measures 379m (1,244ft) along the top and is 14m (46ft) thick at that point.

Immediately to the north, the dam created Lake Mead, one of the largest manmade reservoirs in the world.

Today the lake is run by the National Park Service and used for sailing, boating and other water sports.

North of Lake Mead lies the spectacular 14,165ha (35,000-acre) Valley of Fire State Park, so named because the sandstone rocks here are a fiery shade of red, before toning down to shades of tangerine and lavender. Wind and weather have carved these sandstone rocks into domes, beehives and other weird shapes, including a particularly dramatic example that looks like the head and trunk of an elephant. On some of the rocks are mysterious carvings and paintings made centuries ago by the Anasazi people, ancestors of today's Pueblo people and best known for their remarkable cliff dwellings. Whether the marks are a language or a form of map is not known. Ten thousand or more of these people lived in a 'lost city' on the banks of the Muddy River nearby, in an area now partly covered by Lake Mead.

OPPOSITE PAGE AND LEFT The convex curve of the dam transmits the massive water pressure to the strong rock walls of the canyon. The dam is 200m (660ft) thick at the bottom, narrowing to 14m (46ft) at the top, where a roadway runs across it.

BOULDER CITY

When word of the dam project first got out, legions of unemployed men made their way to the site and camped out in the desert in the hope of being given work. Those who were engaged endured horrific conditions and lived in improvised shelters, some along with their wives and children.

Eventually the long-promised new homes were built for the dam's workforce, giving simple accommodation to 4,000 people, and Boulder City, a pleasant little community, grew up. Part of the motivation for building it was to segregate the workers from the nearby fleshpots of Las Vegas.

SEE ALSO

■ *The Aswan High Dam* page 122
■ *The Itaipú Dam* page 224
■ *The Three Gorges Dam* page 92

THE GOLDEN GATE BRIDGE

■ The bridge is 2.7km (1.7 miles) long.

■ For more than 20 years it had the longest suspension span in the world—1,280m (4,200ft).

■ The towers rise 227m (745ft) above the level of high tide.

■ Each cable is 93cm (36.5in) in diameter and composed of 27,572 separate strands of wire.

WHEN IT OPENED ON MAY 27 1937, the Golden Gate Bridge, linking San Francisco with Marin County, finally silenced all its critics. Many had maintained that the notion of a bridge at the entrance to the bay—one of the largest and safest natural harbors in the world—was impractical. For all the triumph of its final completion, however, the bridge was very difficult to build, and there were many casualties among the workers who toiled for four years to complete it, struggling against high tides, fierce currents and thick fogs.

SHADES OF GOLD

From its earliest days, the Golden Gate bridge has always been painted a distinctive shade known as International Orange. Red or orange is regarded as the traditional shade for steel structures, a consequence of the red lead (a classic anticorrosive substance) added to the paint. In the case of the Golden Gate Bridge, it also helps visibility in the frequent fogs that envelop San Francisco.

By 1968, the original red lead-based finish was severely corroded. An initiative began to replace it with more modern materials, including a vinyl top coat. More recently this was changed to an acrylic emulsion to meet air quality requirements. Today nearly 40 painters keep up the continuous job of retouching the most eroded areas.

GOLDEN GATE PARK

A 405ha (1,000-acre) park lies south of the Golden Gate Bridge and stretches eastward almost halfway across San Francisco. Work on the park began in 1870. The park's original designer, William Hammond Hall, was succeeded by Scotsman John McLaren, who devoted 56 years to its care and nurture. McLaren, who is estimated to have planted two million trees, successfully transformed an unpromising area of shifting sand dunes into mature and thriving gardens.

He is reported to have made a number of rules for the administration of the park. No workman was to wear gloves or to smoke during working hours, signs forbidding people to walk on the grass were outlawed, and garden statuary was treated with suspicion and likely to be hidden behind thick shrubs or bushes.

BELOW The bridge spans the Golden Gate Strait, which gives the bridge its name—it has never been golden in color.

RIGHT The bridge saved drivers a trip of several hours. Its construction was backed by the US automobile industry.

Funds for the building project were raised from a $35-million bond issue, and the bridge was designed by Joseph Strauss, Charles Alton Ellis and Irving Morrow, a consultant architect who introduced some Art Deco detailing. The foundations for the south tower proved the most hazardous part of the job. Workers had to balance on barges, tossed by huge tidal swells, as they constructed a vast concrete fender into which the bridge caissons could be sunk.

Once the two towers were in place, equally courageous workmen had to clamber along catwalks slung between them in order to position the suspension cables. For the first time on a major building project a safety net was installed and as a result 19 men survived after falling off the catwalks. Tragically, on February 17, 1937 a platform fell onto the net and broke it, killing 10 men.

The strength of the bridge is awesome, with each tower carrying a vertical load of 95 million kg (210 million lb) from each cable, and each shore anchorage block required to withstand a pull of 28.5 million kg (63 million lb). The main parts of the tower legs were riveted in place at their manufactories in Pennsylvania to check that they fitted, before being dismantled and transported to the site.

The Golden Gate Bridge has become a key symbol of San Francisco. Despite the noise and pollution generated by the 125,000 cars that cross it every day, the pedestrian path along the bridge is a popular one, and it provides a setting much used by film directors. During a party held to celebrate the 50th anniversary of the bridge in 1987, the whole structure was closed to traffic so that all the party-goers could walk across. As it happened, there were simply too many of them, and the idea had to be abandoned.

SEE ALSO
■ *Kapellbrücke*
page 38
■ *Sydney Harbour Bridge*
page 217

THE DEVIL'S TOWER

- The base of the Devil's Tower is 300m (1,000ft) in diameter.

- From its base the tower is 264m (865ft) tall.

- It rises 400m (1,300ft) above the Belle Fourche River.

- On clear days the tower can be seen from 160km (100 miles) away.

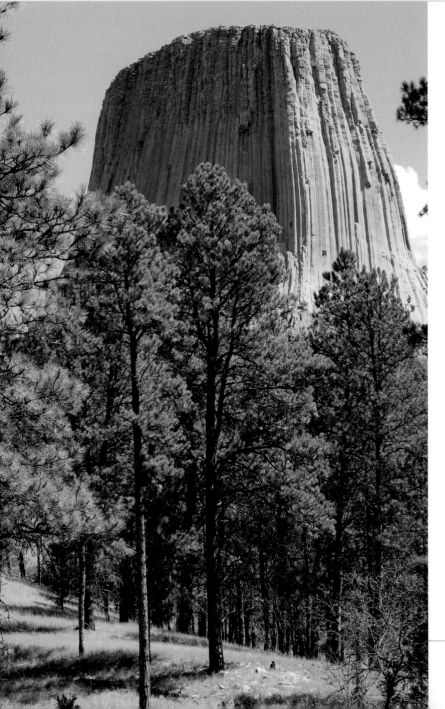

THE DEVIL'S TOWER is truly a giant, rising majestically out of the trees at its base on the rolling plains of Wyoming near the pine forests of the Black Hills. A Native American legend relates how seven maidens fled to the flat summit of the tower to escape a huge bear. The bear, desperate to catch the maidens, scored deep marks in the tower with his claws as he attempted to scramble to the top. When he finally succeeded in reaching the summit, the maidens jumped onto a low rock that saved them from the bear by soaring away into the sky. Another myth suggests that the tower gained its name because an evil demon pounded his drums on the summit, making thunder and terrifying anyone within earshot. In the 1970s the Devil's Tower featured as the backdrop for the landing site for aliens in the film *Close Encounters of the Third Kind*.

The Devil's Tower was formed about 50 million years ago when Wyoming was under the sea, and layers of sedimentary rock such as sandstone, limestone, shale and gypsum were being deposited. At the same time, pressures from deep within the Earth's crust forced a mass of magma to intrude into the sedimentary rock. The magma began to cool and crystallize, and as it did so it contracted and cracked, forming polygonal columns much like those at the Giant's Causeway in Northern Ireland. A similar process is often seen in dried-up streams and ponds, where water has evaporated from the crust, forming small polygonal saucers of mud with slightly upturned edges.

LEFT In 1906 President Theodore Roosevelt declared the Devil's Tower the first United States National Monument.

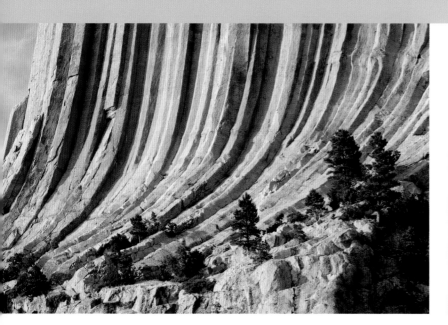

CHIMNEY ROCK

About 25 million years ago a deposit of sandy clay was laid down in western Nebraska. It was later covered with sandstone. Subsequent erosion has removed many of these deposits from the area, and only small, slightly more durable segments remain. One such remnant is Chimney Rock, a dome topped with a sandstone pinnacle 99m (325ft) high. It was a landmark for pioneers heading west on the Oregon Trail, who were able to see it from a distance of 48km (30 miles). Although other geological formations on the route were also named, Chimney Rock is often regarded as the symbol for America's westward migration in the 19th century.

The igneous rock formed by the magma intrusion was much harder than the surrounding sedimentary rock, and over millions of years, as the seabed rose from the water to become solid land, the forces of erosion began to eat away at the sedimentary rocks, leaving this great block of igneous rock standing proud. Water later seeped into the spaces between the columns, expanding and contracting with changes in temperature, and forcing some of the columns to fall away from the main body of rock. Broken columns litter the base of the tower, forming talus slopes. As this process of weathering continues, Devil's Tower will eventually collapse completely—but it is likely to be around for a good few million years yet.

ABOVE LEFT Giant fissures were caused by erosion between the columns.

SEE ALSO

■ *The Giant's Causeway* page 16
■ *Uluṟu (Ayer's Rock)* page 218

MONUMENT VALLEY

Rising dramatically out of the flat desert floor in northeast Arizona are strangely shaped blocks of sandstone, standing up to 300m (1,000ft) high. These towering monoliths were sacred to the Navajo people, and watching them glow red in the setting sun in the empty expanses of desert, it is easy to see how they have inspired a sense of awe for thousands of years. The monuments were formed in a similar way to the Devil's Tower, except that the rock here is sandstone. The entire area was once covered by sedimentary rocks, which were worn down over millions of years, leaving behind only the more resistant parts as free-standing towers and blocks.

YOSEMITE NATIONAL PARK

- **In 1864 Yosemite Valley became the first state park in the United States.**

- **In 1890 the area around the valley was designated a national park.**

- **At 739m (2,425ft), Yosemite Falls is the tallest waterfall in North America.**

ABOVE Snow melt causes the flow at Yosemite Falls to be strongest in spring. In years of little snow it can stop altogether in late summer.

RIGHT Sheer granite cliffs at El Capitan (left) and Cathedral Rocks make Yosemite a world-renowned climbing destination.

FEW PLACES IN THE WORLD can have as many spectacular features in one small area as Yosemite Valley, a 12km (7.5-mile) long natural masterpiece of staggering beauty and diversity nestling in the heart of the Sierra Nevada mountain range of California. It is home to the Merced River, Yosemite Falls and many splendid domes and peaks, with some of the largest rock walls in the world including El Capitan, a granite buttress that rises almost straight up, 1,099m (3,605 ft) from the valley.

The Yosemite Valley is only a small part of the Yosemite National Park, which covers an area of 3,080 sq km (1,189 square miles). Near the southern entrance to the park, Mariposa Grove contains huge sequoia trees that are thousands of years old. To the east is the popular high country of Tuolumne Meadows, where huge rock domes tower over lush, green meadows, and lakes have a pristine clarity. Past Tuolumne Meadows is the 3,031m (9,945-ft) Tioga Pass, the high point in the park, which leads down a steep road through the Inyo National Forest to the eastern side of the Sierra Nevada.

To the north of all of this is the rarely visited High Sierra region, including the Grand Canyon of the Tuolumne River and the Hetch Hetchy Reservoir, which was created in 1913 by flooding a valley almost as beautiful as Yosemite Valley. Campaigners are still calling for the reservoir to be drained and for water supplies to be provided elsewhere, so that the valley can be restored to its former glory.

Yosemite lay unknown to Westerners until 1851, when the volunteers of the Mariposa Battalion entered the valley in pursuit of a number of Ahwahneechee Native Americans, whom they had been assigned to take to a reservation. The park's name came from the corruption of the local Native American word for grizzly bear, *uzumati*.

Within a few years sightseeing parties were coming to admire the views down into the valley, and they are the same views that visitors see today upon emerging from the Wawona Tunnel. To the left the majesty of El Capitan and to the right, the elegant 189m (620-ft) Bridalveil Fall

that pours down from the back of the Cathedral Rocks. There is also the seemingly unassailable Sentinel Rock and, straight ahead, the glacier-carved face of Half Dome.

The man who really made Yosemite part of the American consciousness was the Scottish-born environmentalist, John Muir. He spent a great part of his life here and was key in the establishment of a United States forest conservation policy.

SEE ALSO
- *The Guilin Hills* page 90
- *Redwoods and Giant Sequoias* page 178
- *Zion National Park* page 166

ROCK CLIMBING IN YOSEMITE

Yosemite Valley offers all types of climbing: cracks, chimneys, faces, overhangs, artificial aid, high angle, low angle—whatever a climber could desire, including Sentinel Rock, Royal Arches and El Capitan, one of the largest granite faces in the world.

Yosemite became the focus for rockclimbing in the US in the 1950s and 1960s, when Royal Robbins, Yvon Chouinard and Warren Harding first made ascents on climbs that had previously been thought impossible. Robbins, Jerry Galwas and Mike Sherrick were the first climbers to conquer the sheer, 610m (2,000-ft) northwest face of Half Dome in 1957, and Harding, Wayne Merry and George Whitwore made the first ascent of the Nose Route of El Capitan the next year. Famous climbers in the 1970s and 80s included Bev Johnson, one of the greatest female climbers.

THE GRAND CANYON

- The main canyon is 365km (227 miles) long and about 29km (18 miles) across at its widest point.

- The North Rim Headquarters and Grand Canyon Village, on the south rim, are less than 19km (12 miles) apart across the canyon, but it takes a diversion of 320km (200 miles) to get from one to the other.

OPPOSITE PAGE A dizzying vista: the glass-bottomed pathway of the Grand Canyon Skywalk extends out vertiginously over the drop.

BELOW Nearly two billion years of the earth's geology have been revealed by the downcutting action of the Colorado River.

NO DESCRIPTION CAN EVER truly prepare the visitor for the sheer size and magnificence of this massive gorge, stretching as far as the eye can see in a vast, spectacular complex of canyons, waterfalls, caverns, towers, ledges and ravines. The Grand Canyon never seems to look the same twice, and the sun and the shadows of passing clouds constantly change the shades of the rocks through a delicate spectrum from black and purple-brown to pale pink and blue-grey.

Peering down at the bottom of the canyon from one of the many vantage points, it is difficult to imagine that the tiny brown stream of water up to 1.6km (1 mile) below was responsible for this huge gorge. However, if you can, view the river from the canyon floor itself, where you'll see the Colorado River as a swift and powerful force—the Lava Falls Rapids are said to be the fastest navigable rapids in the world—and where it is easier to envisage how it was able to carve itself a path through the rocks.

THE GRAND CANYON DISCOVERED

Native Americans knew about the Grand Canyon for thousands of years before it was discovered by Europeans. The caves and caverns in the park are rich in archaeological remains, and include rock paintings, pots and wooden figures. In 1540 a small group of Spanish adventurers arrived looking for gold, but finding none they moved on.

An expedition was mounted in 1857 to travel down the canyon by boat, but had to proceed on foot when the boats were wrecked almost before the trip had started. The most famous expedition was led by Major John Wesley Powell in 1869. Powell, a Civil War veteran and college professor, took nine frontiersmen with him to map the huge canyon, but his account of the journey remained unpublished for more than 20 years.

Around 17 million years ago the Colorado River meandered over a huge plain. Then movements in the earth's surface caused the land to rise, and the river began to cut a channel through the rocks. The soft two-million-year-old limestones were the first rocks to be eroded, then the older shales and sandstones lying in layers underneath. The oldest rocks are the two-billion-year-old granites and schists that form the bottom of the canyon today.

The Grand Canyon is not just one gorge. Many other canyons run into it, each one different from the others, and together they make up the Grand Canyon National Park. The Vulcan's Stone, a black cinder cone formed by volcanic activity about 10,000 years ago, stands high above the river, while the Esplanade is a heavily eroded terrace of red sandstone that glows scarlet in the evening sun. In many

places, pinnacles of layered sandstone teeter at the edges of precipices, affording the most incredible views.

Although millions of tourists visit the most famous parts of the Grand Canyon, there are many places where you can find complete solitude. Fern Glen Canyon is famous for its microclimate, and, surprisingly, lush flowers and plants flourish there in the middle of the desert. North Canyon Wash has silent green pools of water that lie at the base of creamy-white canyon walls.

ROOSEVELT AND THE GRAND CANYON

One of the early visitors to the Grand Canyon was President Theodore Roosevelt, who first came in 1903, and made it a national monument in 1908.

Roosevelt was influenced by the writings of the conservation campaigner John Muir, and pursued policies aimed at protecting vast areas of American wilderness and maintaining the balance of their delicate ecology. Even at the turn of the 20th century, Roosevelt was aware of the delicate ecology of the area. He commented that the wisest course was for Americans to 'leave it as it is. You cannot improve on it. The ages have been at work on it, and man can only mar it'.

SEE ALSO
■ *The East African Rift Valley* page 130
■ *Zion National Park* page 166

REDWOODS AND GIANT SEQUOIAS

■ The Californian forests originally covered about 6,200 sq km (2,400 square miles).

■ The coast redwood is the tallest living tree; the giant sequoia is the largest living organism.

■ Redwoods can live for up to 3,000 years and giant sequoias can live for up to 4,000 years.

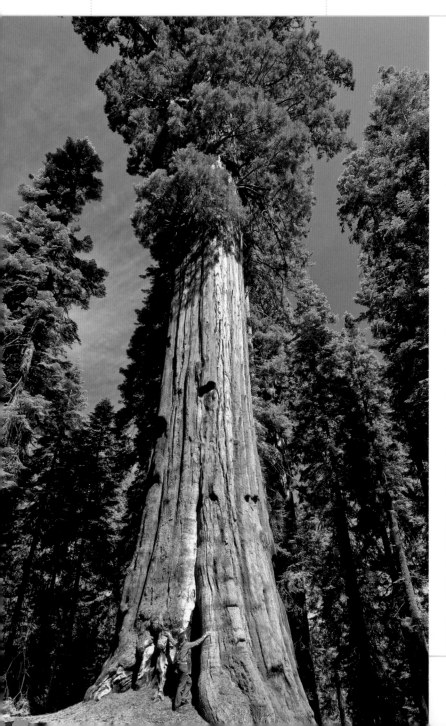

REDWOODS ARE NOW RESTRICTED to a narrow coastal strip stretching from the Klamath Mountains in southern Oregon to Monterey Bay in northern California, and giant sequoias grow on the slopes of the Sierra Nevada Mountains. The tallest redwood trees are in Redwood National Park on the north California coast, and the largest sequoias are in Sequoia National Park in central California. Fossil records show that these giant species were present in the Jurassic period, between 208 and 144 million years ago, when they were distributed over large areas of the northern hemisphere.

The giant sequoia grows to around 95m (312ft), and the trunk can have a diameter of 5m to 11m (16ft to 36ft). The largest of these trees, known as General Sherman, is thought to be between 2,300 and 2,700 years old. In addition to these majestic trees, the forests of the Redwood and Sequoia National Parks are also important for a wide range of animals including moose, elk, black bear, beaver and white-tailed and mule deer.

EXPLOITING THE FOREST GIANTS

The redwood and giant sequoia produce very high-quality timber, prized as a multipurpose wood suitable for a range of uses including the production of houses, furniture and railway sleepers. They are straight-growing, with very few knots and a fine grain, making them light but strong, and a combination of natural oils and resins makes them almost rot-proof and resistant to attack from termites.

In the latter half of the 19th century these trees were heavily exploited, and at risk of extinction. Exploitation continues today, although the US National Park Service continues in its efforts to annex remaining tracts of forest to the existing protected areas.

METEOR CRATER

■ **Meteor Crater is a saucer-shaped hole 1,220m (4,000ft) in diameter and 180m (600ft) deep.**

■ **A recent estimate is that the meteor was about 41m (135ft) across and weighed 272,000 metric tons (300,000 tons).**

■ **The meteor hit the ground with incredible force and parts of it have been found 10km (6 miles) away.**

BIG BANG

Some scientists believe that a meteorite may have been responsible for the mass extinction of dinosaurs that occurred 65 million years ago. According to this theory a huge piece of space debris tore through the earth's atmosphere to cut a crater 40km (25 miles) deep and 200km (125 miles) across, now buried underneath the Yucatán Peninsula in Mexico. The Chicxulub crater, as it is known, is believed to have released volcanic material and hot gases alongside the millions of tons of dust and rock hurled into the air.

The dust rose high into the atmosphere and blocked life-giving solar energy, causing a disruption in plant growth and a shortage of food, and subsequently led to the extinction of many animals and plants, including the dinosaurs.

AROUND 50,000 YEARS AGO a bright trail flared in the sky over northern Arizona. The fireball crashed into the earth at about 42,000km/h (26,000mph), hurling millions of tons of rock into the air and creating Meteor Crater. The destructive energy of the explosion was a thousand times that of the atomic bomb dropped on Hiroshima. Fortunately, such enormous missiles from outer space do not often crash into the Earth—but meteoroids penetrate the atmosphere each day. Most of these are small particles of dust, vaporized before they reach the surface by the heat generated by friction in the outer atmosphere.

Most of the few metereoids that are found contain iron, which is better able to withstand the great heat generated as it plummets downward. A meteorite found at Cape York in western Greenland had been used for many years by the local Inuit people as a source of iron for their tools.

SEE ALSO
■ *Ngorongoro Crater* page 130

THE EVERGLADES

■ The Everglades are freshwater marshlands that once covered around 10,000 sq km (4,000 square miles).

■ The remaining freshwater marshlands are among the three most important wetland areas in the world.

■ Native Americans call this area *pa-hay-okee*, which means 'grassy waters'.

THIS UNIQUE SUBTROPICAL wilderness is fed by water from Lake Okeechobee, the largest lake in North America after the Great Lakes. The water from the lake seeps into the underlying limestone, and from there feeds this vast wetland area through a series of aquifers. The Everglades is dominated by dense, and in places impenetrable stands of sawgrass that grow up to 4m (13ft) high, covering vast areas. The region is criss-crossed by channels and small lakes of open water, where other plants such as water lilies and bladderworts thrive. The bladderworts are specially adapted for living in these nutrient-poor waters; they

ABOVE Flat-bottomed airboats, propelled by a fan at the stern, enable tourists to get close to the mangroves lining the shallow waters.

have small air bladders that trap insects and larvae which the plant then absorbs to obtain vital nutrients.

Small islands, or hammocks, where the underlying limestone rises above the water table, support a variety of hardwoods together with many species of orchids, ferns and animals. At the coast, the freshwater marsh, or glade, gives way to a fringing strip of red mangroves, to form the only forested marine wetland in North America.

The large range of habitats is reflected in the highly diverse flora and fauna of the area. There are more than 1,000 seed-bearing plants, including 25 varieties of orchid and 120 species of tree, which range from tropical palm and mangrove through temperate forest species such as oak and ash to desert plants such as yucca and cactus.

Many creatures depend on more than one element in this mosaic of habitats—for example, colonial birds use the cypress and mangrove forests as nest sites, while feeding in the sawgrass marshes. The Everglades is an exceptionally important area for birds, with more than 320 different species recorded. These include such rarities as the wood stork, the reddish egret and the

THE FLORIDA MANATEE

Among the animals taking advantage of the abundant fish in the Everglades' coastal waters are 12 species of turtle, including the giant loggerhead turtle and the green turtle. The Florida manatee is a gentle, plant-eating mammal and is a member of the group of animals known as the Sirenia, which were once believed by sailors to be mermaids.

Manatees feed on the seagrass beds in the shallow waters fringing the mangrove forests. These harmless creatures face a threat from marina developments, which decrease their feeding area, and bring with them pollution and the increased danger of death or injury from boats.

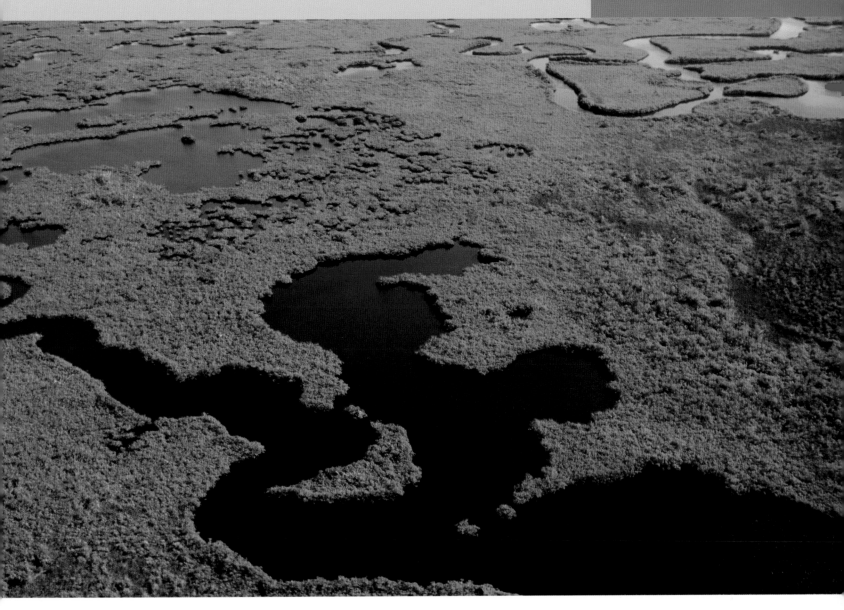

RESTORATION OF A WILDERNESS

Since the early 19th century there has been pressure to reclaim the wetlands of the Everglades for farming crops such as sugar cane; around half the original area of the Everglades has been drained. The threats posed by land reclamation, flood defenses and water pollution to the wildlife of the remaining swamps became widely recognized during the late 20th century. During the 1980s a canal that straightened the Kissimmee River was removed, and in 2000 the US authorities approved an ambitious restoration plan. Over some 30 years, this aims to restore and preserve the freshwater sources for the whole of the ecosystem of southern Florida.

southern race of the bald eagle. The Everglades kite feeds exclusively on snails, using its specially adapted, long, curved and sharply pointed bill to extract the flesh of the snail from the shell. Many species of fish-eating birds also frequent the freshwater swamps, and the coastal mangrove fringe is home to anhingas, roseate spoonbills, pelicans, wood ibis, heron and egrets.

More than 150 fish species are found in the coastal waters, providing good feeding for the many birds, reptiles and mammals. The American alligator is the main predator in the swamp, but there are others such as the American crocodile, the rare Florida panther and various otters.

SEE ALSO
■ *The Camargue*
page 22
■ *The Okavango Delta*
page 144
■ *The Waddenzee*
page 21

THE HAWAIIAN ISLANDS

■ **The Hawaiian Islands stretch for about 2,400km (1,500 miles) across the north Pacific Ocean.**

■ **Mauna Kea is the tallest mountain in the world when measured from its base on the ocean floor, 5,998m (19,680ft) below sea level.**

■ **The first settlers are believed to have arrived from Polynesia around 300 BC.**

THE HAWAIIAN ISLANDS extend from Kure and Midway Island in the west to the island of Hawaii itself in the east. Although volcanic, they seem unrelated to the other volcanoes that lie around the margins of the Pacific. Most of these, known as the Ring of Fire, are associated with deep sea trenches, where the oceanic crust is being dragged under the continental margin. The Hawaiian Islands sit above a hot spot in the Earth's mantle, a major source of heat. Geologists believe there are about 30 such hot spots that are relatively static and produce lines of volcanoes as the oceanic crust passes over them, as has happened with the Hawaiian Islands. The crust of the western part of the Pacific is moving steadily westward, and seems to have shifted about 2,400km (1,500 miles) during the life of this hot spot. All the islands in the Hawaiian chain are volcanic; the oldest are at the western end and the youngest—and hence most active—are on the island of Hawaii itself, at the eastern end of the chain.

The island of Hawaii is shaped like a triangle balancing on one of its points, and is about 130km (80 miles) by 153km (95 miles). Its highest point is the summit of Mauna Kea, at 4,205m (13,796ft) above sea level. Its height and its clear, unpolluted atmosphere have made it an ideal place to site several of the most powerful astronomical telescopes in the world.

Most of the current volcanic activity in Hawaii is at Kilauea, a subsidiary vent on the flanks of Mauna Loa, the second highest mountain, about 32km (20 miles) east of the

HAWAII'S EMERALD ISLAND

Kauai is the lushest and most beautiful of the Hawaiian Islands, with dense green vegetation, golden beaches and turquoise seas. At its heart is an extinct volcano called Mount Waialeale.

This is also one of the wettest places on Earth with an average of 1,170cm (460in) of rain every year. The high precipitation means that Kauai is remarkably green, and more than 70 percent of the island is devoted to plantations, national parks and open space.

The island's main industry was traditionally the growing of sugar cane. The first sugar cane mill opened in 1835 and workers were recruited from China, Japan and the Philippines, as well as from the local population. Many settled in Kauai, which accounts for the island's richly multicultural background.

THE BANZAI PIPELINE

Waves are caused by a combination of winds, currents, and the gravitational pull of the Earth. As they roll toward the land, other factors determine their size and shape, such as the shape of the seabed over which they travel. A gently sloping sandy beach has waves very different from those where the beach rises sharply.

The seabed on the northwest coast of the Hawaiian island of Oahu gives rise to huge Pacific waves that roll toward the shore, growing taller as they reach shallower waters, eventually toppling over themselves. The toppling effect occurs at a slight angle, forming a blue-green tunnel known as the Banzai Pipeline. As a result, Oahu is a popular place for surfers, who use great skill to skim along the inside of the tunnels, surrounded by the translucent walls.

BELOW LEFT The steep slopes of the Kalalau Valley, on Kauai, make it accessible only by hiking, or by kayaking around the coast.

ABOVE Lava has been flowing from Kilauea continuously since 1983, creating a new area of land where the flows meet the sea.

BELOW Hot vapours rise from a cinder cone on Kilauea. Volcanic gas emissions can cause air pollution across the region.

summit. This volcano was in virtually continuous eruption during the 19th century and has been active since 1983. The volcanic crater is 150m to 180m (490ft to 590ft) deep and covers an area of 10sq km (4 square miles).

Kilauea is believed to be the home of Pele, the Hawaiian goddess of volcanoes, and anyone detecting the low-pitched humming or roaring noise that precedes some Hawaiian eruptions is said to be 'hearing Pele'.

Another detectable sign of imminent eruption is a change in the local magnetic and electrical fields: magma heated above about 600°C (1,100°F) loses its natural magnetism, indicating that a large body of molten rock has developed within the volcano.

SEE ALSO

■ *Deception Island* page 236
■ *Volcanic Iceland* page 14

CENTRAL & SOUTH AMERICA

Teotihuacán **186**

Chichén Itzá **188**

Great Civilizations **190**

Tikal **192**

Angel Falls **194**

The Nazca Lines **195**

Machu Picchu **196**

The Amazon Basin **200**

Iguaçu Falls **202**

Galapagos Islands **204**

The Inca Trails **206**

Tierra del Fuego **208**

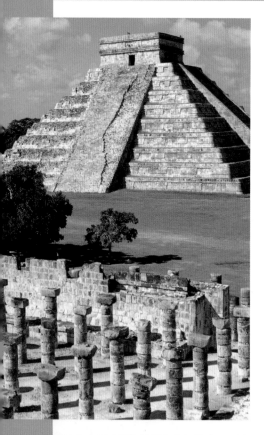

CENTRAL AND SOUTHERN AMERICAN HISTORY REMAINS enigmatic, though early inhabitants left an impressive legacy of art, treasures and monuments. From the fourth century AD to the tenth the Maya civilization reached its apogee in Guatemala, eastern Mexico and the Yucatán, with Tikal as perhaps its largest city. Farther west, the city of Teotihuacán was larger than imperial Rome. The Aztecs built up their empire and by 1450 they controlled almost all of modern Mexico from their capital at Tenochtitlan. They were infamous for starting wars, capturing prisoners for sacrifice and enslaving the peasantry. Local resentment of Aztec oppression helped the Spanish in their conquest of Mexico in 1521, after which they ruled Mesoamerica for 300 years.

Spanish and Portuguese rule was also imposed on South America, a 7,403-km (4,600 mile) long landmass embracing a remarkable range of climates and landscapes, from the jungles of the Amazon to Tierra del Fuego, near the icebergs of the Antarctic. In the Andes, snow-capped peaks rear up close to the equator,

Chichén Itzá ■

Teotihuacán ■

Tikal ■

Angel Falls ■

Galapagos Islands ■

Amazon Basin ■

Machu Picchu ■

Nazca Lines ■ ■ Inca Trails

Iguaçu Falls ■

Tierra del Fuego ■

BELOW LEFT The Pyramid of Kukulkan (background) and the Temple of a Thousand Columns at Chichén Itzá (see pages 188–189).

BELOW The lost Inca city of Machu Picchu, set high amongst the peaks of the Peruvian Andes (see pages 196–197).

running parallel to the western coast like a great wall. In Peru and Bolivia there are two parallel ranges, and between them is the Altiplano, a high plateau of plains, hills and valleys, where some of the first city–states developed. The Nazca people created astonishing works of art in the barren plain near the southern coast of Peru, forming huge patterns and animals clearly visible only from the sky.

From their capital at Cuzco the Incas built up the largest empire in the Americas, linked by an efficient road system. In 1531 Francisco Pizarro landed on the Peruvian coast in search of the gold city of El Dorado and conquered the empire in a few months. But the Inca Empire did not give up all its secrets, as became apparent when the settlement of Machu Picchu, a site whose purpose is still unknown, was uncovered in the Andes in 1911.

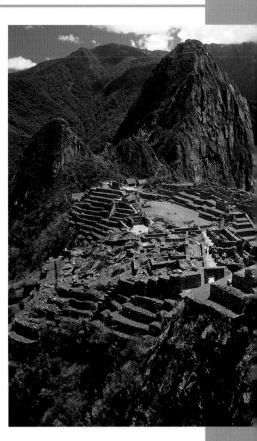

TEOTIHUACÁN

- ■ Teotihuacán is an Aztec name meaning 'place of the gods'.
- ■ It covers an area of more than 21 sq km (8 square miles).
- ■ The city's population may once have numbered more than 200,000.
- ■ According to local legend, the sun and the moon were born in Teotihuacán.

THIS REMARKABLE SITE dates back to the first century BC. By AD 500 Teotihuacán had grown larger than the imperial city of Rome and was the biggest city in Mesoamerica. It was a sophisticated city, with wide streets, monumental religious buildings, artisans' quarters and private houses, but despite tireless archaeological investigation, little evidence has been uncovered revealing the daily life and customs of its people. It has, however, been possible to determine by studying the engravings and statues on religious temples that this highly developed civilization worshipped a rain god and revered the jaguar.

Teotihuacán was meticulously planned according to a grid system so strict that a river was diverted into a channel to prevent it from interrupting a network of parallel streets. The main axis, which runs north–south, is a vast avenue 40m (130ft) wide and 2.3km (1.5 miles) long, known as the Street of the Dead. Lined with temples and shrines, it is dominated by two pyramids: the Pyramid of the Moon—actually several interlocking pyramids with an overall height of 46m (150ft)—at the north end, and the Pyramid of the Sun standing farther south. Two monumental public places of assembly stand at the heart of the city: the Citadel and the Great Compound.

The Great Compound, with two large platforms on which a number of buildings once stood, seems to have had an administrative function, while the Citadel clearly played a religious role. Approached by a grand stairway, the Citadel platform, 365m (400 yards) square, supports another pyramid, the Temple of Quetzalcoatl (the Feathered Serpent, a major god), which originally rose to a height of about 21m (70ft) in tiers of richly carved sculpture. Stone serpents, their heads projecting menacingly from the tiers, appear alarming even today—they must have made an even greater impression when their shining obsidian eyes were still in place. Local supplies of obsidian were an important trading commodity in a chiefly agricultural economy.

High-quality murals suggest that the people had artistic talent, but evidence of human sacrifice during the years of decline points to a more barbaric side of their culture. No one knows precisely how Teotihuacán came to an end, but by the eighth century the city had been sacked and burned.

ESPERANZA CULTURE

Esperanza culture is the term used to describe an amalgam of Teotihuacán and Maya culture that can be seen at Kaminaljuyu, near the heart of modern Guatemala City. Once an important Maya site, it was apparently conquered by the people of Teotihuacán at the beginning of the fifth century AD. The area lacked suitable stone for building so the victors built a planned city—an imitation of Teotihuacán—from the local clay.

Rather than wipe out Maya culture, the new inhabitants absorbed and developed aspects of it and furnished their tombs with Maya-style pottery.

Teotihuacán influenced art and architecture elsewhere in the Maya region, and Teotihuacán deities can be seen on Maya ceramics.

ABOVE Details from wall paintings at Teotihuacán. Structures such as the Temple of Quetzalcoatl were once covered in stucco and paintwork.

LEFT The view from the Pyramid of the Moon along the Avenue of the Dead, with the Pyramid of the Sun in the background dwarfing all the other structures in the complex.

PYRAMID POWER

Extravagant claims have been made regarding the mystical power of pyramids. It is said, for example, that organic material can be preserved, razor blades sharpened and a person's mind stimulated when they are positioned close to the ancient monument's apex.

Some believe that ancient cultures had an understanding of cosmic energies that we lack today, and that there is a significance in the way monuments were aligned in relation to the sun, the moon, and the stars. Certainly the orientation of the grid plan at Teotihuacán is very precise, and it does seem likely that the people of Teotihuacán were aware of the movements of the celestial bodies and attatched considerable importance to them.

SEE ALSO
■ *Chichén Itzá* page 188
■ *The Great Pyramid* page 118
■ *Tikal* page 192

CHICHÉN ITZÁ

■ The site at Chichén Itzá was inhabited by the Maya and later by the Toltecs.

■ The days and months of the year are represented on the pyramid temple, El Castillo, by the number of steps and terraces; 52 panels symbolize the Maya 52-year cycle.

■ El Castillo has nine tiers and 91 steps up each side.

CHICHÉN ITZÁ WAS AN IMPORTANT Maya site until the tenth century AD. At some later point, as Maya civilization went into decline, Toltec warriors appear to have seized control and turned Chichén Itzá into a bigger version of their own capital, Tula. The extensive remains at the site today are neither purely Maya nor purely Toltec, but rather an intriguing fusion of the ideas and motifs of both cultures.

Chichén Itzá is thought to have been built as a new capital for the ruler-god Topiltzin Quetzalcoatl, known here by the Maya name Kukulkan. A pyramid temple dedicated to him, called El Castillo (The Castle), dominates the complex. The careful alignment of the building, whose stairways face exactly north, south, east and west,

HUMAN SACRIFICE AND THE SACRED CENOTE

Chichén Itzá's sacred cenote, or well of sacrifice, is approached along a 274-m (900ft) causeway. A natural well, 23m (75ft) deep, it supplied fresh water and was treated as a place of pilgrimage.

In times of drought, victims were thrown alive into the well in an attempt to provoke the rain god into action, and offerings of precious metals, jade and sacred images have been retrieved from its depths. Many children drowned during the ritual, but those who survived the ordeal were treated with respect, as it was believed that they had communicated with the gods.

creates an extraordinary effect at the spring and autumn equinoxes, when shadows fall on the serpent god's carved head and tail at the bottom and the top of the main staircase, supposedly bringing it to life.

Chichén Itzá has perhaps the finest ball court in Mesoamerica. It is vast, with two parallel walls 83m (272ft) long and 8.2m (27ft) high, set 27m (90ft) apart. Temples stand at each end of the court, but the exact religious significance of the game is not known. Bas-relief

ABOVE The Temple of the Warriors is surrounded by rows of carved columns depicting warriors.

RIGHT A carved head of a jaguar, a creature was revered by the Maya and the Toltec people.

panels on the side walls showing decapitated players suggest that these were contests fought to the death. A later account of the game indicates that the winner was the player who got the ball through one of the stone rings high up on each side wall. The victor was rewarded with the spectators' clothes.

The Temple of the Warriors is approached through a colonnade, and countless such pillars, carved to represent Toltec warriors, once supported a roof. The temple is decorated with carvings and frescoes, and the familiar jaguar and eagle motifs of Toltec art are both in evidence. Chichén Itzá also has a Temple of the Jaguars, with a fine specimen of the species carved out in stone guarding the approach.

The overgrown area known as Old Chichén contains several buildings, including an observatory—a tower supported on a double platform—and a pyramid in which a number of tombs were found. The settlement is thought to have been abandoned in about 1224 after an attack by a rival power.

TOLTECS

The Toltecs were a nomadic people who are believed to be behind the destruction in the eighth century AD of the civilization based at Teotihuacán (see pages 186–7). Their own capital was established at Tula, but this in turn was destroyed by enemies, and for a long time their future was in doubt.

Despite this they went on to rule over Mexico from the mid-10th to the mid-12th century AD.

Their legendary skills and achievements survived them. Toltec art, dismissed by some as crude, is full of representations of warriors and illustrates the power and extent of their empire, but the line between myth and fact is unclear.

SEE ALSO

■ *Tikal* page 192

GREAT CIVILIZATIONS

Great civilizations rise and, however mighty their rulers and cities, they eventually fall. Our landscapes are littered with the remains of civilizations that, at their height, must have seemed all but indestructible to those who lived within them. All we know of some of these ancient societies are the monuments they left behind.

■ The four primary civilizations of the Old World (in Mesopotamia, Egypt, the Indus Valley and northern China), all developed at a similar latitude.

■ The Roman Empire extended north to Britain, south to North Africa and east as far as modern-day Syria.

AGE OF STONE
Popular myth once dismissed the people of the Stone Age—covering hundreds of thousands of years, from the earliest humans to around 4000 BC—as cave-dwelling savages. But over millennia they developed sophisticated societies with highly developed craft industries, international trading and large-scale symbolic structures.

Remnants of the Stone Age can still be found in Europe, from cave paintings more than 30,000 years old to great stone circles created up to the dawn of the Bronze Age.

ANCIENT EGYPT
While Stonehenge was receiving its third or fourth renovation, the pharaohs of Egypt's Old Kingdom (2686–2181 BC) were building their pyramids at Giza. The Egyptian Empire that grew from the Nile's fertile banks lasted nearly 3,000 years and recorded its history in writings that baffled the modern age until Jean Barthélemy cracked the hieroglyphic code in 1785.

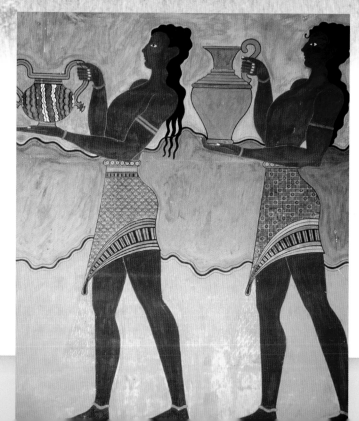

Above *Recent discoveries place Stonehenge in a vast landscape among other circles of stones and wooden posts.*

Left *The frescoes at Knossos, Crete, date from around 1500 BC. They were restored in the early 20th century.*

Right *Minoan civilization, as depicted in the Knossos frescoes, celebrated human beauty, wine and sport.*

Above *Huge elephant statues guard the entrance to the Tomb of Hongwu, in Nanjing, China. It was completed in 1405.*

Right *The Pyramid of the Sun at Teotihuacán in Mexico dates from 100 BC and is one of the largest ancient structures in Mesoamerica.*

CHINA

Ancient Chinese dynasties flourished over 11,000 years, producing, among other things, gunpowder, paper, the compass and the philosophies of Confucius.

In the third century BC the cruel but successful Qin Shihuangdi overcame rival warring kingdoms to create a unified empire, securing its boundaries with the Great Wall. The name of the unified empire, China, derives from the name Qin.

OLD AND NEW WORLDS

The first Spanish adventurers to reach Central and South America were astonished to find the impressive cities of the Maya, Aztec and Inca civilizations. However, within the space of only a few years these peoples were to disappear, helpless against the new diseases and superior weaponry introduced by the European conquerors.

Today fabulous gold museum pieces and the ruins of settlements such as Tula and Chichén Itzá in Mexico, Tikal in Guatemala, and Machu Picchu in Peru survive as clues to the histories of once formidable and wealthy empires.

Left *Aztec civilization used a calendar based on a 20-day ritual cycle. It is depicted on this stone mosaic.*

Right *Stone carvings of human heads are typical of the British Iron Age, from around 700 BC until the Roman invasion of AD 43.*

SEE ALSO
■ *Chichén Itzá*
page 188
■ *Machu Picchu*
page 196
■ *The Pont du Gard*
page 30

TIKAL

- A total of 16 temples remain in Tikal today.

- The ceremonial area covered 2.5 sq km (1 square mile).

- Tikal's largest pyramid, known simply as Pyramid IV, is 70m (228ft) high.

- At its peak the settlement's population is thought to have numbered between 10,000 and 45,000.

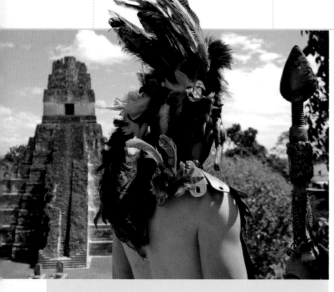

THE MAYANS

The Maya people, ancestors of the present-day Maya Indians, belonged to a civilization that inhabited a wide area of highland and lowland Mesoamerica. Their culture, dominated by religious ceremony, was presided over by ruler-priests.

The highly elaborate Maya calendar, the Long Count, involved a cycle of 52 years, and attempts to reconcile this with the European system have produced conflicting results. Radiocarbon dating supports the view that the Classic Maya period, when the civilization reached its peak, was between the fourth and the tenth century AD.

TIKAL LIES ON THE YUCATÁN PENINSULA, in a region first entered by Europeans in 1517 and gradually conquered by Spain over the next 30 years. Set in the northern lowland area of Maya territory, Tikal was perhaps the largest settlement of Classic Maya civilization. At its heart was a huge square, bordered by pyramid temples on the west and east sides and an acropolis on the north. Beyond this complex there were some 3,000 buildings within an area of 16 sq km (6 square miles). The acropolis shows signs of having been occupied continuously for 11 centuries, and the temples to be seen there now stand on the buried remains of countless other earlier buildings, including some elaborate painted tombs.

The word *city* is perhaps not the best description of Tikal; rather, it was an important ceremonial center on whose outskirts large numbers of people chose to live. Although the majority of people did not live in any great affluence, the Maya devoted tremendous energy to the construction of their tombs and temples. In paying tribute to their gods, their elite and their dead, they created monuments that are still awe-inspiring today.

The buildings occupying the large, central ceremonial area were linked by causeways to more squares and their associated structures. There are many so-called palaces: single-story complexes and rooms, plastered, decorated, and, like almost every Maya building, standing on a platform. Religious structures may have been elevated with the intention of increasing the onlooker's sense of awe, but relatively modest houses in the outlying areas were also built on mud platforms, presumably as a safeguard against floods during the rainy season.

Glimpses of Maya rulers and their religious ceremonies can be seen in stone sculpture as well as in fine carvings on sapodilla wood. This woodwork was used for decorative beams in some of the palaces and for ornate lintels over the doorways of the pyramid temples. Stone

BELOW LEFT The main plaza lies in front of Temple II, which was dedicated to a queen, though no tomb was ever found.

BELOW Temple I, a giant tomb, was completed around AD 750 and stands 47m (154ft) high. It was once crowned by a seated statue.

stelae in front of the palaces and temples were often symbolic, depicting a ruler or warrior trampling an enemy underfoot.

Tikal has six steep pyramids, with chambers at the top approached by steps and crowned with elaborate 'roof combs'. The pyramids were tombs for the wealthy and important, who were buried with sumptuous grave goods and food for their journey to the next world.

SEE ALSO
- *Chichén Itzá*
  page 188
- *Teotihuacán*
  page 186

THE CONQUEST OF THE YUCATÁN

In 1526 Francisco de Montejo was authorized by the King of Castile to lead an expedition to the Yucatán, with certain conditions for the conduct of this expedition laid out in a formal document known as a *requerimiento*. It stated that the aim of the King of Castile was to convert the natives of the New World to Christianity by means of understanding and good treatment. These intentions were to be explained clearly to the natives through an interpreter. If they failed to comply, the Spaniards would declare war against the land and subject the people to the authority of Crown and Church.

There followed years of guerrilla warfare, and resistance to the *conquistadores* and their ways continued long after they had imposed their rule on the Yucatán.

ANGEL FALLS

- Salto Angel in the Venezuelan jungle is the highest waterfall in the world, with a total fall of 979m (3,212ft).

- The first drop is 807m (2,648ft) to an obstruction; a second stage plunges 172m (564ft) into a jungle pool.

- The falls are named for an American pilot, Jimmy Angel.

IN THE REMOTE southeastern corner of Venezuela, close to the borders with Guyana and Brazil, torrential tropical rains feed the Rio Churún, a tributary of the Caroní River that winds slowly over Auyán Tepuy, a high plateau above the jungle, until it reaches the cliff on the northern edge. The river then gathers pace down a short incline and rushes into space. From a distance the thin white line at the cliff edge gradually broadens into a blur of spray, until the water drops out of sight into the jungle.

For a long time the entire area was virtually inaccessible and was reached only by the most determined jungle explorers, but today it is possible to get to the falls in a motorized dugout canoe or in a light aircraft. Adventurous modern-day explorers also come here to leap off the plateau in a hang-glider or sail off the cliff under a paraglider.

FINDING THE FALLS

The existence of the falls has always been known to local indigenous people, who call them Churún-Meru. Their name for the plateau, Auyán Tepuy, means Devil's Mountain.

The first documented sighting of the falls was in 1910, when Ernesto Sánchez la Cruz reported his discovery, but it was an American pilot, Jimmy Angel, who brought them to the attention of the wider world. Angel was seeking gold in 1933 when he noted the falls in his logbook. Shortly after the falls were given his name: Salto Angel in Spanish, Angel Falls in English. Jimmy Angel failed to find gold, but he did achieve lasting fame.

THE NAZCA LINES

■ In 1926 Alfred Kroeber and Mejia Xesspe were the first scientists to report the existence of the lines.

■ Stone cairns mark the points where the lines converge, possibly indicating a ceremonial purpose.

■ The German scholar Maria Reiche spent 30 years in the pampas studying the lines.

GEOMETRIC SHAPES, birds and animals are etched in the Pampa Ingenio desert in the Nazca Valley in Peru. From the ground they seem to be a network of pathways, but from above they appear as a gigantic menagerie— a 50m (164ft) spider, a giant condor, a hummingbird, a lizard and a monkey 100m (328ft) long.

This maze of designs, spread over 500 sq km (193 square miles), was created by removing the surface crust of stones to expose the yellowish-white layer beneath. Archaeologists estimate that the Nazca Lines date back to the first century AD, but their purpose remains a mystery. One theory is that the patterns represent constellations, another (and fanciful) theory is a suggestion by Erich von Däniken in his 1968 best-seller *Chariots of the Gods*, that the lines mark entry ports for visitors from outer space.

SEE ALSO
■ *Easter Island* page 212

THE PYRAMIDS OF CAHUACHI
The Pyramids of Cahuachi are part of an extensive archaeological site in the Nazca Valley. Among workaday constructions of adobe and quincha (mud-covered cane) rise several public or ceremonial buildings, the most prominent being the Great Temple, a stepped pyramid 20m (66ft) high, faced and capped with walls made of elongated adobes. Around the base are adobe-walled rooms and plazas, the largest measuring 45m by 75m (148ft by 246ft). Burial pits on the site were found to contain offerings of food and pottery.

In the early stages of Nazca culture, which lasted from AD100 to 800, the priestly function seems to have been important. Portrayals of animals on Nazca pottery and textiles imply that certain creatures, such as felines, were regarded as sacred.

ABOVE AND LEFT Hundreds of animal depictions in the Nazca Lines echo the decorative themes to be found on pottery from the same society.

SUPER SITE
MACHU PICCHU

- Machu Picchu covers an area of 2ha (5 acres).

- There is 18 sq km (7 square miles) of terraced stonework on the site, linked by 3,000 steps.

- Machu Picchu has about 200 buildings, including residences, temples and storehouses.

- According to one estimate, as few as 1,500 people may have lived here.

A long-lost ceremonial site sits high in the Peruvian Andes, 475m (1,500ft) above the Urubamba River. This mysterious place, perched on the saddle between two mountains, is known today as Machu Picchu—The Old Peak— but its name gives no clues to its origins, having been borrowed from a nearby mountain and attached to the remarkable settlement. The real name of Machu Picchu, its origin and purpose, are matters for speculation.

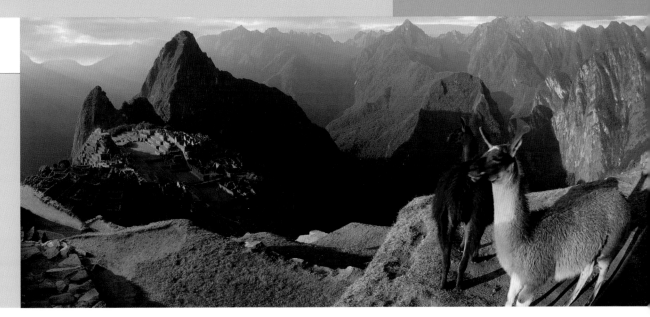

RIGHT Llamas, the only beasts of burden used by the Incas, gaze over Machu Picchu. They also provided meat and wool.

BELOW Machu Picchu lies nearly 2,400m (8,000ft) above sea level. The surrounding cliffs and mountains provide natural defenses.

WHEN MACHU PICCHU was rediscovered in the early 20th century it was first thought to be Vilcabamba, where the Incas survived for 36 years after Spanish conquerors had driven their emperor from his capital at Cuzco. However, the identification of the site as the Incas' last refuge is now thought to be wrong. Machu Picchu appears to have been an important ceremonial or religious complex rather than a city. The date of its construction is uncertain, but it probably originates from the rapid period of expansion of the Inca Empire at the end of the 15th century.

BELOW More than 100 flights of steps link the terraces. Fields and houses were served by a complicated system of irrigation channels leading from a sacred spring.

An unknown purpose

Little is known about the purpose of the site, but it is possible to determine that Machu Picchu was a place of gardens and terraces, grandiose ceremonial buildings and palaces. The different levels and terraced gardens were connected by hundreds of steps and there is evidence of aqueducts, fountains and bath buildings and the cultivation of maize, potatoes and other vegetables. Skeletons discovered on the site suggest that the female–male ratio was 10:1, leading to the theory that Machu Picchu was a place of sun-worship and a sanctuary for women known as Virgins of the Sun.

THE HISTORY

- **1460–70** Machu Picchu is built, probably for the Incan ruler Pachacuti Inca Yupanqui.
- **1527** Incan population is reduced by half, mainly due to smallpox brought by Spanish invaders.
- **1911** Hiram Bingham, an archaeologist from Yale University, rediscovers the site.
- **1983** Declared a World Heritage Site by UNESCO.
- **2010** Floods destroy roads into the area; several thousand people are airlifted out.

BELOW LEFT Most Inca buildings used mortar-free construction. The dry stone walls can move slightly in an earthquake without collapsing.

BELOW RIGHT Inca walls were designed to help avoid earthquake damage, for example, by bracing corners with L-shaped blocks.

MIRACULOUS MASONRY

One of the most remarkable aspects of Machu Picchu is its amazing stonework, and the skill with which the huge white granite blocks were laid without the use of mortar. Many of the shaped stones are locked together, their edges carefully contoured so that one stone fits into another with perfect precision. The result is a wall with joints of almost imperceptible width, and the buildings constructed in this way have proved remarkably resilient, with many still standing.

Machu Picchu lay abandoned for several hundred years before its rediscovery, but although the jungle had encroached during that time and much clearance work was necessary, structural damage to the site was surprisingly limited. Some observers question how the Incas, who apparently had no iron tools, whose only beast of burden was the lightweight llama, and who used wheels only in toys, could have produced masonry of such quality, and suggest that this is the work of some pre-Inca community.

Whatever the method used to build it, Machu Picchu provides a tantalizing glimpse into the way of life of an enigmatic people.

Further evidence of the importance of the sun at Machu Picchu is provided by the Intihuatana (Hitching Post of the Sun). This curiously shaped stone structure seems to have been a complex astronomical device. Nothing else like it survives, but it is thought to have been used to calculate significant dates, such as the solstices. Its name seems to refer to a ceremony in which the sun was said to be tethered to the post at the winter solstice.

Solar observation also seems to have taken place at the Tower of the Sun—a building with a horseshoe-shaped plan and a special window oriented to catch the sun's rays at the winter solstice—and the Temple of the Three Windows. The alignment and arrangement of these windows, with an upright rectangular stone at the center of the building, has clearly been carefully thought out. An Inca sun festival, known as Inti Raymi, is known to have taken place here during the summer and winter solstices.

BELOW An aerial view; tourist helicopter flights were banned in 2006 because of concerns about the impact on wildlife and on the atmosphere of the site.

SEE ALSO
■ *The Inca Trails* page 206

THE AMAZON BASIN

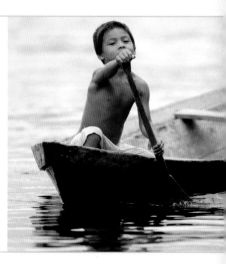

- **The Amazon River flows for 6,565km (4,080 miles)—the second longest river in the world after the Nile.**

- **Its area of tropical rainforest covers nearly 6 million sq km (2.3 million square miles).**

- **A 10sq km (3.9 square mile) area of rainforest can contain 1,500 species of flower and 400 bird species.**

THE AMAZON BASIN contains the world's largest tropical rainforest and extends into nine countries. The lifeblood of this vast expanse of rainforest is the mighty River Amazon and its tributaries, which together contain about 25 percent of all the water carried by the world's rivers.

This vast expanse of tropical rainforest contains over a million species of plant and animal life and is the repository of the genetic inheritance of the world. Even within a relatively small area the diversity is staggering, with many species still to be recorded and identified.

The Amazon and its tributaries support over 2,000 species of fish, and many unusual mammals and reptiles, including the Amazonian manatee, the pink river dolphin, the giant otter and the spectacled caiman. The diversity of fish is extraordinary, ranging from the small but infamous red-bellied piranha—a feared and voracious carnivore that occurs in large shoals—to other, closely related species that eat seeds and fruits that fall into the water from the fringing trees. The arowana, which can grow up to 1m (3ft) in length, leaps out of the water to pick off beetles from low-hanging branches of trees. The giant otter, a gentle, curious creature, is now one of the rarest animals on Earth, as a result of overhunting and the destruction and pollution of its habitat. It lives in extended family groups, containing as many as 30 individuals, and an adult male can measure up to 1.8m (6ft) in length.

Since the 1960s it has been estimated that almost 20 percent of the Amazon rainforest has been cut down. Illegal logging for prized hardwoods and clearing land for raising cattle or soy beans reached a peak in 2004, but by 2010 the rate of clearance in Brazil had halved, possibly as a result of better surveillance and law enforcement using improved satellite technology.

Governments in the Amazon region are grappling with the problem of reconciling conservation and development, and have called on the international community for economic assistance, such as converting debt into conservation funds. A controversial bridge near Manaus, Brazil, the first bridge in the entire Amazon region, opened in 2010, aiming to bring prosperity to an isolated area, but opponents fear the associated highways will make it easier for illegal deforestation to take place along them.

LEFT A tourist boat in the Tambopata National Reserve, Peru, which was created in 1990 to protect the ecosystems along the Heath and Tambopata rivers.

TOP The dugout canoe: still a useful means of travel. Until the early 1960s, when the first major roads were built, access to the Amazon Basin was almost entirely by boat.

GARDENS IN THE FOREST

Local indigenous people live in harmony with the Amazonian rainforest, exploiting it in a sustainable way by mimicking nature. The traditional farming custom involves clearing small areas known as *chagra*, or 'gardens in the forest', where the inhabitants cultivate yuccas, peppers, mangoes and other crops. After a short period of fertility the tribe moves on to clear another *chagra*, leaving the old one to revert to rainforest.

A natural clearing that may have been caused by fire will revert to mature natural forest in as little as 40 years; a *chagra* may take as long as 200 years. Nevertheless, this is still far preferable to the complete, irreversible destruction caused by clear felling.

NOT ENOUGH TREES

Exploitation of the forests has resulted in the loss of many tree species, with others brought to the brink of extinction. By 1990 it was being reported that only 12 mature Rio Palenque mahogany trees, prized for their beautifully colored and durable timber, were left. Trading in threatened Amazon woods was restricted under the international CITES agreement in the late 1990s. Commercial plantations in Asia have since been set up to meet world demand for mahogany, while in the Amazon new saplings are being raised.

Brazilian rosewood, used for furniture and musical instruments, is another highly protected timber, now used only as a very thin veneer over other woods.

ABOVE The Amazon rivers rise by more than 9m (30ft) in the rainy season, flooding the surrounding forest to create a unique habitat.

LEFT The River Purus is one of the most winding rivers in the world. Straightened out, it would cover twice as far as its present course.

SEE ALSO
■ *The Congo River* page 138

IGUAÇU FALLS

■ **The River Iguaçu rises in the Serro do Mar, close to the Brazilian coast south of São Paulo.**

■ **It flows inland (westward) for about 1,320km (820 miles).**

■ **Just as Niagara Falls straddle two countries (the USA and Canada), Iguaçu Falls form part of the boundary between Brazil and Argentina.**

THE RIVER IGUAÇU follows a winding course across the Paraná Plateau until, swollen by tributaries, it drops down via 70 waterfalls that punctuate its path. Where the river eventually reaches the edge of the plateau it plunges over the Iguaçu Falls, shortly before joining the Paraná River. The water here is about 4km (2.5 miles) wide, and the whole width of the river tumbles down a magnificent crescent-shaped cliff. There are as many as 275 separate cascades, some plunging directly 82m (270ft) into the cauldron below, others crashing over a series of smaller cataracts before reaching the river. These smaller cataracts are broken by ledges of resistant rock that disperse the tumbling water into clouds of mist and spray; sunlight then completes the display, creating brilliant ever-changing rainbows.

ABOVE Iguaçu Falls have some of the most spectacular public viewing of any great waterfall. At one point a visitor can be surrounded by falling water on three sides.

FAREWELL TO A WATERFALL

Until 1982, one of the world's greatest waterfalls was to be found on the Alto Paraná River, about 160km (100 miles) upstream of the confluence with the Iguaçu. Known as the Seven Falls of Guairá, or Sete Quedas, this was a span of 18 waterfalls with a lip 5km (3 miles) wide.

With an average height of only 34m (110ft), it seemed an unlikely contender for the largest waterfall in the world, but when measured on its flow of water it was easily the world's most powerful by volume, with more than double the average annual flow of Niagara Falls. The falls were submerged when the Itaipu Dam (see below) was filled.

Between the cascades the rock outcrops are covered in trees and dense foliage—palms, bamboo and lacy tree ferns forming outposts to the surrounding jungle. Beneath the trees, wild tropical flowers—begonias, bromeliads and orchids—splash vivid colors through the undergrowth, and parrots, macaws and other gaudily feathered birds fly through the canopy.

National parks in both Brazil and Argentina flank the falls, and access to the area is normally through one of these. Perhaps the best view is achieved from a helicopter, when the whole breathtaking panorama is spread out below. But the most thrilling way to experience the falls is from the catwalk that extends over the river, passing the falls at close range and crossing to the far side. At these close quarters you can feel the immense power of the water as it plunges into the abyss below.

ABOVE The falls have the second-highest annual average flow in the world, after Niagara Falls.

The falls are at their most spectacular during the rainy season, from November to March, but there is usually a good show at any time of year. Despite the impression of permanence given by the constant rush of water, the falls have been known to stop. In May and June 1978, during a period of particularly dry weather, the river gradually ceased to flow, and for 28 days not a drop of water passed over the lip. Again in 2006 the flow was severely reduced in a drought, but normally the effects of a dry season last for only a few weeks.

SEE ALSO
- *Angel Falls* page 194
- *Niagara Falls* page 152
- *Victoria Falls* page 142

THE WORLD'S SECOND-LARGEST DAM

The power of the Paraná River, the second-longest in South America, was harnessed in the 1980s by the construction of the Itaipu Dam, on the border between Paraguay and Brazil. At the time of opening in 1988 it was the world's largest dam, but it was overtaken in 2008 with the completion of the Three Gorges Dam in China (see page 92).

The massive Itaipu Dam project took 14 years to build. Once the construction work had been completed, sluice gates closed for 40 days to allow the reservoir to fill, creating a new lake 160km (100 miles) long, and submerging an area of 1,550sq km (600 square miles). The dam's hydroelectric generators power the whole of Paraguay and the industrial cities of Rio de Janeiro and São Paulo in Brazil; a transmission failure in 2009 briefly blacked out this entire region, affecting some 50 million people.

GALAPAGOS ISLANDS

■ The Galapagos Islands are on the equator in the Pacific Ocean, and cover about 7,800 sq km (3,000 square miles).

■ There are 15 main islands, 42 islets and a further 26 rocks or reefs.

■ The archipelago extends 300km (185 miles) from north to south.

A UNIQUELY VARIED ECOSYSTEM, the Galapagos Islands are now a highly protected environment. When Charles Darwin came to the islands in 1835 during his epic voyage of discovery on HMS *Beagle* he was particularly inspired by the peculiar nature of the flora and fauna. Darwin saw much here that would subsequently inspire his great thesis, *On the Origin of Species* (1859), in which he formulated his theory of evolution, based on observations made during the voyage.

ISLAND REPTILES

The Galapagos Islands are the only place on Earth where you can find marine iguanas. These lizards feed exclusively on seaweed, and have adapted to their marine way of life by developing partially webbed feet. Seven different species of marine iguana, each showing marked variations, have evolved on the different islands. On six of the islands there is also a species of land iguana peculiar to the Galapagos.

The islands are also famous for another reptile, the giant tortoise. Fully grown, they can weigh up to 180 kg (400lb). Fifteen distinctive subspecies have evolved to adapt to niches for which there are no other competitors—despite this four of them are now extinct and a fifth is today represented by a single male.

The Galapagos are a group of oceanic islands formed from lava rising from the seabed. More than 96 percent of the archipelago is now a national park, with a surrounding marine reserve of 79,900sq km (30,850 square miles).

The contrast in island habitat is notable. The lowland coastal fringes are arid and dry, and the vegetation here is dominated by cacti. The humidity increases with altitude, and the hillsides between 200m and 500m (650ft and 1,600ft) are covered with lush evergreen forest, while the higher regions have open areas dominated by sedges and ferns.

The flora and fauna of these islands, as with all oceanic archipelagos, depends on chance arrivals by sea or air, although recently humans have also played their part. Many of the animal species found on the islands are unique not only to the archipelago but also to specific islands in the group. Two species of seal are found in the waters around the Galapagos Islands, both of which are found only in the area. The Galapagos fur seal is the only tropical representative of a sub-Antarctic genus and is active by night, while the other, the Galapagos sea lion, is active by day. Even more remarkably, there are two species of bat that are also endemic to the islands,

DARWIN'S FINCHES

Galapagos finches are descended from common ancestral stock that arrived by chance from South America. They found a large number of vacant niches in various habitats throughout the islands, and have evolved into 13 species of distinguishable size, shape of bill, plumage, song, diet and habits.

This adaptive variation is best illustrated by the differences in the beaks of the various species. Some have the typical seed-eating bill; others, which feed on cacti, have developed a long, pointed bill; and yet more have a small titlike bill for feeding primarily on insects. The woodpecker finch has developed not only a specialized bill, but also a complex behavior pattern that includes the ability to use a cactus spine to prize larvae out of cracks and crevices.

BELOW The Galapagos giant tortoise is one of the longest lived of all vertebrates. In the wild they can be expected to survive for 150 years.

BELOW LEFT Bartolomé Island is home to Galapagos penguins, the only equatorial penguin species. They thrive in the cool water currents that flow around the islands.

together with three species of native rat, including a recently discovered giant rat, previously known only from fossil remains.

The bird populations of the Galapagos include migratory sea birds, such as the waved albatross, which visits the islands to breed, and 28 native species of land bird. More than 750,000 pairs of breeding sea birds make the island their home, including the largest known colony of masked booby in the world, the indigenous Galapagos penguin and the Galapagos dark-rumped petrel.

SEE ALSO
■ *Madagascar* page 140
■ *The Great Barrier Reef* page 220

THE INCA TRAILS

■ Half of the Takesi Trail's length of 40km (25 miles) is made of irregular pieces of stone fitted together.

■ Altogether the Inca Empire had about 40,000km (25,000 miles) of roads, varying in width from 50cm (20in), where there were steps, to 6m (20ft), where the land was flat.

THE INCA ROAD NETWORK
Good communications were key to establishing and administering the Inca empire; roads traversed their territories from the Amazon in the east to the coastal plain in the west, and from what is now Colombia in the north to Argentina in the south.

All roads led to Cuzco, the capital. From there the Sun King sent his messengers (*chasquis*) to the farthest outposts. The *chasquis* ran in relays, covering nearly 320km (200 miles) a day, exchanging the baton in rest houses (*tambos*) at regular intervals along the trails. The baton was a knotted llama wool string called a *quipu,* and different shades and thicknesses of wool, along with the number of knots tied, conveyed different messages.

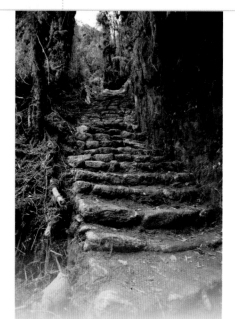

CLEARING THE WAY
The most well-trodden Inca trail is the two- to four-day walk leading to Machu Picchu in Peru from a point outside Cuzco. The number of hikers increased more than tenfold between the early 1980s and 2000, and there have long been concerns about erosion of the path and the amount of litter being left.

Since 2003 there have been tight controls on the number of people allowed on the trail. They must be in an accompanied group, and camp fires are forbidden. Visitors are expected to act responsibly and take their waste away with them. As the whole trail is part of the Machu Picchu UNESCO World Heritage Site, intrusive facilities such as litter bins and public lavatories are not provided.

THE INCAS, like the Romans, were builders of roads. Like the Romans, too, they preferred to take the most direct route, but unlike them they had to surmount the obstacle of the Andes. This meant that engineers had to perfect techniques that could cope with the often precipitous mountain terrain: where the gradient was steep, they cut steps; where outcrops of rock impeded the shortest route, they bored tunnels.

They even cast suspension bridges over gorges. In the uplands, retaining walls were built of stone to keep back the snow; in the desert, adobe walls protected the roads from drifting sand.

Strictly speaking, however, it is incorrect to attribute every mile of paved trail to the Incas, because they inherited roads built by earlier civilizations. Whoever was first responsible for the construction of the roads, many can still be walked today. The finest preserved stretch of Inca paving is in Bolivia, on the Takesi or Inca Trail. During the two days required to complete the hike, the scenery shifts between extremes from black, bare granite mountains brooding over the start of the route to the jungle vegetation of the humid Yungas Valley on the final stretch.

From Ventilla the trail rises steeply to the pass at 4,650m (15,255ft). Although the steps up the mountainside are shallow, this is an arduous and chilly section, but once completed, you are rewarded with magnificent views of snow peaks and the Yungas below. The trail then descends to the village of Takesi, after which encouraging signs of plant life reappear, beginning with carpets of moss on the rock. The trail follows the Rio Takesi, then curves

ABOVE Heading for the hills: the trail between Cuzco and Machu Picchu, looking toward ruins of the Inca site of Phuyupatamarca.

RIGHT Local porters lead a party of hikers along a well-preserved section of trail. Altitude sickness is a risk for visitors unaccustomed to the conditions.

around Palli Palli hill to Kakapi and heads down to the Rio Quimasa Chata. From here it crosses the Takesi again, the lowest point at 2,100m (6,890ft), and finishes at Chojilla.

The longer but less strenuous hike from La Cumbre (The Summit), at 4,725m (15,500ft), to Coroico offers a similar scenic contrast over four days. It begins where a statue of Christ helpfully points to a path leading to the highest point at 4,850m (15,910ft), marked by a stone cairn. From there it is downhill all the way along a clear trail to the village of Achura. After passing the tree line the path narrows and becomes progressively more overgrown as the vegetation becomes more tropical.

SEE ALSO
■ *Machu Picchu* page 196

TIERRA DEL FUEGO

RIGHT Grey Glacier, at the southern end of the Patagonian ice field, flows into a lake in the Torres del Paine National Park, Chile.

■ The total area of the Tierra del Fuego archipelago is 72,500 sq km (28,000 square miles).

■ Chile owns 70 percent of the land; the rest belongs to Argentina.

■ In the 1830s, 3,000 Yahgan people lived here. Many died due to disease and the loss of hunting grounds.

BELOW Gentoo penguins lay their eggs in nests of stones. Males and females take turns to keep them warm over a 35-day incubation period.

TIERRA DEL FUEGO forms part of the hook at the tip of the South American continent, a finger of land reaching toward the vast icy wastes of Antarctica just 965km (600 miles) away. In winter fierce storms lash the desolate coast at the southern tip of South America, driven by the freezing, snow-laden winds from the Antarctic seas. In the summer the land near the coast is balmy and mild, though sudden squalls are a threatening reminder that Tierra del Fuego is not far from the wild shores of Antarctica.

Tierra del Fuego and the Antarctic Peninsula once formed a continuous stretch of land, but the continents began to move apart 25 million years ago. Corresponding rock structure and formations provide strong evidence that they were once joined, and fossils suggest that many animals and plants lived both in South America and in Antarctica.

Tierra del Fuego was discovered in 1520 by the Portuguese navigator Fernando Magellan (1480–1521), who named the land after the fires lit by the Indians along the coast as he sailed down what is now the Strait of Magellan. In 1578 Sir Francis Drake caught a glimpse of the small group of islands, later named by Dutch explorers as Cape Hoorn (Cape Horn). A full survey was

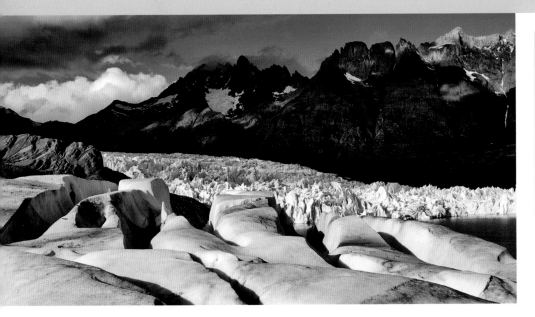

THE ANDES

The Andes, which form the western part of Patagonia, make a rocky spine that runs the length of South America. The range is about 650km (400 miles) across at the widest part and 8,850km (5,500 miles) long. The highest peak is Aconcagua (6950m/22,800ft), which is the tallest in the western hemisphere.

Surprisingly, the Andes mountain range is still growing—movements in the Earth's crust are forcing the mountains up at an estimated rate of 10cm (4in) every 100 years. Glaciers from the last Ice Age also remain, and are still shaping peaks and scraping out U-shaped valleys in some parts of this magnificent mountain range.

not undertaken until the 19th century, when the British Admiralty sent two expeditions. The second of these voyages was undertaken by Captain Robert Fitzroy in a small barque named HMS *Beagle*. Fitzroy wanted to take a naturalist with him when he charted these little-known coasts, and he chose 22-year-old Charles Darwin.

On December 27, 1831, the *Beagle* set sail from Plymouth in England on a journey that was to last almost five years. Tierra del Fuego was reached in December 1832. Darwin disembarked and remarked of the mountains and glaciers that it was 'scarcely possible to imagine anything more beautiful'. Fitzroy named the snow-dusted mountains that range down the Beagle Channel after Darwin.

As the tiny ship made its way down the channel, Darwin looked for Native American Indians. He came across the Yahgan tribe and noted their harsh life. They survived by eating the plant life and taking fragile canoes into the cold and often mountainous seas.

SEE ALSO
■ *Galapagos Islands* page 204

PATAGONIA

Tierra del Fuego is sometimes counted as part of Patagonia, in the southern part of South America. This is a region of rugged beauty, shaped by spectacular mountains, two little-known ice fields and desolate plains. Geographically, the region is roughly divided into two: the Andes and the tablelands.

The tablelands rise from the coast to the foothills of the Andes in a series of steps, and the overlay of soft sedimentary rocks is deeply incised by a number of gorges that run from west to east. In some gorges salt-water lakes have formed, but few carry permanent rivers, and most of the canyons have dried up. The Chilean part of Patagonia on the other hand has magnificent fjords, carved out by the glaciers that once covered the region.

AUSTRALASIA & OCEANIA

Easter Island 212

Sydney Opera House 214

Uluru (Ayers Rock) & Kata Tjuta 218

The Great Barrier Reef 220

Feats of Engineering 224

Glaciers of the Southern Alps 226

Rotorua 228

BELOW The Sydney Opera House was designed by Danish architect Jørn Utzon and completed in 1973 (see pages 214–217).

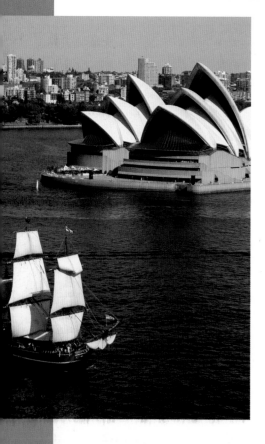

THE PACIFIC OCEAN IS LARGER THAN THE ENTIRE LAND area of the globe, covering an area of about 166 million sq km (64 million square miles). Scattered about it, mere specks of land in this vast sea, are more than 10,000 volcanic and coral islands. This was the last part of the earth to be permanently settled by human beings, the last to be colonized by Europeans, and the last to be freed from colonial dependence.

The Pacific Islanders rank among the greatest long-range seafarers of all time. They sailed their outrigger canoes confidently over enormous distances of empty ocean, navigating by the sun, the stars, sea currents and swells and the flight of birds. Over many centuries they populated all the habitable islands of Oceania. The first human beings in Australia arrived from the southeast of Asia perhaps as long as 40,000 years ago. They were the ancestors of the Australian Aborigines, who, when the first European colonists arrived, are thought to have numbered about 300,000. The earliest people to settle Oceania—maybe 20,000 years ago—were probably

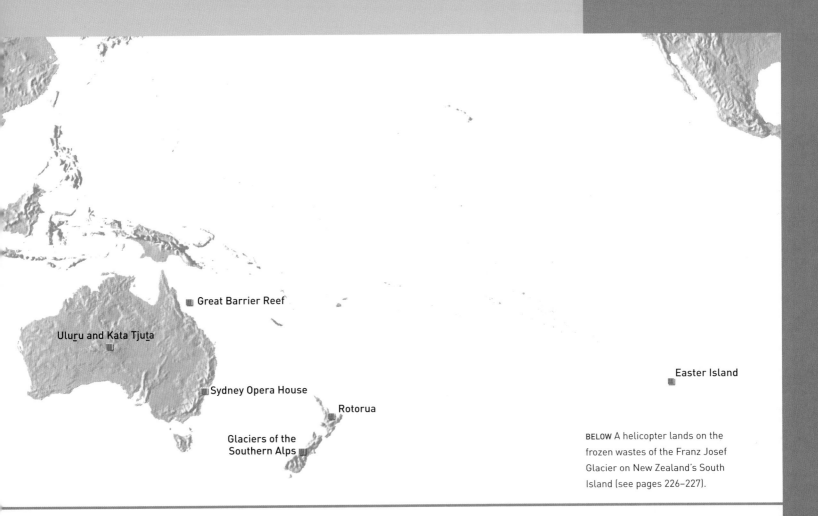

Great Barrier Reef

Uluru and Kata Tjuta

Sydney Opera House

Rotorua

Glaciers of the
Southern Alps

Easter Island

BELOW A helicopter lands on the
frozen wastes of the Franz Josef
Glacier on New Zealand's South
Island (see pages 226–227).

also of southeast Asian origin. Most of the main island groups
in the western Pacific had been occupied by the first century AD.

Between the fifth and tenth centuries groups moved eastward
across the Pacific in canoes tied together to form rafts. They
brought bananas, breadfruit and pigs, and set up new homes
in New Zealand and Hawaii. On Easter Island, over a period of
centuries, enormous statues were set up and remain an enigma
to this day.

From the early 16th century European ships were charting
these waters in search of gold and a navigable route to the Far
East, and in 1788 a British colony was established at Sydney
Cove in Australia. The dynamic city that grew from these small
beginnings is now graced by one of the most striking buildings
of modern times: the Sydney Opera House.

EASTER ISLAND

■ Easter Island is volcanic and roughly triangular in shape, measuring 16km by 18km by 24km (10 miles by 11 miles by 15 miles).

■ It lies 3,200km (2,000 miles) southwest of the Galapagos Islands and 4,200km (2,600 miles) west of Valparaíso in Chile, the country by which it was annexed in 1888.

RIGHT Statues (*moai*) embedded in the ground at the volcano quarry of Rano Raraku, where they were carved mostly between the 12th and 16th centuries.

BELOW At Ahu Tongariki a line of 15 *moai*, one fitted with a red stone *pukao* ('hat' or 'topknot'), stand facing away from the sea.

EASTER ISLAND (RAPA NUI) offers convincing evidence that truth can be stranger than fiction. It lies in the Pacific Ocean, thousands of miles from any other habitation. The first Europeans to approach it, on Easter Sunday 1722, were confronted by a line of massive statues on a stone platform, facing away from them. The inhabitants had lit fires, which Captain Roggeveen and his Dutch crew saw as a welcoming sign. The visitors observed that the people, who were indeed friendly, showed a great variety of hair and skin color. Some had curiously extended earlobes, into which large discs were fitted and they showed particular reverence for the giant statues, which also had long ears. Very few women were seen, and a large part of the population kept out of sight, probably hiding in underground caves.

In 1770 a Spanish expedition from Peru made similar observations; the people were friendly and the land well cultivated. But Captain Cook, only four years later, encountered a very different scene. The land was neglected, the people listless and demoralized, and they now carried wooden clubs and obsidian-tipped spears. The huge statues had been overturned, and no one seemed to worship them any more. In the 19th century the island became a target for slave traders, and a massive Peruvian slave raid in 1862 proved appallingly destructive.

After coming close to destroying the Easter Islanders, the Western world finally began to study the people and their culture. Christian missionaries worked to convert the

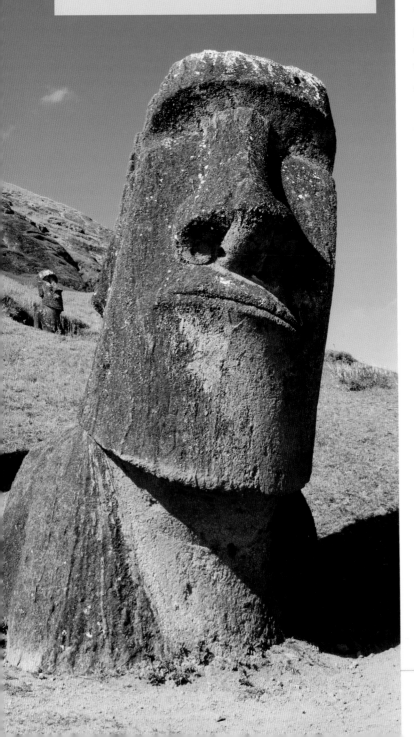

THE STATUES

Many of Easter Island's statues (*moai*) stand 3.7m to 4.6m (12ft to 15ft) high. Some are up to 9.8m (32ft) tall and weigh 91.5 tons (101 tons). There has been much speculation about how the islanders managed to move these bulky figures into place. Local tradition fiercely insists that the statues 'walked'. Archaeologists have shown that 'walking' the *moai* in an upright position, using rocks or logs as pivot points, could have been done with just a few dozen people and two ropes, but at the cost of damage to the base of the figure. The most efficient method would have been to drag it on rollers, slung horizontally in a frame.

surviving population from their existing beliefs in a god called *Make-Make*, and in doing so discovered miniature idols that were kept in the people's homes, but apparently not worshipped with any great ceremony. When wooden tablets carved with hieroglyphic signs were discovered, it became clear that this had been a society that had known how to write. Some of the tablets were destroyed as instruments of paganism, but a few survived. Known as *Rongorongo* tablets, they used signs representing humans, birds, fish and other items. Their precise meaning is still disputed by experts.

The most obvious questions about Easter Island concern the thousand or so *moai*. Who do they represent? Why were so many left at the quarry or seemingly discarded? What ceremonies were associated with putting their eyes and *pukao* in place? And why do they face away from the sea? Much still remains to be discovered.

SEE ALSO

■ *The Nazca Lines* page 195

ANCESTRAL VOYAGERS

The idea of a connection between Easter Island and Peru was popularized by the writer and explorer Thor Heyerdahl. His celebrated 1947 Pacific voyage on the *Kon-Tiki*, a replica Inca raft, supported the theory that early South American societies could have made such journeys. Peruvian and Easter Island oral traditions and the existence of crops such as the sweet potato in both locations also seemed to support this interpretation.

Only in the late 1990s were tests available for scientists to study DNA from the bones of ancient Easter Islanders. The results clearly showed that their ancestors originated from the Polynesian islands to the west, rather than from South America. Further experimental voyages showed that Polynesian boats were equally capable of having made the journey.

SUPER SITE
SYDNEY OPERA HOUSE

■ The Sydney Opera House complex covers a total area of 1.8ha (4.5 acres).

■ The highest roof vault, above the concert hall, is 67m (221ft) above sea level.

■ The roof shells are supported by 350km (217 miles) of cables.

■ The concert hall organ is the world's biggest mechanical organ and has 10,500 pipes.

In 1957 the competition to design an opera house for Sydney attracted 222 entries from 32 countries. The winner, a Danish architect named Jørn Utzon, had never seen the site and, like many other entrants, had to work from photographs. His design, inspired partly by the sails of yachts on Sydney's immense and beautiful harbor, and partly by Maya and Aztec temples in Mexico, was to give Australia its most celebrated and recognizable manmade landmark.

RIGHT Constructing the shells was one of the most difficult engineering tasks ever undertaken. Utzon was re-engaged in 1999 to oversee renovations and to develop a set of design principles for future work.

TECHNICALLY, UTZON'S was the most difficult design to realize, though by far the most unusual and exciting. Both the appearance of the proposed building and its escalating cost provoked heated public debate. The opera house was supposed to open in 1963 and cost $7 million. It actually took 10 years longer to construct and cost more than $100 million. Most of the extra money was raised by lotteries.

Somehow the project kept moving forward amid incessant argument and violent storms of hostility and Utzon resigned in disgust in 1966. The beautiful concrete shells or 'sails'—elliptic paraboloids—proved impossible to construct as originally conceived and the design had to be modified. Thousands of hours of computer time went into solving the difficulties, and the final building is as much a triumph of Ove Arup's engineering as of Utzon's design.

A titanic white swan

The end result is arguably one of the most beautiful major buildings raised in any country since World War II—and one of the most distinctive constructions of any era. It is seen at its best from the waters of the harbor, where it suggests a titanic white swan that might be about to take to the air. On the sails are more than a million Swedish antifungal ceramic tiles, which glint in the sun and never need cleaning, and after dark the building is floodlit.

RIGHT The design and construction of the shell structure took eight years to complete, requiring 2,400 ribs and 4,000 roof panels.

LEFT The special ceramic tiles on the shells are a mixture of glossy white and matte cream, although they appear white from a distance.

The opera house stands by the harbor on Bennelong Point, named after an Australian Aboriginal friend of the colony's first governor. Inside, the effect has been dubbed Space Age Gothic, with steel ribs and concrete fans and 6,200 sq m (67,000sq ft) of tinted glass. The biggest theatre curtains in the world are hung here, each covering close to 90 sq m (1,000 sq ft) and needing six men to lift them. Woven from wool in France in the Aubusson manner, they were designed by an Australian, John Coburn, to represent the sun and the moon. Within the building are five performing halls, an exhibition hall, a restaurant and a bistro. The opera hall seats 1,550 people, the concert hall 2,700, and the Sydney Symphony Orchestra, the Sydney Philharmonia Choir and Sydney Theatre all have their homes here.

SEE ALSO
■ *Feats of Engineering* page 224

LEFT Sydney Harbour provides a dramatic urban waterside setting for the revolutionary architecture of the opera house.

RIGHT The Concert Hall is designed for acoustic performances, with a high vaulted ceiling and finishes of pale Australian timbers.

THE HISTORY
- **1954** *Government sets up committee and appeal fund for new opera house.*
- **1957** *Jørn Utzon's design wins competition.*
- **1959** *Construction of the opera house begins.*
- **1966** *Jørn Utzon resigns.*
- **Sept 28, 1973** *First performance in Opera Theatre.*
- **Oct 20, 1973** *Sydney Opera House officially opened by Queen Elizabeth II.*

THE COATHANGER

Sydney Harbour Bridge, near the opera house, was previously the city's best-known landmark. Functional in gray steel, its curving arch—locally nicknamed the Coathanger—has immense strength and a certain elegance. It was designed by an Australian railway engineer, John Job Crew Bradfield. The road across the bridge, which also carries trains, was named Bradfield Highway in tribute to him.

Demand for a bridge across the harbor goes back almost to Sydney's earliest days; some called for a tunnel, rather than a bridge. (Congestion on the bridge later prompted the building of a tunnel, which opened in 1992.) Approval was eventually given to Bradfield's design in 1923 and it was completed in 1932.

Work had progressed through the Depression years, hence the gray paint, the cheapest available. The bridge has a total length of 1,150m (3,770ft), the single main span being 503m (1,650ft) long. The crown of the arch is 134m (439ft) above the water of the busy bay. The walkway along the eastern side commands excellent views of both the harbor and the city.

RIGHT Abseilers descending one of the sails as part of the Opera House's 25th birthday celebrations, held in 1998.

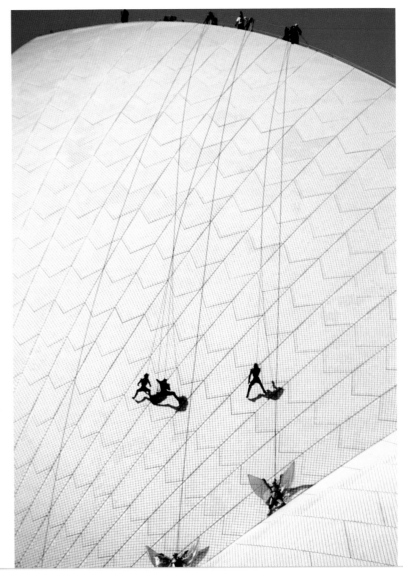

ULURU (AYERS ROCK) & KATA TJUTA

- ■ Uluru is 2.4 km (1.5 miles) long, 1.6km (1 mile) wide and towers 348m (1,143ft) high above the desert plain.

- ■ Uluru is the largest exposed monolith in the world.

- ■ The custodians of Uluru and Kata Tjuta are Anangu, the local Aboriginal people who live within Uluru-Kata Tjuta National Park.

ULURU (AYERS ROCK) lies near the southwestern corner of Northern Territory in the dry, red heart of Australia. Most visitors now stay at the Ayers Rock resort, from where they can experience the spectacle of the rock in the changing light of morning and evening. As the sun sets the rock appears to glow from an inner fire as it changes from the dry brown of the day to an intense, fiery red, before becoming a black silhouette in the fading light. The dawn light reveals Uluru in even more beautiful pastel shades.

Uluru is an example of an inselberg, or 'island mountain', and is the last remnant of what was once a larger mountain range. It survived in the landscape through being an exceptionally solid single piece of rock, or monolith, with few joints to allow erosion to take hold.

Uluru was first seen by a European in 1872, when the Australian explorer Ernest Giles crossed this part of the desert. However, long before Europeans came to Australia, and the British created settlements, Uluru had been a significant part of Anangu (local aboriginal) culture, and there are many Anangu paintings around the base of the rock. The Anangu regard climbing the rock as disrespectful, and request visitors not to do so. It may be closed to climbers in future.

The Uluru-Kata Tjuta National Park in which Uluru stands is governed by the Anangu principle of *Tjukurpa*, which conveys 'law, tradition, ceremony, creation stories, religious philosophy and everything that has ever been, is and always will be'.

GEOLOGICAL HISTORY

Uluru (Ayers Rock) is made from a coarse-grained sandstone, a sedimentary rock called arkose sandstone. Kata Tjuta is formed of conglomerate, a sedimentary rock that is a mix of boulders, pebbles and gravel held together by mud and sand. As a result it contains many minerals and different types of rock, including granite and basalt.

The distinctive red color of Uluru can be attributed to weathering of the rock. Time and environmental factors such as rainwater and oxygen affect the iron minerals in the rock (imagine how iron looks when it rusts). The weathering of the feldspar minerals inside the sandstone also contributes to the beautiful color. It is interesting to note that both Uluru and Kata Tjuta extend for several kilometres underground.

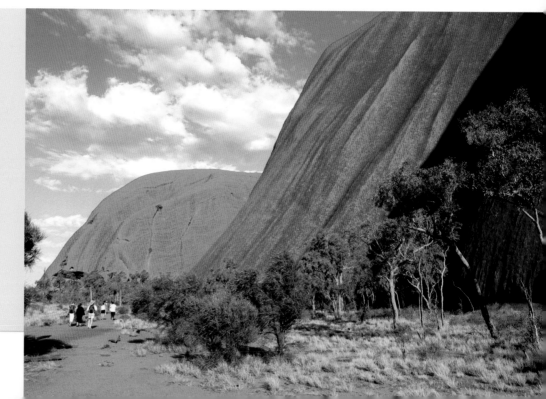

The strata at Uluru are approximately vertical, while those at Kata Tjuta (Mount Olga), some 26km (16 miles) away to the west, are close to horizontal, a contrast that may explain the difference in patterns of erosion between the two outcrops. Two main types of erosion have affected both areas: rain and thermal erosion. Despite their desert locations, they do have a measurable rainfall of a few inches per year, but this tends to fall in one or two major storms every few years. During these storms, raging torrents of water flood down the sides of the rocks, washing away any loose particles in their path. Thermal erosion, on the other hand, is caused by the extreme temperature variation between very hot days and very cold nights, when the constant expansion and contraction of the rock eventually causes fragments to break away.

SEE ALSO
■ *The Devil's Tower* page 172

ABOVE Uluru is part of the traditional belief system of the Anangu, one of the oldest human societies in the world.

BELOW Kata Tjuta, also a sacred site to the Anangu, is said to be the home of the great snake king, Wanambi.

SUPER SITE
THE GREAT BARRIER REEF

- The Great Barrier Reef extends for a distance of more than 2,000km (1,250 miles).

- It comprises around 2,900 reefs, ranging in size from a few square metres to 100sq km (38.6 square miles).

- The total area of the reef is 348,700sq km (134,600 square miles) —greater than the land area of Great Britain.

- The coral's limestone skeletons create walls up to 100m (330ft) high.

The Great Barrier Reef extends along the east coast of Australia from Lady Elliot Island to the tip of Cape York. This area of shallow coastal waters, where a staggering diversity of species thrives, is biologically, geologically and scenically one of the greatest natural wonders in the world. Its recognition as a World Heritage Site, a Biosphere Reserve and a marine park reflect the vital importance of this beautiful but vulnerable area.

BELOW The Great Barrier Reef, showing pale against the blue of the water, is the only living thing visible from outer space.

ABOVE One of the world's premier destinations for scuba diving, the reef offers warm clear waters and the brilliant colors of tropical fish such as the clownfish (below right).

LIVING ANIMALS, OR CORAL POLYPS, make up the Great Barrier Reef, similar in design to the fossilized anemones found on the shore. These tiny, primitive animals live in vast colonies, each of which was derived from an individual polyp that has undergone innumerable divisions. The coral is actually made up of a soft body surrounded by a skeleton of limestone, which creates the fabric of the reef. A living reef is the product of thousands of years of life and death; the bulk of it is made up of the empty skeletons of past generations of polyps, which are covered by a thin veneer of living organisms.

Creature comfort

Coral reefs are restricted to waters that maintain a temperature of between 22°C and 28°C (between 72°F and 82°F) throughout the year. This tropical habitat is capable of supporting very complex life systems—the most diverse ecosystem known on Earth. The Great Barrier Reef contains over 400 species of hard and soft coral. Hard, reef-forming corals occur in many different shapes and sizes, and include mushroom corals, brain corals and staghorn corals, in shades ranging from vivid red to dazzling yellow to black. More than 4,000 species of mollusc have been identified—including chitons, snails, giant clams and octopus—as well as countless numbers of sponges, anemones, worms, crustaceans and echinoderms.

More than 1,500 species of fish live in and around the Great Barrier Reef, presenting a kaleidoscope of colors and patterns as shoals

THE HISTORY

- **17 million years ago**
  Reef-building corals begin inhabiting Australia's eastern coastal waters.

- **1768** *First report of reef, by explorer Louis-Antoine de Bougainville.*

- **1770** *Captain Cook's ship* Endeavour *is grounded on reef.*

- **1960s** *Mass tourism has adverse effects on reef.*

- **1975** *Great Barrier Reef Marine Park is established to manage and protect reef.*

- **1981** *Declared a World Heritage Site by UNESCO.*

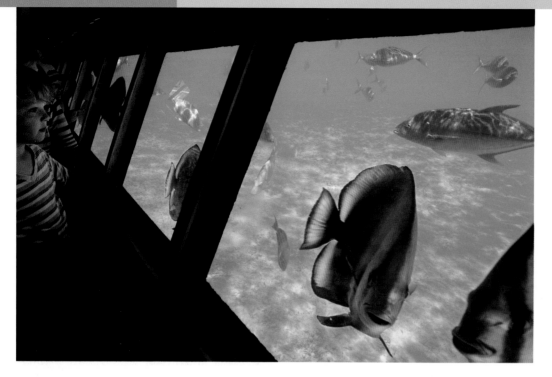

LEFT Viewing the reef from a semi-submarine, a glass-bottomed boat in which passengers sit below the surface of the water.

BELOW LEFT A diver with soft coral, which does not form a reef. It is related to the sea anemone and the jellyfish, and may sting.

BELOW RIGHT The clear waters of the reef are threatened by runoff from agriculture and industry; plans to improve the management of these activities are underway.

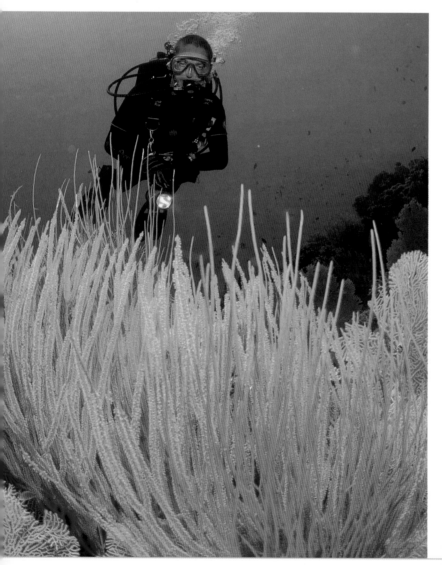

dart one way and then another. The reef is also important for its numerous species of whale, including minke, killer and humpback. These waters are an important breeding area for the humpback whales, and mothers and suckling calves are sighted regularly. This is also a home to six of the seven species of sea turtle in the world, all of which are endangered and depend on the remote islands of the reef for safe nesting sites.

More than 240 species of wader and sea bird nest on the low islands of sand and coral, with shearwaters, tropicbirds, frigatebirds, six species of tern, including roseate terns, as well as noddies, white-bellied sea eagles and ospreys among their number.

TRAPPED ON THE REEF

The great British explorer Captain James Cook (1728–79) accidentally stumbled across the Great Barrier Reef during his epic voyage in 1770, which involved charting the waters off the east coast of Australia.

The reef was very nearly the downfall of the expedition, for Cook had in ignorance sailed northward for over 998km (629 miles) inside the reef itself. It was only when he reached Cape Tribulation that he became aware of the labyrinth of reefs that lay to his seaward side and the consequent danger to him and his crew. Their ship *Endeavour*, a converted coalship weighing 334 metric tons (368 tons), eventually grounded not far from Cape Tribulation on June 12, 1770. Over the following weeks guns, ballast, ammunition, old food, water and wood were jettisoned and a plug was made of a sail spread with sheep dung to mend the hole made by the reef.

Boats were dispatched to find the best routes out and on August 4 the ship set off, though it was still leaking. Not until August 13 did the Endeavour eventually sail clear of the reef.

LEFT Green Island is the only coral island on the reef to have a tropical rainforest. In 1937 it was the launch site for the world's first glass-bottomed boat.

SEE ALSO

- *Galapagos Islands* page 204
- *Madagascar* page 140

FEATS OF ENGINEERING

The urge to conquer distances, heights and inhospitable terrain has inspired some remarkable engineering achievements. Behind every new construction lies the imagination and invention of its designer, and the blood, sweat and toil of hundreds or thousands of workers who made the idea a reality.

- The Itaipu Dam in South America generates 75 billion kW of electricity a year and stands 643ft (196m) high.

- The Channel Tunnel between France and England is the world's longest underwater tunnel.

- The Incas transported huge blocks of stone to the site at Machu Picchu without using wheels.

WATER SUPPLY

Ancient Rome's expert engineers built not only long, straight, well-drained roads to carry the imperial troops, but also sturdy aqueducts and reservoirs to supply the ever-growing population of Rome and other cities across Europe.

The growth of modern conurbations has led to a demand for water-supply on a far greater scale, resulting in awe-inspiring projects such as the vast Hoover Dam on the Colorado River in the US and the Three Gorges Dam in China.

Crossing water presents a different set of difficulties. Pontoon (floating) bridges were used as early as the fifth century BC by Persians crossing the Bosphorus. Stone-arch bridge technology goes back to Roman times.

Ironmaster Abraham Darby III (1750–91) sparked an engineering revolution with the first cast-iron bridge, across the River Severn in England. San Francisco's Golden Gate suspension bridge, the longest in the world when completed in 1937, used cables made of thousands of separate wire strands to secure its immense span.

Above Roman examples probably inspired the construction of the aqueduct in Nerja, Spain, built in the late 19th century to supply a nearby sugar factory.

Below The biomes, domed greenhouses at the Eden Project in Cornwall, England, consist of inflated plastic cells supported by steel frames.

Right Taipei 101 was the world's tallest building from 2004 to 2010. As well as highly advanced engineering, its design incorporates traditional symbols and feng shui philosophy.

Above The Sydney Harbour Bridge spans 503m (1,650ft) with a single steel arch, the ultimate in bridge design when it was completed in 1932.

Below At 24m (79ft) deep, the Suez Canal can take all but the largest supertankers. It carries around 7.5 percent of the world's shipping.

REACH FOR THE STARS

Building high presents unique engineering problems. Gustave Eiffel's decorative lacy ironwork in the Eiffel Tower was designed to minimize wind force. Malaysia's twin 452m (1,482ft) Petronas Towers, built in 1996, use an innovative high-strength concrete and a damper on each tower. They have since been overtaken, first in 2004 by Taiwan's 509m (1,670ft) Taipei 101 Tower and by Dubai's 828m (2,717ft) Burj Khalifa, which opened in 2010.

But perhaps the greatest construction jobs were those carried out by ancient civilizations, whose enormous structures were erected without the help of sophisticated machinery and computer-aided design.

LAND

Before the advent of the railways, canals—artificial waterways punctuated by locks to allow for fluctuations in the terrain, which could take hours to negotiate—were the speediest means of commercial transport. The Suez Canal, built in the 1860s to provide a direct 190km (118 mile) route from the Mediterranean to the Red Sea, was excavated by 1.5 million Egyptian workers without the aid of any sophisticated equipment—just picks and shovels.

Inconvenient geography is a constant challenge to rail engineers. On the Canadian Pacific Railway, for example, they had to navigate a 1:22 gradient through the heights of Kicking Horse Pass to complete the connection between Montréal and Vancouver.

SEE ALSO
■ *The Eiffel Tower* page 26
■ *The Great Wall of China* page 84
■ *The Three Gorges Dam* page 92

GLACIERS OF THE SOUTHERN ALPS

- ■ Only 24km (15 miles) separate the Fox and Franz Josef glaciers.

- ■ Westland National Park, which contains both glaciers, covers an area of 87,800ha (217,000 acres).

- ■ The Tasman Glacier is the largest in New Zealand. In places it is 610m (2,000ft) thick.

THE SOUTHERN ALPS form a high mountain barrier along the western side of the South Island of New Zealand. The highest point is Mount Cook at 3,764m (12,349 ft); it is only 32km (20 miles) from the summit westward across the coastal strip to the Pacific Ocean. To the east the land descends more gradually for 130km (80 miles) across the Canterbury Plains to the coast. The westerly winds that blow in from the Tasman Sea are laden with moisture, and as the damp air rises against the mountains it drops heavy snowfalls along the range that feed the glaciers. The three most famous are the Tasman, Fox and Franz Josef glaciers.

The glaciers on the western side of the mountains are short and steep, tumbling downward like frozen cataracts that reach into the dense, subtropical evergreen rainforests in an extraordinary juxtaposition. On the eastern side of the range the glaciers are quite different in character, with the higher reaches typically steep and rugged, patterned by networks of crevasses that make travel difficult. Lower down, these glaciers flow to low altitudes, and the Tasman Glacier reaches almost as far as the central plain.

THE CHANGING CLIMATE OF NEW ZEALAND

The climate of New Zealand, like that of many other regions, has gone through change over time. More than 500 million years ago New Zealand was a part of the ancient super-continent of Gondwana, and lay about 35 degrees north of the equator. During the next 250 million years Gondwana drifted southward until Australia and New Zealand lay close to the South Pole, where they experienced widespread glaciation.

The continuing rotation of Gondwana over the next 120 million years took New Zealand northward again into warmer temperate or subtropical regions, and the ice sheets disappeared. At about this time Gondwana began to break apart to form the different continents that we know today.

The Fox and Franz Josef glaciers flow to the west, the latter reaching 12km (7 miles) in length. They have both been advancing since the mid-1980s. Both are within the Westland National Park, an area that includes alpine peaks, snowfields, glaciers, forests, rivers and lakes. Lake Matheson provides a famous view of the three major peaks—Cook, Tasman and La Perouse—reflected in its calm waters.

The Tasman Glacier, which flows down from Mount Cook, is its crowning glory. The glacier forms a narrow tongue of ice 27km (17 miles) long that widens in places to as much as 3km (2 miles), and is very active, flowing as fast as 51 to 64cm (20 to 25in) per day. Despite its high speed, the glacier is gradually retreating: its snout is only 760m (2,500ft) above sea level, where temperatures are relatively high, and the rate of melting and evaporation is greater than its flow. New Zealand underwent its most recent process of glaciation in the last Ice Age, and was covered in ice until the Earth began to warm again about 10,000 years ago. Today, most of New Zealand's glaciers continue to retreat, and the long-term effects of current global warming may be to melt them completely.

NAMING THE GLACIERS

Tasman Glacier takes the name of the Dutch explorer Abel Tasman, who was sent on an expedition in 1642 by the Dutch East India Company to settle the vexed question of whether a great southern continent existed. No other European set foot in New Zealand for more than 100 years.

British explorer Captain James Cook arrived in 1769–70 and noted the existence of the Franz Josef Glacier, but another hundred years or so passed before its exploration by geologist Julius von Haast in 1865. He named the glacier—then 3km (2 miles) closer to the coast than it is now—in tribute to Emperor Franz Josef of Austria.

Fox Glacier was originally known as the Victoria Glacier, but was renamed during a visit by New Zealand's Prime Minister, Sir William Fox, in 1872.

OPPOSITE Fox Glacier ends its journey only 300m (980 ft) above sea level, among lush rainforest. Along with Franz Josef, it is one of the few New Zealand glaciers to be advancing.

ABOVE A climber at sunset above Franz Josef Glacier in Westland National Park, which extends from the alpine peaks down to the rugged coast.

ROTORUA

■ **Pohutu is the greatest geyser in New Zealand, usually spouting every 20 minutes or so to a height of 30m (100ft).**

■ **When the Waimangu Geyser appeared in 1900 it was the most powerful in the world, firing a mixture of mud, steam and water as high as 450m (1,500ft) into the air.**

BELOW Pohutu Geyser—its name means 'big splash' or 'explosion'—spurts two to three times an hour and can reach up to 100m (330ft).

GEOTHERMAL ACTIVITY AT ROTORUA, near the heart of New Zealand's North Island, has drawn tourists for many years, and the Maori settlement and Maori Arts and Crafts Institute provide an added attraction, giving an insight into the customs of the earliest people to settle New Zealand. The Maoris have traditionally used the hot springs for cooking, washing and heating, but the springs are also reputed to have healing properties, particularly for arthritis and rheumatism, and the local Queen Elizabeth Hospital still uses the sulfurous waters in its treatment regime.

GEYSERS

Geysers work on a principle similar to that of hot springs, but they erupt scalding hot water fountains. Some spout every few minutes, some are separated by hours or even days—and they are not always regular.

The essential factor that changes a hot spring into a geyser is an obstruction in the passage leading to the surface. As the water in the reservoir heats it expands: if that expansion is confined by an obstruction, the pressure increases, as does the temperature of the water. The water becomes super-heated until the pressure can no longer be contained and the water rushes upwards. The reduction in pressure promotes instant boiling and an explosive release of steam in the reservoir that forces the water upwards ever faster.

BOTTOM RIGHT Colourful formations at the Champagne Pool at Wai-O-Tapu Thermal Wonderland are caused by mineral deposits.

HOW HOT SPRINGS WORK

There are three basic criteria for hot springs: a good supply of ground water, a source of heat, and a suitable vent from the underground reservoir to the surface. New Zealand's wet climate ensures plentiful ground water, and the molten rock below ground provides a steady supply of heat. After a volcanic eruption, residual lava frequently slips back into the magma chamber, leaving voids in the rocks above that can be filled with water, providing reservoirs for hot springs.

If there is no obstruction in the passage from the reservoir to the surface, a hot spring will form, gently bubbling as the hot water continually rises towards the surface.

Nowhere in Rotorua is far from thermal activity of some sort. The town's many spas include the former Bath House, founded in 1908, and now a museum. A popular boat trip takes visitors to Mokoia Island, in the middle of Lake Rotorua, where they can take a dip in Hinemoa's hot pool. On the edge of the town is the Whakarewarewa thermal area and Geyser Flat, where Pohutu, the splashing geyser, can be seen. Normally the smaller Prince of Wales Feathers geyser close by gives a display shortly before Pohutu erupts, like a prelude to the main act. Nearby are bubbling sulphurous mud pools, and the rock is hot underfoot.

Terraces in Waimangu covered an area of more than 5ha (12 acres) and attracted crowds of curious tourists. Tragically, an eruption of nearby Tarawera Mountain destroyed this famous landmark on June 10, 1886, along with several villages, burying everything under a huge shower of hot ash and debris, and killing 150 people. However, hot springs continued to bubble in the area, and in 1900 a new geyser, the Waimangu Geyser, appeared. In four years its power had decreased, and by 1908 the geyser had become extinct once more.

SEE ALSO
■ *Beppu* page 105
■ *Pamukkale* page 70
■ *Volcanic Iceland* page 14

About 10km (6 miles) southeast of Rotorua along Highway 5 are the famous blue and green lakes of Waimangu—hot-water lakes in an extinct volcano crater. The water is heated at depth and dissolves different minerals in its upward passage, coloring the water various vivid shades. The source of the water in each lake is probably different, and each has a separate route to the surface, leaching various minerals from the rocks to make the different colors. Iron oxides in the low cliffs surrounding the lakes produce a contrasting red, and in some places yellow is the result of sulfurous deposits. Throughout most of the 19th century the famous Pink and White

ANTARCTICA

Mount Erebus 232
The Elements 234
Deception Island 236

IN 1820 THE CAPTAIN OF A RUSSIAN SHIP, THE *VOSTOK*, SIGHTED A SERIES OF ICY hillocks from the Southern Ocean. A couple of days later a British ship, the *Williams*, arrived and confirmed his sighting—the first record of the Antarctic mainland. There had been talk of a 'southern land' for hundreds of years, but not until 1840 was it established that this was a continent, rather than a group of islands.

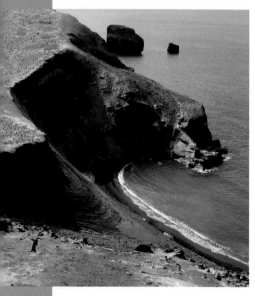

In fact this cold continent is the fifth largest, exceeding Australia and Europe in size. Of its 14 million sq km (5,404,000 square miles), 13.72 million sq km (5,295,920 square miles)—about 98 percent—is made up of thick ice; the rest is barren rock. Its mountainous terrain ranges from the Bentley Subglacial Trench, at 2,555m (8,382ft) high, to the 4,987m (16,361ft) Vinson Massif. About half the 17,968km (11,165 mile) coastline is formed of glacier shelves, and over 10 percent of the whole continent is made up of floating ice.

Even this mainly uninhabitable region has not escaped human attention. Whalers have been active around the South Shetland Islands since the 18th century, and in the 1920s a sealing

Deception Island ■

Mount Erebus

LEFT ABOVE Approaching
Coulman Island in calm
weather on the Ross Sea.

LEFT BELOW Deception Island
was formed from an extinct
volcano (see pages 236–237).

BELOW Midnight in Antarctica,
a scene on Ice Tower ridge
Mount Erebus (see pages
232–233).

expedition set up a hut in Bouvetøya, one of the most inhospitable islands on Earth as well as being the most remote. The late 20th century saw a flurry of scientific research stations established by several different countries. The Antarctic Treaty, which came into force in 1961, provides a code for all nations operating in the area, without giving any one nation territorial rights.

This is the coldest, highest, driest and windiest of the continents—yet in summer it receives more radiation from the sun than the equator. It is also a changing continent: the scientists based there discovered a hole in the atmospheric ozone layer over Antarctica in 1985, and are now monitoring the shrinking of ice shelves and other results of global warming.

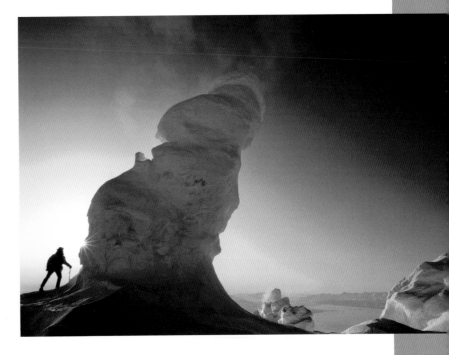

MOUNT EREBUS

- The summit of Mount Erebus is 3,794m (12,448ft).

- Its crater is 805m (2,640ft) across and 275m (900ft) deep.

- At the bottom of the crater is a small lake of molten lava.

- The name *Erebus* comes from the Ancient Greek word *erebos*, which means darkness.

MOUNT EREBUS ON ROSS ISLAND forms a beacon for anyone venturing into this daunting area of Antarctica. The presence of an active volcano amid the ice and snow of a frozen continent seemed extremely enigmatic in the days when the science of geology was in its infancy, but today's geologists are no longer surprised by such phenomena. Volcanic rocks are quite common in Antarctica, although most of them are geologically very old and represent activity at times when the continent was not in its present polar position.

Volcanic rocks are important indicators of continental movements and can be a useful aid to plotting the ancient wanderings of the continents over the surface of the globe. The geologically young McMurdo Volcanic Province in the Ross Sea region and the related volcanoes of Marie Byrd Land are simply indicative of recent continental movement in Antarctica. Some Antarctic volcanoes—particularly the island volcanoes of the Southern Ocean—have been active during the past 200 years. Many eruptions have gone unwitnessed, to be recorded toward the end of activity or after the event, simply because the region is so sparsely populated. Only on Deception Island are there stations within the damage radius of the volcano.

Climbing this dramatic landmark rising above the sea ice has been a goal for explorers and mountaineers since its discovery. During Ernest Shackleton's 1907–9 expedition, a party of six men made the first ascent of the mountain. They

ANTARCTIC VOLCANOES

Mount Melbourne, just across McMurdo Sound from Ross Island, has fumarole activity on its summit. The combination of steam and subzero temperatures has formed many delicate ice pillars, and despite the altitude, there is a unique bacterial flora living around the fumaroles.

In 1893 the Norwegian C. A. Larsen, making a rare voyage south into the Weddell Sea along the east coast of the Antarctic Peninsula, reported seeing volcanic activity at Seal Nunataks. For many years this distant observation was regarded with scepticism by many geologists, who argued that it was probably a cloud that he had seen, but recent work has found evidence of fumarole activity in the area.

ABOVE Mount Erebus viewed across a sea of pack ice. The present summit has grown out of an earlier crater, which appears as a plateau to its left.

RIGHT Icebreakers keep the supply route open for scientists working on Mount Erebus by clearing a channel to the remote port of McMurdo Station.

reached the summit on March 10, 1908. Each Antarctic summer a party of scientists and students set up camp near the top to monitor volcanic activity. The lava lake is permanently active. Periodic eruptions of lava bombs—aerated globules of lava that collapse once they hit the ground—have been recorded since 1972, and have probably been occurring for much of the volcano's recent history.

But it is not only geologists who are drawn to Mount Erebus. Modern explorers cannot resist the temptation to photograph the mountain in all its moods, and the early explorers—including Edward Wilson, doctor and naturalist on both of Captain Scott's expeditions—were compelled to commit its beauty to paper in watercolors. Botanists, too, have a special interest in Tramway Ridge, high on the mountain's flanks, where an area of fumaroles supports rich vegetation on the warm ground.

LEFT The lava lake is unusual in being continuously, but not violently, active.

SEE ALSO

■ *Mount Fuji* page 106
■ *Mount Kilimanjaro* page 136

THE DISCOVERY OF EREBUS

On January 9, 1841, James Clark Ross and Francis Crozier, in their ships HMS *Erebus* and HMS *Terror*, emerged with relief from the dangers of the pack ice into the open water of the Ross Sea. Three days later they saw a magnificent mountain range with peaks rising to 2,400m (8,000ft), which Ross christened the Admiralty Range.

The ships continued south, following the mountains. On January 28, 1841, the explorers were astonished to see, according to *Erebus* surgeon Robert McCormick, 'a stupendous volcanic mountain in a state of high activity'. The scientists on board were stunned to find an active volcano in this frozen land. The smoking volcano was duly named Mount Erebus, and a smaller extinct cone to the east Mount Terror, after the two ships.

THE ELEMENTS

For those who live in temperate climates the weather is usually little more than a handy topic of conversation or, at worst, an inconvenience. However, extreme weather seems to be occurring more frequently worldwide as a result of climate change, and earthquakes, floods or tornadoes can strike with devastating effect.

- Antarctica's lowest recorded temperature ever was -89.4°C (-129°F).

- Some parts of the Atacama Desert have had no rain for more than four centuries.

- The hottest place in the world is El Azizia in the Sahara. In 1922 the temperature reached 57.8°C (136°F).

Left A tornado strikes in Kansas, in 'Tornado Alley'. The US state experiences around 50 tornadoes a year. Residents are warned by sirens, and take refuge in storm cellars.

Below When Mount St Helens erupted in 1980, it was the first significant eruption on the US mainland since 1915. The entire top of the volcano was pulverised and ejected into the air.

AIR

Hurricanes develop over tropical oceans, taking their energy from evaporating water and moving at speeds of more than 120km/h (75mph) before gradually losing their energy when they meet land. Tornadoes are violently spinning funnels of air that have been known to travel up to 480km/h (300mph), leaving wide trails of destruction.

The US and Canada are especially vulnerable to tornadoes, which gather humid air from the Gulf of Mexico. The Great Plains area of the US, between the Rocky Mountains and the Appalachians, has so many tornadoes that it has become known as Tornado Alley.

Left Wind and water have eroded the soft sedimentary rocks at Bryce Canyon, Utah, into spectacular fluted formations known as hoodoos.

Below Wave Rock, Western Australia, is a 2,700 million-year-old granite cliff shaped by underground chemical action, followed by water erosion.

SEE ALSO

- *Antarctica* page 230
- *The Great Sahara* page 128
- *Volcanic Iceland* page 14

EARTH AND FIRE

Mount St Helens volcano in Washington State in the US erupted with devastating force on May 18, 1980. A vast area was affected by the volcanic ash and 100 people were killed.

Earthquakes are closely associated with volcanoes and the volcanic islands on the Pacific Rim, known as 'The Ring of Fire', mean that countries such as Japan are particularly vulnerable. In 1906 the San Andreas Fault caused a quake that devastated San Francisco.

WATER

Cherrapunji, 1,290m (4,232ft) above sea level and overlooking the plains of Bengal, has the world's heaviest rainfall, with an annual average of 1,163cm (458in). Seasonal monsoons hit it with full force and ironically, since much of the torrential rains run into the valley below, residents often have to walk long distances for fresh water.

Antarctica is not only the coldest continent but also the windiest, the highest and, surprisingly, the driest. It has so little precipitation that it is technically as dry as the Sahara. The Atacama Desert, on the coast of Chile, has the lowest known rainfall, with less than 0.01cm (0.004in) a year.

DECEPTION ISLAND

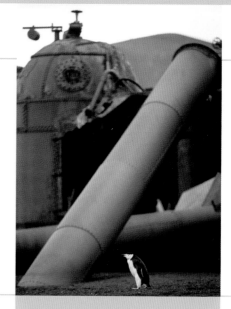

■ Sir Hubert Wilkins made the first powered flight in the Antarctic on November 16, 1928 from Deception Island.

■ Between 1912 and 1931 a post office operated on the island, and the first stamp was cancelled on March 6, 1913.

WHALING AND DECEPTION

Whalers operated in the Southern Ocean in the 18th century, and it is conceivable that American sealers knew about the South Shetland Islands for some years before their official discovery, but kept it secret for commercial reasons. In 1819 news of the islands' existence reached the sealers working in South Georgia, who were quick to exploit the new, more profitable beaches farther south.

In the hunting seasons of 1819–20 and 1820–1 the level of slaughter was so great that the fur seals were virtually extinguished, making further voyages unprofitable. However, Deception Island was now firmly on the map, and the scene was set for its future role in Antarctic exploration and exploitation. Today it is a popular stop for tourist ships.

SITTING AMONG THE SOUTH SHETLAND ISLANDS, Deception Island is shaped like a horseshoe, a roughly circular ridge open to the sea on its southern side. It is an ancient volcano whose central cone has collapsed to form a caldera, now occupied by a crater lake breached by the sea. Many minor vents have since been active around the rim of the caldera, reinforcing the island's shape. The South Shetland Islands are largely volcanic, formed in response to the oceanic crust descending beneath their northwestern margin. Bransfield Strait is also volcanic in origin, but formed by sea-floor spreading behind the volcanic arc of the islands. Penguin and Bridgeman islands are young volcanoes but, unlike Deception Island, are no longer active.

A shore station, Aktieselskabet Hektor, was established at Whalers Bay on Deception Island in 1912. A Stipendiary Magistrate had been appointed by the Falkland Islands government for the 1911–12 and 1912–13 whaling season, and he was resident on Deception during the seasons until the station closed; whaling from the island ceased in 1931.

ABOVE A visiting expedition reenacts hauling a ship through ice, as the explorer Ernest Shackleton attempted to do in 1916.

A British base was built at Deception Island in 1944, followed by Argentine and Chilean stations in 1948 and 1955. On December 4, 1967, a sudden eruption in the northwest corner of Port Foster showered ash and pumice over the Argentine station, and everyone was quickly evacuated onto the nearby Chilean vessel *Piloto Pardo*. Subsequent visits revealed that a new island had been formed by the eruption. Some personnel returned to Deception Island the following season to assess the damage, and the bases were partly reoccupied.

In 1969 and 1970 there were more eruptions and activity on Mount Pond, near the British and Chilean bases. The entire Chilean station collapsed except for the brick-built entrance arch. A lahar, a river of mud, ash, blocks of ice and slurry triggered by the heat of the eruption, flowed through the British base, knocking down one wall and creating a window with a view of the bay as it left. Earthquakes shook the ground and tilted some of the oil storage tanks. Once again the *Piloto Pardo* came to the rescue. Evacuees were grateful that the volcano had chosen to erupt during the summer season, while ships were about; had the eruptions occurred during the winter the story might have been quite different.

SEE ALSO
- *Mount Erebus* page 232
- *The Hawaiian Islands* page 182
- *Volcanic Iceland* page 14

ABOVE Deception Island has large colonies of chinstrap penguins, named for the narrow black band that passes under their chins.

BELOW Tourists on the rim of the volcano. It is still so active that steam rises through the beach sand and warms the sea water.

DISCOVERY OF DECEPTION ISLAND AND THE ANTARCTIC MAINLAND

The South Shetland Islands are so-called because they lie in the same latitude south as the Scottish Shetland Islands in the north. It is possible that Dirck Gherritz, a Dutchman, sighted the islands in 1599. They were rediscovered in February 1819 when William Smith's brig *Williams* was blown off course while rounding Cape Horn, en route from Buenos Aires to Valparaíso.

The Admiralty chartered the *Williams* and placed her under the command of Edward Bransfield, with Smith acting as the pilot. Charged with charting the South Shetland Islands, they sighted Deception Island on January 29, 1820. The following day, they sighted 'Trinity Land' (now known as Trinity Peninsula) and became, arguably, the first men to sight the Antarctic mainland.

INDEX

Page numbers in *italic* refer to illustrations

A

Aboriginal people 218
Aeneid (Virgil) 124
Africa 114-147
Alberti, Leon Battista 53
Alexandrovsky Palace 65
Alhambra 58-59, *58-59*
Alps 40-41
Amazon Basin 200-201, *200-201*
American Falls 152
Anangu people 218, 219
Anasazi people 168
Andes mountains 209
Angel Falls 194, *194*
Angkor Thom 109
Angkor Wat 109, *109*
Antarctica 230-237
Antiochus I 74
aqueducts 30, 224
architecture 164-165
Argentina 202-203, 208-209
Arlington Memorial Bridge 159
Arsameia on Nymphaios 74
artificial islands 83
Arup, Ove 215
Asia 68-113
Aswan High Dam 122
Atacama Desert 235
Athens 54-55
Aughrabies Falls 142
Aurangzeb 97
Australasia & Oceania 210-229
Australia 214-223
Austria 37
Avebury Stone Circle 20
Ayutthaya 112-113, *112-113*
Aztecs 191, *191*

B

Bali *135*
Banff National Park *151*
Banqueting Hall, London 52, *52*
Banzai Pipeline 183
baobab forests 140
Baptistry, Florence *53*
Barcelona 60-61
Bartholdi, Frédéric-Auguste 154
basalts 16, 17, 18
Battle of Little Bighorn 161
Beijing 88-89
Belgium 31
Benin 143
Bentinck, Lord William 96
Beppu 105, *105*
Bergen 12
Bernini, Giovanni 50
Bhutan 102-103
Black Hills 161
Blondin, Charles 153
Blue Mosque 72-73, *72-73*, 165

Blue Nile 122
Bolivia 206-207
Borglum, Gutzon 160-161
Borobudur 108, *108*
Botswana 144-145
Boulder City 169
Brahms, Johannes 37
Bramante, Donato 53
Brazil 202-203
bridges 38-39, 170-171, 217, 224
brine shrimps 22, 23
Brunelleschi, Filippo 53
Brussels 31
Bryce Canyon National Park 167, *235*
Buddhism 99, 101, 108, 109, 110-111
Burj Al Arab hotel *164*
Burj Khalifa 82-83, *82-83*, 164, 225
Burkina Faso 143
Burton, Richard 123

C

Ca' d'Oro, Venice 46-47
Camargue 22-23, *22-23*
Cambodia 109
Canada 150-153
Canadian Pacific Railway 150-151, *150-151*, 225
canals 225
Cape Town 146, 147
Cappadocia *135*
Carthage 124-125, *124-125*
Castle of Good Hope 147
Cathedral of St Michael the Archangel 63
caves 90, 91
centaurs 57
Central and South America 184-209
Champagne Pool *229*
Chankasem Palace 113
Channel Tunnel 224
Chartres Cathedral 165
Checkerboard Mesa 166
Chedi Phu Khao Thong 112
Cherrapunji 235
Chicago 82
Chichén Itzá 188-189, *188-189*
Chicxulub crater 179
Chile 208-209
Chimney Rock 173
China 84-93, 191
church architecture 52-53, 100
Church of the Holy Sepulchre 79, *79*
civilizations 190-191
climate change 9
CN Tower 82
Colorado River 168, 176, 177
Colosseum 42-43, *42-43*, 164
Colossi of Memnon 117
Congo River 138-139, *138-139*
continental drift 102, 226
Cook, Captain James 212, 223, 227
coral 221
Córdoba 59

Crazy Horse Memorial 161
Curzon, Lord 96, *96*, 98
Cuzco 206
Czar Cannon 62, *62*
Czech Republic 34

D

Dalai Lama 99
dams 92-93, 122, 168-169, 203
Danube Delta 36, *36*
Darwin, Charles 204, 209
Dead Sea 75, *75*
Deception Island 236-237, *236-237*
Deir 80
Delhi 97, 98
Denmark 21
desertification 129
Devil's Tower 172-173, *172-173*
Diaz, Bartholomew 147
Dido 124
Dome of the Rock 77, *77*, 79, *79*
Doric architecture 55
Dubai 82-83, 164, *164*

E

earthquakes 130-131, 235
East African Rift Valley 130-131, *130-131*
Easter Island 212-213, *212-213*
Ecuador 204-205
Eden Project 224
Edinburgh Castle 18-19, *18-19*
Edinburgh Military Tattoo 18
Egypt 116-123, 190
Eiffel, Gustave 26-27, 29, 154, 156
Eiffel Tower *7*, **26-29**, *26-29*
Eiger 40
El Capitan *8*, 174, 175, *175*
Elgin Marbles 54
Ellis Island 156
Emerald Buddha 110-111
Empire State Building 162-163, *162-163*
engineering feats 224-225
England 20
Ephesus *165*
Esperanza culture 186
Ethiopia 130-131
Europe 10-67
Everglades 180-181, *180-181*
extreme weather 234-235

F

Fez Medina 126-127, *126-127*
Fingal's Cave 17
fjords 12-13, 209
flamingos 23, *23*, 130, 132, 133
Forbidden City 88-89, *88-89*
Fox Glacier 226, 227, *227*
France 26-30, 165
Franz Josef Glacier 226, 227, *227*
Frasassi Caves 90
French, Daniel Chester 159

G

Galapagos Islands 204-205, *205*
Galileo Galilei 45, *53*
Garmisch-Partenkirchen 40
Gaudí, Antoni 60-61
Geirangerfjord 12, *13*
Generalife 59
General Sherman 178
geothermal activity 15, 70-71, 75, 105, 228-229
Germany 32-33, 164
geysers 15, 105, 228, 229
Ghiberti, Lorenzo *53*
giant pandas 93
Giant's Causeway 16-17, *16-17*
giant tortoises 204, *205*
Giza 118
glaciers 15, 40, *134*, *209*, 226-227, *226-227*
Goat Island 152
Golden Gate Bridge 170-171, *170-171*, 224
Golden Gate Park 171
Golden Lane, Prague 34, *34*
gondolas 46
Gondwana 102, 226
Göreme Valley 135
Gothic architecture 100
Granada 58-59
Grand Canal 46-47, *46-47*
Grand Canyon 176-177, *176-177*
Grand' Place, Brussels 31, *31*
Great Barrier Reef 220-223, *220-223*
Great Buddha of Kamakura *101*
Great Buddha of Nara 100
Great Palace, St Petersburg 64-65
Great Pyramid *8*, 83, **118-121**, *118-121*
Great Wall of China *6*, **84-87**, *84-87*
Greece 54-57
Greenland 14-15, 16
Grimsvötn 15
Guatemala 192-193
Guggenheim Museum, Bilbao 164
Guilin Hills 90-91, *90-91*
Guinea 143

H

Hagia Sofia 73
Hall of Mirrors 24
Hall of the Great Buddha 100
Hannibal 125
Hapsburg dynasty 37
Hawaiian Islands *134*, **182-183**, *182-183*
Hearst Castle 164
Helmcken Falls 153
hermits 56
Herrenchiemsee 32
Heyerdahl, Thor 213
Hillary, Sir Edmund 103

Himalayas 102-103, *102-103*
Hindu architecture 101, 109
Hiroshima 104
Hofburg, Vienna 37, *37*
Hoover Dam 168-169, *168-169*
Horseshoe Falls 152
Humayun's Tomb 97
Hunlen Falls 153
hurricanes 234
Hurtigruten 12
Hvannadalshnúkur 14

I

ice caps 12-13, 15
Iceland 14-15, *14-15*, 134
Iguaçu Falls 202-203, *202-203*
iguanas 204
Incas 197, 198, 206-207, 224
Inca Trails 206-207, *206-207*
India 94-98, 102-103
Indonesia 108
Industrial Revolution 11
Ireland 16-17
Ironbridge 224
Israel 75-79
Istanbul 72-73
Itaipu Dam 203, 224
Italy 40-51
Itsukushima Shrine 104, *104*
Ivan IV, 'the Terrible' 63

J

Japan 100, 104-107
Java 108
Jerusalem 76-79, *76-79*
Jigokudani Hot Springs 105
Jin Mao Tower 82
Jones, Inigo 52
Jordan 80-81
Jugurtha Tableland 147
Jungfrau 40

K

Ka'ba 100, *100*
Kano 129
Kapellbrücke 38-39, *38-39*
Karakoram Mountains 102
Karouyine Mosque 126, *127*
karst landscapes 90, 91
Kata Tjuta 218-219, *219*
Kauai 182
Kenya 130-133
Khmers 109
Kilauea 182-183, *183*
Knossos *190*
Kremlin 62-63, *62-63*

L

Lake Chad 129
Lake Mead 168
Lake Nakuru 132-133, *132-133*
Lake Natron 130
Lake Okeechobee 180
Lake Tanganyika 130, 131
Lake Victoria 123, 131
Lamayuru *103*
landscapes 134-135

Laurasia 102
Lava Falls Rapids 176
Leaning Tower of Pisa 44-45, *44-45*
Le Nôtre, André 24
Leifur Eiríksson 15, *15*
lemurs 140, 141
Lengai 131
Lenin, Vladimir Ilyich 63
Leonardo da Vinci 52, *53*
Lhasa 99
Library of Celsius 165
Lincoln Cathedral 83
Lincoln Memorial 158-159, *158-159*
Linderhof 33
Livingstone, David 123, 142-143
Livingstone Falls 139
Lofoi Falls 142
Louis XIV of France 24-25
Lucerne (Luzern) 38-39
Ludwig II of Bavaria 32, 33

M

Machu Picchu 196-199, *196-199*, 224
Madagascar 140-141, *140-141*
Magellan, Fernando 208
Malebo Pool 138
manatees 180
Manneken Pis 31
Maoris 228
Marie Antoinette 24, 25, 37
Mary, Queen of Scots 19
Matterhorn 40-41, *40-41*
Mauna Kea 182
Maya culture 186, 188, 192-193
McLaren, John 171 Mecca 100
medressahs 126
Mesa Verde 147
Metéora Monasteries *2-3*, **56-57**, *56-57*
Meteor Crater 179, *179*
Mexico 186-189
Michelangelo 50, 51, 52
Ming tombs 86
Minoans *190*
Miyajima Island 104
Moghul architecture 97
Mons Meg 19
monsoons 235
Mont Blanc 40
Monument Valley *134*, 173
Moorish Spain 58-59
Morocco 126-127
Moscow 62-63
mosque architecture 100
Mount Cook 226
Mount Erebus 232-233, *232-233*
Mount Etna 134
Mount Everest 103
Mount Fuji 106-107, *106-107*
Mount Kilimanjaro 136-137, *136-137*
Mount Melbourne 232
Mount Meru 108
Mount Rushmore 160-161, *160-161*

Mount St Helens *234*, 235
Mountains of the Moon 139
Muhammad, Prophet 77, 126
Muir, John 175, 177
Mumtaz Mahal 94

N

Nabataeans 80, 81
Nanga Parbat 9
Nasrid dynasty 58, 59
Nazca Lines 7, **195**, *195*
Nefta 129
Nemrut Dag 7, *7*, **74**, *74*
Nepal 102-103
Nerja *224*
Netherlands 21
Neuschwanstein 32-33, *32-33*, 164
New York City 162-163
New Zealand 134, 226-229
Ngorongoro Crater 130
Niagara Falls 152-153, *152-153*
Niger River 129
Nile crocodile 123
Nile Delta 122
Nile River 122-123, *122-123*
Noh theater 104
North Africa 128-129
North America 148-183
Norwegian fjords 12-13, *12-13*

O

oases 129
Okavango Delta 144-145, *144-145*
Ol Doinyo Lengai 137
Olduvai Gorge 130
Orange River 142

PQ

Pakistan 102-103
Palladio, Andrea 52
Palm Jumeirah 83
Pamukkale 70-71, *70-71*, 135
Pangaea 102
Paraná River 203
Paris 26-29, 165
Park Güell 61
Parthenon 54-55, *54-55*
Patagonia *134*, 209
Pavlovsk 65
peacock throne 98
Peru 195-199, 206-207
Peterhof 64-65
Peter the Great, Czar 64, 65
Petra 80-81, *80-81*
Petronas Towers 225
Philosopher's Stone 34
Piazza San Marco, Venice 47
Pisa 44-45
Poland 35
Pompidou Center 165, *165*
Pont du Gard 30, *30*
Potala Palace 99, *99*
Prambanan 108
Punic Wars 125
Pyramids of Cahuachi 195
Pyramids of Chichén Itzá 188-189
Pyramids of Egypt 8, 83, 118-121, 190

Pyramids of Teotihuacán 186, 187, *191*
Pyramids of Tikal 192, 193
Qin Shihuangdi 84, 85, 87, 191

R

railways 66-67, 150-151
rainforest 9, 139, 200-201
Red Fort 98, *98*
Red Sea 130
Red Square 63
redwoods 178, *178*
Reed Flute Cave 91
Reichstag 164
Renaissance 52-53, 100
Réseau Jean-Bernard 90
Reykjavik 14, 15, *15*
rift valleys 130-131
Ring of Fire 106, 107, 182, 235
River Purus *201*
Roman Empire 30, 80, 125, 126, 190, 224
Romania 36
Rome 42-43, 48-51
Rotorua 228-229, *228-229*
Rudolf II of Bohemia 34
Russia 62-67

S

Sagrada Família 60-61, *60-61*
Sahara Desert 128-129, *128-129*
St Anthony of Egypt 56
St Athanasios 56
St Peter's Basilica 48-51, *48-51*
St Petersburg 64-65, 164
St Simeon Stylites 56
salt mines 35
salt pans 22, 23
salt pillars 75
San Francisco 170-171, 235
San Lorenzo 52
Santa Maria della Salute 47
Scotland 18-19
Scottish National War Memorial 18
seals 21, 204
sequoias 178
Seven Falls of Guairá 203
Shah Jehan 94, 95, 97, 98
Shanghai 82
Shinto 101, 104, 107
Siberia 66-67, 134
Silk Road 87
Sistine Chapel 50
skyscrapers 82-83, 162-163, 225
Smeerenburg fjord *12*
Sognefjord 12, *13*
Sokoto 129
Somnath *101*
Southern Alps glaciers 226-227, *226-227*
South Shetland Islands 236, 237
Spain 58-61
Spanish Riding School 37

Speke, John Hanning 123
Sphinx 120
Spreuerbrücke 39
Staffa 17
Stanley, Henry Morton 123, 138
Statue of Liberty 154-157, *154-157*
Stone Age 190
Stonehenge 20, *20*, *190*
Stóri Geysir 15
Suez Canal 225
Surtsey Island 14
Suryavarman II 109
Switzerland 38-41
Sydney Harbour Bridge 217, *225*
Sydney Opera House *1*, **214-217**, *214-217*
synagogue architecture 100

T

Table Mountain 146-147, *146-147*
Tagbaladougou Falls 143
Taipei 101 83, *225*
Taiwan 82-83
Taj Mahal 7, **94-97**, *94-97*
Tambopata National Reserve *200*
Tannogou Falls 143
Tanzania 130-131, 136-137
Tasman, Abel 227
Tasman Glacier 226, 227
Temple of Heaven 89
Temple of Karnak 116-117, *116-117*
Temple of Solomon 77
Temple of the Golden Pavilion *165*
Tenzing Norgay 103
Teotihuacán 186-187, *186-187*, *191*
Thailand 110-113
Thebes 116
Thessaly 56-57
Three Gorges Dam 92-93, *92-93*
Tiananmen Square 89
Tibet 99, 102-103
Tierra del Fuego 208-209, *208-209*
Tikal 192-193, *192-193*
Tinkisso Falls 143
Tisisat Falls 122
Tokyo *107*
Toltecs 188-189
tornadoes 234, *234*
Toronto 82
Trans-Siberian Railway 66-67, *66-67*
Trump Tower 82
Tsarskoe Selo 65
Tuareg *128*
Tugela Falls 142
Tunisia 124-125, 147
Tuolumne Meadows 174
Turkey 70-74, 135
Tutankhamun 117

U

Ulm Minster 100, *101*
Uluru (Ayers Rock) 218-

219, *218-219*
USA 152-163, 166-183
Utzon, Jørn 214–215

V

Valley of Fire State Park 168
Valley of the Kings 117
Van Horne, William 150, 151
Vatican City 50
Vatnajökull 15
Venezuela 194
Venice 46-47
Versailles 24-25, *24-25*, 164
Victoria Falls 142-143, *142-143*
Vienna 37
Virginia Falls 153
Virunga Mountains 131
Vitruvius 52
Vladivostok 67
volcanism 15, 17, 105, 106-107, 131, 136-137, 182-183, 232-233, 235, 236-237
Volubilis 126

W

Waddenzee 21, *21*
Wailing Wall (Western Wall) 77
Waimangu 229
Washington, D.C. 158-159
Wat Chai Watthanaram *113*
Wat Phra Keo 110-111, *110-111*
Wat Phra Mahathat 113, *113*
Wat Phra Si Sanphet 112
Wat Ratburana 113
Wat Yai Chai Mongkhon 112
Wave Rock 235
Wegener, Alfred 130
wetlands 21, 22-23, 36, 144-145, 180-181
whaling 236
White Nile 122, 123
Whymper, Edward 41
Wieliczka Salt Mines 35, *35*
Winter Palace 164

XYZ

Xuankong Si *100*
Yahgan people 208, 209
Yangtze dolphin 93
Yangtze River 92-93
Yekaterinsky Palace 65
Yosemite National Park *8*, **174-175**, *174-175*
Yucatán Peninsula 192, 193
Zambezi River 142
Zambia 142-143
Zimbabwe 142-143
Zion National Park 166-167, *166-167*
Zugspitze 40

ACKNOWLEDGEMENTS

The Automobile Association would like to thank the following photographers, companies and picture libraries for their assistance in the preparation of this book. Abbreviations for the picture credits are as follows – (t) top; (b) bottom; (c) centre; (l) left; (r) right; (AA) AA World Travel Library.

001c AA/Paul Kenward; 002/003 AA/R Surman; 004tl AA/Michael Moody; 004tr AA/Ingrid Morejohn; 005tc AA/Clive Sawyer; 005c AA/Clive Sawyer; 005tr AA/Rick Strange; 005cr Gavin Hellier/Robert Harding; 005br Nigel McCall/Alamy; 006tl AA/Ian Burgum; 006b AA/Gordon D R Clements; 007tl AA/karl blackwell; 007tr AA/Douglas Corrance; 007br AA/Paul Kenward; 008t AA/Richard Ireland; 009br Wolfgang Kaehler/Alamy; 010bl AA/Peter Wilson; 011br AA/Michael Moody; 012cl Photolibrary; 013t Philippe Body/Photolibrary; 013bl Kuttig - Travel/Alamy; 014cl Photolibrary; 014r Photolibrary; 015tl AA/James Tims; 015tr AA/James Tims; 015b Photolibrary; 016b Photolibrary; 017tl Jeremy Pembrey/Alamy; 017tr Tony Waltham/Robert Harding; 017bc Photolibrary; 018tc Photolibrary; 018bl Photolibrary; 019tr AA/Jonathan Smith; 019b AA/Jonathan Smith; 020bl Photolibrary; 021tr blickwinkel/Alamy; 021cl Buiten-Beeld/Alamy; 021b imagebroker/Alamy; 022cl Javier Tajuelo/Photolibrary; 022bl Photolibrary; 022br blickwinkel/Alamy; 023t AA/Yadid Levy; 023br imagebroker/Alamy; 024cl Kevin O'Hara/Photolibrary; 024br Jochen Schlenker/Robert Harding; 025tr Photolibrary; 025b Photolibrary; 026bl ND/Roger-Viollet/TopFoto; 026r AA/karl blackwell; 027tc Mary Evans Picture Library/Alamy; 027tr Mary Evans Picture Library/Alamy; 027b Henri Roger/Roger-Viollet/TopFoto; 028 Kord.com/Photolibrary; 029tr Jim Zuckerman/Alamy; 029bl bilwissedition Ltd. & Co. KG/Alamy; 029br Lourens Smak/Alamy; 030r AA/Barrie Smith; 031tr Paul Shawcross/Alamy; 031bl Arterra Picture Library/Alamy; 031br Rohan Van Twest/Alamy; 032c Photolibrary; 033tr Sylvain Grandadam/Photolibrary; 033bl Photolibrary; 033cr Peter Widmann/Alamy; 034tr SHEILA TERRY/SCIENCE PHOTO LIBRARY; 034cl Richard Nebesky/Robert Harding; 034br AA/Simon McBride; 035b AA/James Tims; 036tl imagebroker/Alamy; 036c Wilmar Photography/Alamy; 037tr AA/Michael Siebert; 037b Photolibrary; 038tr imagebroker/Alamy; 038cl VERNIER JEAN BERNARD/CORBIS SYGMA; 038br/039b AA/Steve Day; 039tr Photolibrary; 040cl Pictorium/Alamy; 041l Walter Bibikow/Photolibrary; 041tr Images & Stories/Alamy; 41br funkyfood London - Paul Williams/Alamy; 042b AA/Alex Kouprianoff; 043tl North Wind Picture Archives/Alamy; 043cl AA/Clive Sawyer; 043br AA/Mockford & Bonetti; 044l Image Source/Alamy; 044br Simon Bowen/Alamy; 045tl CuboImages srl/Alamy; 045tr NDP/Alamy; 045cr Photolibrary; 046tc ROUSSEL BERNARD/Alamy; 046bl Photolibrary; 047t David Robertson/The Travel Library; 047br John Lawrence/The Travel Library; 048b/049l John Lawrence/The Travel Library; 049t Ivern Photo/Photolibrary; 049br Photolibrary; 050tl AA/Mockford & Bonetti; 050br Photolibrary; 051tl Photolibrary; 051tr AA/Clive Sawyer; 051cr AA/Peter Wilson; 052cl CuboImages srl/Alamy; 052cr AA/James Tims; 052bc JTB Photo Communications, Inc./Alamy; 053tl Photolibrary; 053tc mediacolor's/Alamy; 053tr Massimo Listri/Corbis; 053bl AA/Simon McBride; 054l AA/Richard Surman; 054br AA/James Tims; 055tl Alvaro Leiva/Photolibrary; 055c AA/Peter Wilson; 055cr AA/James Tims; 056b Petr Svarc/Photolibrary; 057l Kevin Schafer/Photolibrary; 057cr Kuttig - Travel/Alamy; 058tr J.D. Dallet/Photolibrary; 058b Gavin Hellier/Robert Harding; 059tr age fotostock/Robert Harding; 059br Michael Busselle/Robert harding; 060bl imagebroker/Alamy; 060cr Johan Furusjo/Alamy; 061tl AA/Max Jourdan; 061tr AA/Myriam Bonnet; 061br Author's Image Ltd/Alamy; 062tr MARK SYKES MOSCOW/Alamy; 062b Alex Segre/Alamy; 063t Photolibrary; 063cr Photolibrary; 063bl IFstock/Alamy; 064c Gavin Hellier/Robert Harding; 065tl David Parker/Alamy; 065tr AA/Ken Paterson; 065bl Stuart Black/The Travel Library; 066tr Iain Masterton/Alamy; 066b Picture Contact/Alamy; 067tl Dominic Harris/Alamy; 067bl Philip Game/Alamy; 067bc Bill Bachmann/Alamy; 068bl AA/Anna Mockford & Nick Bonetti; 069br AA/David Henley; 070cl Marco Simoni/Robert Harding; 070bl/071b Philippe Michel/Photolibrary; 071tr Marco Simoni/Robert Harding; 072cr Photolibrary; 072b/073b John Lawrence/The Travel Library; 073tl Art Kowalsky/Alamy; 073tr Images & Stories/Alamy; 074tr Adam Woolfitt/Robert Harding; 074bl Adam Woolfitt/Robert Harding; 075l AA/Pat Aithie; 075tr Eitan Simanor/Alamy; 076b/077l Russell Kord/Alamy; 077tc Eitan Simanor/Robert Harding; 077br Photolibrary; 078tr Kord.com/Photolibrary; 078bl AA/Pat Aithie; 078br Eddie Gerald/Alamy; 079tr AA/Julian Loader; 079bl Michael DeFreitas/Robert Harding; 079br Photolibrary; 080tr Jon Arnold Images Ltd/Alamy; 080bl Giuseppe Trombetta/Alamy; 080r/081l Photolibrary; 081br Jon Arnold Images Ltd/Alamy; 082r Timothy Swope/Alamy; 083tl philipus/Alamy; 083cr Picture Contact/Alamy; 084 AA/Gordon D R Clements; 085tr imagebroker/Alamy; 085br AA/Anna Mockford & Nick Bonetti; 086tl AA/Anna Mockford & Nick Bonetti; 086bl JTB Photo Communications Inc/Alamy; 087tc Photolibrary; 087b AA/Ingrid Morejohn; 088tl Photolibrary; 088br/089bl Tibor Bognar/Alamy; 089t Photolibrary; 089br AA/Anna Mockford & Nick Bonetti; 090t AA/A Kouprianoff; 091tr AA/David Henley; 091bl AA/David Henley; 092cl Photolibrary; 092br/093bl John Henshall/Alamy; 093tr Ed Brown/Alamy; 093tr Verge Images/Alamy; 094b AA/Douglas Corrance; 095t Ben Pipe/The Travel Library; 095cl The Granger Collection, NYC/TopFoto; 096t ann stevens/Alamy; 096bc Bill Bachmann/Alamy; 096br/097b Photolibrary; 098tr Mary Evans Picture Library/Alamy; 098cl P. Narayan/Photolibrary; 098b PhotoStock-Israel/Alamy; 099cr AA/Ingrid Morejohn; 099bl Rebecca Havekost/Alamy; 100cl AA/Ingrid Morejohn; 100br JTB Photo/Photolibrary; 101t John Wilson/Robert Harding; 101bl Bildarchiv Monheim GmbH/Alamy; 101br Jon Arnold Images Ltd/Alamy; 102cl Roger Cracknell 14/Asia/Alamy; 102br/103bl Loraine Wilson/Robert Harding; 103tr Jochen Schlenker/Robert Harding; 103br AA/Lee Karen Stow; 104tl yannick luthy/Alamy; 104bl Photolibrary; 104br Photolibrary; 105cr Photolibrary; 105bl Yukihiro Fukuda/naturepl.com; 106cl Hideo Kurihara/Alamy; 106r/107l Jose Fuste Raga/Robert Harding; 107tr Jon Arnold Images Ltd/Alamy; 107br Photolibrary; 108l Philippe Michel/Photolibrary; 108tr Images & Stories/Alamy; 108bl Photolibrary; 109tr Olga Khoroshunova/Alamy; 109b Gavin Hellier/Robert Harding; 110b Jose Fuste Raga/Robert Harding; 111tl Mikel Bilbao/Photolibrary; 111cr Nico Tondini/Robert Harding; 111bc Jonathan Gordon/Alamy; 112cl AA/Rick Strange; 112bl Pep Roig/Alamy; 113tr Tim Whitby/Alamy; 113b Ellen Rooney/Robert Harding; 114bl AA/CLIVE SAWYER; 115br AA/Ian Burgum; 116cl AA/Rick Strange; 116b Photolibrary; 117tl AA/Rick Strange; 117tr Robert Harding; 117br AA/Rick Strange; 118/119l AA/Rick Strange; 119t AA/Rick Strange; 119br Photolibrary; 120tl Photolibrary; 120tr AA/Rick Strange; 120bl AA/Clive Sawyer; 120br Andrew McConnell/Robert Harding; 121t Photolibrary; 121br Jochen Schlenker/Robert Harding; 122tc AA/Rick Strange; 122bl Robert Harding; 123l Photolibrary; 123tr Hemis/Alamy; 124tr North Wind; 124b AA/Steve Day; 125tr AA/Steve Day; 125br Photolibrary; 126bl Sarah Galambos/Alamy; 126tr/127tl Sylvain Grandadam/Photolibrary; 127tc Petr Svarc/Alamy; 127tr AA/Ian Burgum; 127bl Jeronimo Alba/Photolibrary; 128c Photolibrary; 128b Photolibrary; 128tr/129tl Authors Image/Robert Harding; 129br isifa Image Service s.r.o./Alamy; 130cl AA/Paul Kenward; 130r/131b Photolibrary; 131tr Images & Stories/Alamy; 132tc Photolibrary; 132tr Wilmar Topshots/Alamy; 132br/133bl Images of Africa Photobank/Alamy; 133t Photolibrary; 134c Richard Rickard/Alamy; 134b Jordi Cami/Photolibrary; 135tl Richard Maschmeyer/Robert Harding; 135cr AA/Clive Sawyer; 135br Gavin Hellier/Robert Harding; 136b AA/William Gray; 137tl Martin Harvey/Alamy; 137tr Photolibrary; 137bl Photolibrary; 138tc Marion Kaplan/Alamy; 138bl Andrew McConnell/Robert Harding; 139t Robert Caputo/Getty; 139bl Photolibrary; 140cl Wolfgang Kaehler/Alamy; 140tr The Africa Image Library/Alamy; 140br/141bl David Pickford/Robert Harding; 141tl Photolibrary; 142cl Andrew McConnell/Robert Harding; 143l Ken Welsh/Photolibrary; 143cr Galen Rowell/Mountain Light/Alamy; 144bl Karin Duthie/Alamy; 144tr Gary Dublanko/Alamy; 145tr imagebroker/Alamy; 145b Karin Duthie/Alamy; 146c Photolibrary; 147tl Photolibrary; 147bl Bleyer/FRIEDRICHSMEIER ARCHIVE/Alamy; 148bl AA/CLIVE SAWYER; 149br AA/Ken Paterson ; 150bl AA/Chris Coe; 151t Justin Prenton/Alamy; 151br AA Picture Library; 152c Photolibrary; 153tr Bruno Perousse/Photolibrary; 153bl Photolibrary; 154cl Gavin Gough/Alamy; 154r/155l Travel Pix/Robert Harding; 155t Kord.com/Photolibrary; 155c Corbis; 155r The Art Archive/Alamy; 156b Rafael Ben-Ari/Alamy; 156r/157l AA/James Tims; 157tr AA/James Tims; 158l AA/Clive Sawyer; 158br/159bl AA/Julian Love; 159t AA/Julian Love; 159cr Photolibrary; 160b Photolibrary; 161tl Photolibrary; 161br Photolibrary; 162l AA/James Tims; 162cr Photolibrary; 162r/163l Mathias Beinling/Alamy; 163tr Kord.com/Photolibrary; 164cl Visions LLC/Photolibrary; 164cl AA/Simon McBride; 164b Amanda Hall/Robert Harding; 165t Jon Arnold Images/Photolibrary; 165bl AA/Wyn Voysey; 165bc AA/J F Pin; 166cl AA/Manon Van Vark; 166tr/167t P. Narayan/Photolibrary; 167br Medio Images/ImageState; 168c Photolibrary; 168r/168l Photolibrary; 169br WoodyStock/Alamy; 170/171l Photolibrary; 171tl Paul Andrew Lawrence/Alamy; 171cr Jim Goldstein/Alamy; 172l Ethel Davies/Robert Harding; 173tl Clint Farlinger/Alamy; 173b AA/Manon Van Vark; 174cl inga spence/Alamy; 174tr/175bl AA/Richard Ireland; 175br Photolibrary; 176b AA/Clive Sawyer; 177tl AA/CLIVE SAWYER; 177cr Photolibrary; 178l Photolibrary; 179cr Lonely Planet Images/Alamy; 180tc James Schwabel/Alamy; 180bl Reinhard Dirscherl/Alamy; 181t Marvin Dembinsky Photo Associates/Alamy; 181bl AA/James Tims; 182br James Osmond/Alamy; 183tl Andoni Canela/Photolibrary; 183cr Mauro Ladu/Alamy; 183br AA/Kirk Lee Aeder; 184bl AA/Rick Strange; 185br AA/Guy Marks; 186bl AA/Rick Strange; 186/187l R H Productions/Robert Harding; 187tr R H Productions/Robert Harding; 188b/189l AA/Rick Strange; 189t Photolibrary; 189cr AA/Rick Strange; 189bl Aphra Pia/Photolibrary; 190c AA/Jon Wyand; 190bl PjrTravel/Alamy; 190br AA/Philip Enticknap; 191tl AA/David Henley; 191cr Dmitry Rukhlenko - Travel Photos/Alamy; 191bl AA/Rick Strange; 191br AA/S & O Mathews; 192cl Jon Arnold Images Ltd/Alamy; 192br/193bl Sergio Pitamitz/Robert Harding; 193tr Photolibrary; 194l Photolibrary; 195bl STOCKFOLIO/Alamy; 195br AA/Guy Marks; 196/197l AA/Guy Marks; 197tr Andrew Newey/The Travel Library; 197br stephen horsted/Alamy; 198tc Alvaro Leiva/Photolibrary; 198bl First Light/Alamy; 198b Kuttig - Travel/Alamy; 198br/199b Tono Labra/Photolibrary; 200tr Octavio Campos Salles/Alamy; 200bl Kuttig - Travel - 2/Alamy; 201l Photolibrary; 201cr Jacques Jangoux/Alamy; 202 AA/James Tims; 203tl AA/James Tims; 203cr Images & Stories/Alamy; 204cl Photolibrary; 204tc WorldFoto/Alamy; 204r/205b Sybil Sassoon/Robert Harding; 205l Celia Mannings/Alamy; 205cr AA/Guy Marks; 206cl Rob Cousins/Robert Harding; 206tr/207t AA/Guy Marks; 207bl AA/Guy Marks; 208b Photolibrary; 208tr/209tl Photolibrary; 209br imagebroker/Alamy; 210bl AA/Paul Kenward; 211br AA/Paul Kenward; 212cl Gavin Hellier/Robert Harding; 212r/213l Gavin Hellier/Robert Harding; 213br Gavin Hellier/Robert Harding; 214b Mark Mawson/Robert Harding; 215tr Jose Fuste Raga/Robert Harding; 215bc David Jacobs/Robert Harding; 216tr redbrickstock.com/Alamy; 216b/217l Sergio Pitamitz/Robert Harding; 217tr Photolibrary; 217br AA/Steve Day; 218tr Susanna Bennett/Alamy; 219t Photolibrary; 219br AA/Adrian Baker; 220b/221l Photolibrary; 221t digitalunderwater.com/Alamy; 221br David Wall/Alamy; 222tc David Wall/Alamy; 222bl digitalunderwater.com/Alamy; 222br Kurt Lackovic/Alamy; 223l David Wall/Alamy; 224cl Klaus-Peter Wolf/Photolibrary; 224b AA/John Wood; 225tl Michele Falzone/Photolibrary; 225tr AA/Paul Kenward; 225br AA/Rick Strange; 226cl David Bowman/Alamy; 226r/227l Colin Monteath/Photolibrary; 227br AA/Mike Langford; 228 Photolibrary; 229tl Photolibrary; 229br Henk Meijer/Alamy; 230t Nigel McCall/Alamy; 230bl Accent Alaska.com/Alamy; 231br Galen Rowell/Mountain Light/Alamy; 232br/233bl Galen Rowell/Corbis; 233t Steve and Donna O'Meara/Corbis; 233cr John Higdon/Photolibrary; 234cl Weatherstock/Photolibrary; 234br Photodisc; 235tl Gavin Hellier/Robert Harding; 235br David Jacobs/ Robert Harding; 236tr Alex Benwell/Alamy; 236cl Photolibrary; 237tr Accent Alaska.com/Alamy; 237b Geoff Renner/Robert Harding

Every effort has been made to trace the copyright holders, and we apologise in advance for any accidental errors. We would be happy to apply the corrections in the following edition of this publication.